Making A Rose After the Diaspora

Making A Rose After the Diaspora

An Autobiography by
Eva E. Ross

iUniverse, Inc.
New York Lincoln Shanghai

MAKING A ROSE AFTER THE DIASPORA
AN AUTOBIOGRAPHY

iUniverse books may be ordered through booksellers or by contacting:

iUniverse
1663 Liberty Drive
Bloomington, IN 47403
www.iuniverse.com
1-800-Authors (1-800-288-4677)

Because of the dynamic nature of the Internet, any web addresses or links contained in this book may have changed since publication and may no longer be valid. The views expressed in this work are solely those of the author and do not necessarily reflect the views of the publisher, and the publisher hereby disclaims any responsibility for them.

Any people depicted in stock imagery provided by Thinkstock are models, and such images are being used for illustrative purposes only.

Certain stock imagery © Thinkstock.

ISBN: 978-0-5953-7842-5 (sc)
ISBN: 978-0-5956-7573-9 (hc)
ISBN: 978-1-4697-9613-0 (e)

Printed in the United States of America

iUniverse rev. date: 2/28/2013

This book is dedicated with all my love and gratitude to my parents, Paula and Herman Madarasz and my husband, John Ross.

Contents

PREFACE xi

Part I   AUSTRIA, 1929–1939

CHAPTER ONE. 3

CHAPTER TWO 13

CHAPTER THREE 20

CHAPTER FOUR. 31

Part II   URUGUAY, 1939–1966

CHAPTER ONE. 39

CHAPTER TWO 49

CHAPTER THREE 63

CHAPTER FOUR. 73

Part III   MEXICO, 1960–1966

CHAPTER ONE. 97

CHAPTER TWO 109

CHAPTER THREE 115

CHAPTER FOUR. 125

CHAPTER FIVE 131

CHAPTER SIX 144

CHAPTER SEVEN 165

Part IV   SEATTLE, 1966–1977

CHAPTER ONE 173

CHAPTER TWO 183

CHAPTER THREE 188

Part V   SAN DIEGO, 1977–1980

CHAPTER ONE 211

CHAPTER TWO 219

CHAPTER THREE 231

Part VI   STANFORD, 1980–2000

CHAPTER ONE 241

CHAPTER TWO 263

CHAPTER THREE 269

CHAPTER FOUR 276

CHAPTER FIVE 290

CHAPTER SIX 294

CHAPTER SEVEN 301

CHAPTER EIGHT 310

EPILOGUE 317

ACKNOWLEDGEMENTS

I thank my husband for all his help and support. I couldn't have done it without him.

Judith Reuss provided steady and close help in writing this book, for which I am very grateful.

PREFACE

The twentieth century was one of world wars, genocides, and major upheavals of political systems. With all these disasters the century is filled with millions of personal tragedies, including those of the many refugees displaced by political turmoil. This is my story: one of these refugees who, as a young child at the age of nine, had to flee Austria with her parents due to persecution. In spite of many sorrows experienced, fortunately the story ends well, though it certainly did not for so many others.

I was part of a large family and we had many friends. Some were killed and others escaped to different parts of the world. This is a record of one of the numerous paths taken by the multitude of refugees as a witness to those events. This Diaspora of the twentieth century is part of my life and part of this story.

I have arbitrarily made chapters depending on the place where I lived because my life was quite different in each, and each required a new start.

PART I
AUSTRIA

✦

1929–1939

CHAPTER ONE

I was born in Austria on August 13, 1929, three years after my parents were married. I must have known that life was not going to be easy because I took my time to come into this world. I had to be pulled out by forceps, and my mother had a very difficult time. My father was so scared of losing her that he decided they'd never go through that again, which was the reason that I grew up an only child.

My mother, Paula Stoessl, was one of eleven children born to an orthodox Jewish family in Austria. Like so many women of the times, her mother died giving birth to her tenth child. Left with ten children and no wife, my grandfather quickly remarried and had yet another child!

My grandfather was in the leather business, and he was a leader of the Jewish community in Klagenfurt, which was situated near a beautiful body of water called the Woerthersee. He was equally respected by his fellow Jews as well as by the gentiles with whom he came into contact. He was active in civic issues and a significant benefactor for a number of charities. His reputation was such that he received a medal from Emperor Franz Joseph for his contributions to Austrian society. I often thought he should have received an award for managing to raise eleven children successfully!

He was a kind, but strict father, insisting that all his children receive a good education, with the boys learning to play the violin and the girls the piano. Each had to learn a second language, their only choice being whether it would be English or French. When any one of his children was reported to have missed religious school, he would march up to the offending child, and if it was a boy, grab hold of his ear, or if it was a girl, grab hold of a pigtail. With a melodramatic, thunderous voice, he would wag their head back and forth, demanding with each wiggle:

"Why—Did—You—Not—Go—To—School—Today?"

In a rush of giggles and squirming, the child would come up with some unrealistic story to explain his or her poor behavior, while my grandfather threatened them with all sorts of dire punishments—which the children did not take seriously.

The leather business must have been good, because my grandfather owned the family's large house in Klagenfurt and a vacation home at a resort on the shore of the Woerthersee. The family spent every summer there, and each child learned to swim in the lake.

My mother was a very pretty young woman. She was of medium height with a good shape, and a lovely and kind face. She had beautiful big brown eyes, a well-shaped mouth with pearl white teeth, which did not need straightening. Her thick auburn hair was curly and she often told me how she suffered as a child when her hair had to be combed through after a shampoo. She laughed easily and loved to tell jokes. She had a very warm personality and was loved by everyone. In spite of having lost her mother at the age of seven and having to put up with a step-mother and older brothers who never missed a chance to heckle her, she was easy going and happy. As she told me later, there were a few bad moments which would bring her to tears: One time when a brother was trying to beat her, a man-servant shouted at her brother: "Will you leave her alone; if you beat her she will get dumber." Dumb she was not. To my mind, she was much smarter than I, and had many more talents: doing well at tennis and bridge as well as playing the piano.

She adored her father, and in order to help him with his business correspondence she learned Italian, ultimately becoming fluent.

My grandfather died the same week I was born, and his community honored him by burying him in a special grave with a beautiful headstone on which, among other things, was the following inscription in his own handwriting: "As long as somebody lives who thinks of you, you are not dead." A few years ago, my husband and I went to that cemetery and found the grave in good condition and well cared for. You were right, dear Grandfather, someone is still thinking of you!

My father, Hermann Madarasz, was also born into an orthodox Jewish family, in Bratislava, Slovakia, and had three siblings. He went to the university in Budapest, Hungary; he spoke German, Czech, Slovakian and Hungarian perfectly. He was a handsome man, tall, thin, with blond hair. His well-shaped face was lined even when he was young, which gave him a mature and masculine look. He had smiling hazel eyes, a straight nose over a long pair of lips. Unfortunately his teeth were crooked, something which I inherited from him. He had an aristocratic bearing and was always immaculately dressed, though he smoked a lot and I never saw him without a cigarette or pipe. He was a wonderful human being, a kind and loving husband and father. I still think of him often and have never stopped missing him.

When he met my mother he was living in the village of Pernegg, where he was director of a large distillery. Right after their honeymoon in northern Italy and the French Riviera, my father took his young bride back to his home in Pernegg, located in Styria in the southeastern part of Austria. It was a little village, sitting between

Bruck, a small town, and Graz, a pleasant city, which was also the capital of Styria. The river Mur ran from Bruck to Graz, and Pernegg was built along this river.

My parents' wedding picture

Although my father would have been willing to live in Graz and drive to work in Pernegg, my mother did not want him to commute two hours by car every day. She wanted him to be able to come home for regular meals. Yet she worried about the great change this new home would make in her life. She was used to living in a city, even if not a large one, surrounded by a big family and many friends. Upon marrying, however, she had to live in this modest village. It was not what she had expected and she often felt quite lonely and forsaken.

My earliest memories are of this little village, Pernegg, with its one main street that was also the only road going from Bruck to Graz. There were two grocery stores, a butcher, a pharmacy, a bakery, a school and an inn on that main street. The private homes and summer villas of the shareholders of the distillery were spread out on the hills around the village.

On the other side of the river Mur was the train route. The Distillery was on the main street/highway and our house was a converted schoolhouse located nearby. The house had been nicely rebuilt, giving us big rooms and a lovely covered terrace room overlooking the neighbor, the Lustigs' garden. This veranda, as we called it, had windows on all three sides, which made it possible for us to eat our lunch there. Since it also had a heater, we were able to use it in winter as well. Our home comprised the whole second floor, while the first floor served as an apartment for the steward of the farm that was attached to the Distillery.

Our upper story was large enough to accommodate an ample living room-dining room, four bedrooms and three baths, a large kitchen and the veranda. All the rooms were spacious with high ceilings. It was a very comfortable home. There was a door leading to an attic, which always scared me especially because the maid would tell me that if I didn't behave she would send me to the attic where the boogeyman was waiting! My room was between the maid's room, which had its own bathroom, and the guest room and I had to share my bathroom with any visitors.

My father walking towards our house.

There were a few interesting characters around the village; for instance the baker, a small man with a large belly and a big mustache, who liked his beer, would come home drunk almost every night, irritating his wife so much that she would frequently lock him out. One evening he was so angry that he stood on the street and bellowed loud enough for the whole village to hear:

"Old woman, let me in or I'll throw you out!"

The only partners of the distillery who lived in Pernegg all year were the Kraus family, who lived across the street from us. They had four children, all of whom were much older than I, so there was never a question of my having a playmate. The oldest son was Franzl, who was studying the business of distillery with my father, then came Anni, a vivacious young woman, after her was Ernest and the youngest son was Fritzl. He was a funny boy who once, when entrusted to my mother when his parents were gone, came crying to my mother: "*Tante* Paula I have a bad tooth ache, but please don't take me to the dentist here. He always pulls the wrong tooth." Of course my mother didn't know what else to do, so they went to the local dentist. When they were all done and the dentist had pulled Fritzl's tooth, he started to cry and said: "I told you, *Tante* Paula, he always pulls the wrong tooth!"

Frankly, my mother was not fond of the parents. Richa Kraus, who had not been blessed with anything pretty was a morose and jealous woman, and Emil Kraus, her husband, a pot-bellied older man with a white mustache and fierce-looking brown eyes, did not have a better disposition. However, their company was better than nothing, so we socialized with them. In the evenings, my parents would often go to their house to play bridge. There was not much else to do in town and, though my mother didn't enjoy it, she felt that she had to play because they needed a fourth partner. Some evenings, the mayor, the town doctor and the local priest would take part in card games with my father. They would play *Tarok,* a common card game in many European countries, mainly played by men.

Despite my mother's willingness to live in Pernegg, she was often lonesome. And while I loved to be her companion, I was a little girl and the conversation of a child is not as stimulating as that of an adult. Fortunately, her cousin Mira Hafner and her husband, Fritz, who was an attorney, would visit us frequently on weekends. They lived in Graz, which was only an hour away. Mira was my mother's favorite cousin. She was a charming, sophisticated, cultured and vivacious lady, good looking but not pretty with a good figure. Fritz was completely bald even as a young man but had a nice face with the obligatory mustache. He was very intelligent and was a successful lawyer.

It was always a holiday for us when they came. We loved them and they brought life: news from the city, new books, and toys for me. They enjoyed our company, our cooking, the doubles tennis games and the long, wonderful walks they took in the countryside.

The mountains and woods around our village were spectacular. What I remember most was the fragrance of the resin of the trees. Years later, when I finally smelled the woods of California I was surprised how much it reminded me of my early childhood.

My early years weren't what one would expect for a child growing up in the country. I didn't have the freedom to run around and play in the mud or roll in the hay. There were constant admonitions of "Stay clean! Be careful! Don't get your good clothes dirty!" All my relatives and friends kept bringing lovely dresses for me from the city and I had to wear them quickly before I outgrew them. As a result I hesitated to let myself go, and became rather fearful and shy. Furthermore, my mother, who was always worried about my health, kept telling me to put on a sweater whenever she felt cool. So I turned out rather pampered and sensitive to the climate. Though at the time I often didn't feel like it, I believe I was a beautiful little girl, well loved and indulged by everyone.

My mother and I.

The high points for me came when we would go on vacation somewhere in Austria or Italy or my beloved Woerthersee. The first time I saw its magnificent blue expanse, I was 4 years old. Of all the memories I have of Austria, it is the times I spent in a resort on the shores of the Woerthersee that remain the most vivid and poignant. It was a beautiful, verdant area, filled with majestic mountains and gigantic, gnarled trees that seemed to march up and down the hills and valleys, creating an Eden-like peacefulness that inspired the soul. Such was the splendor of the environment, that when Johannes

Brahms, so the story goes, came to visit he was so moved that he composed a symphony on the spot.

Though it seemed immense to me as a child, my mother boasted that she had swum the entire width of the lake when she was only 16 years old. I was astonished and quite impressed with her aquatic skills. Looking back, I can see that the same determination that gave her strength to swim so far, ultimately gave us our chance for survival.

One of the highlights of my early childhood was the wedding of my father's brother in Bratislava. I was chosen to carry the bride's veil and felt terribly important to be part of this elegant wedding. Everything looked like a fairy tale to me but of course I had no idea what the near future would bring to us and to the world.

Me at the wedding

CHAPTER TWO

On vacations we would often meet up with one of my mother's sisters and her children. Very often it would be my Aunt Elsa, one of my mother's older sisters, not as pretty as my mother and therefore a little jealous of her, but with beautiful blue eyes and blond hair and a very good figure. She had married a German Jew, Emil Jawitz, and moved to Breslau, Germany. Emil was very bossy, with a face that could have been good-looking if it hadn't been for his obtrusive nose. They had two children, Elfi and Heini. Elfi was four years older than I and had beautiful blond hair and blue eyes. Heini was two years her junior. He was a handsome young boy with blond hair, which his mother didn't cut, making him look almost like a girl, but he was a gorgeous boy and I was secretly in love with him.

Sometimes the Jawitz family came to stay with us in Pernegg. It was such a good experience for me to be with children even if they were a little older than I. My mother told me I was always asking for a little sister so I would have someone to play with. When none appeared, apparently I thought that I was asking for too much. Never one to give up, one day I said: "Mother, rather than nothing, I would settle for a little brother!" Oh, how easy everything looks to a child!

Unfortunately, my wish was not fulfilled. Even after my father died and my mother faced hard times, it seems to me it might have been easier with two children, especially for me. I wouldn't have had all the responsibility on my shoulders.

Summer also brought the shareholders of the distillery, the Brauns, the Steiners and the Lustigs, who would come from Vienna to stay with their families for a few months in their villas in Pernegg.

This was a pleasant and sociable time. We would get together for meals, often going swimming in a pool nearby.

Zora Braun was a tiny and delicate woman who was very careful with her health, taking long naps after lunch. Her husband, Moritz was a feisty old gentleman, ready to flirt with every girl or woman and not taking life too seriously. Their daughter, Clara Steiner, a beautiful young woman was married to Lacy Steiner. Lacy was tall and handsome, but had black beady eyes, which made him look hard and greedy.

Lacy and Clara had a little girl, Madeleine Doris, four years younger than I, whom I decided to make "my little sister." Dorita, as she was called much later on, was a cute but spoiled child, a little, pudgy devil, and her parents obeyed every one of her commands. The older she got the worse it was. Nonetheless, since I had decided she was my "little sister" I often played with her. This friendship lasted until she died at the age of 60 of cancer.

My mother's favorite family, the Lustigs, lived in the villa next to us. I remember with pleasure their lovely garden filled with flowers and fruit trees. They had a Fox Terrier, who was so jealous that he bit me once when *Tante* Hedi, as I called her, carried me in her arms. Julius Lustig had died at a young age, so Hedi Lustig and her daughter Hanni were alone. Hedi was a lovely, refined and elegant woman, who kept a warm and welcoming home. Her daughter Hanni was tall and pretty with big black eyes and black hair and a figure like a model. She was 11 years older than I, but we have remained friends. It turned out the Steiners with Dorita, and Hanni and her husband also imigrated to Uruguay, a month before us. Hanni's mother,

Hedi married a Czech man, thinking that this would save her from the Nazis. They stayed in Czechoslovakia and, as so many unfortunate Jews who had not left in time she died in a concentration camp. What a terrible tragedy for poor Hanni who had been hoping to get her mother to join her in Argentina! Hanni had moved there after divorcing her first husband and had married again in Buenos Aires. Amazingly, through pure coincidence, Hanni is living near me again.

◆　　　◆　　　◆

One summer—I think I was 6 years old—my parents took me to Yugoslavia. The plan was that I would be left with my mother's oldest brother and his wife in a small town called Zellie, while my parents went to visit a younger brother of my mother in Belgrade. Uncle Mundi was a wonderful human being, but had a congenital problem with his spine. He walked with a cane and had a lot of pain. I can't remember his wife Dora very well, but she was a good wife to him all his life. Unfortunately, after only one day with my relatives I fell ill with scarlet fever. I felt terribly sick and was crying for my parents. My aunt and uncle wanted to put me in the hospital but my protests were so fierce that they finally decided to keep me in their apartment. The doctor put me in quarantine in a separate room and hired a nurse to take care of me. She was a nun who only spoke Yugoslavian, so we had to communicate with sign language.

Of course, my uncle immediately called my parents, but the phone connection was so bad they heard only the words "scarlet fever." This was enough for my mother and father to take the next train to come to their child. They were so worried, I think, they were sicker than I was! When they arrived, they were not allowed into my room, so I could only talk with them through the door. The nun was not allowed to leave the room either and she was my only companion during the entire quarantine. She prayed a lot, at which time she would pull a curtain between us, so she could have her privacy. Sometimes this frightened me and sometimes it made me very curious. What was she doing that she did not want me to see?

Thus we remained, I think, almost three weeks incommunicado. I was devastated that I could not be with my mother and I missed her terribly. My father went back home, but my mother, of course, could not have been moved from that apartment and sent letters, toys and books into the room on a daily basis. As the disease was a light case, I did not feel too sick, often just bored and lonesome. I was always sad when I was away from my mother. When they finally let me out I was so overjoyed that I jumped up and down. However, before being allowed into the rest of the apartment, I had to suffer through a decontamination bath. My mother put me in a bathtub with some terrible smelling disinfecting solution and scrubbed me down for a long time. As soon as I was allowed to travel we went back to Pernegg. I was elated to be back in my own surroundings.

It was during one of my father's business trips to Yugoslavia that Anni, the daughter of the Kraus family, asked my mother whether she wanted a ride to Graz. Of course my mother accepted. She took every opportunity to go to the city, so we piled into their car. My mother and I sat in the back with a very heavy (actually, a very fat) lady. Emil Kraus sat next to his daughter. Although it was a rainy day and the streets were slippery, Anni drove. A few miles before Graz, on a road carved into the mountain, (one side rock, the other side down into the river Mur), a tire blew out and Anni lost control of the car. The car tumbled down towards the river. I was terrified! My mother told me later that her thoughts at that instant were: if we crash into the rock wall we are doomed, if we fall into the river it will be no different. Through a miracle, the vehicle was caught by a large bush, but ended upside down. Luckily, a man who was traveling behind us was able to pull us out through the windows. The fat lady had saved our lives. Because we were packed like sardines none of us was hurt! The police drove us home but I was in shock, and although my mother took me into her bed where I felt protected, I kept crying out in my sleep.

The next morning my father, still in Yugoslavia, read the shocking headline in an Austrian paper: "Through a miracle, the wife of Director Madarasz of Pernegg with her little daughter Eva, escaped death!" He couldn't get fast enough to the nearest phone and came home the same day. With tears in his eyes he embraced me and didn't want to let me go.

◆   ◆   ◆

My father was an excellent driver. He never had an accident, and with his philosophy being: "Expect other drivers to be stupid," he drove defensively. Only once did he have a problem. One foggy night while he was driving with my mother, suddenly, out of the dark, a chicken flew into the windshield! Before they had a chance to recover from that, the poor chicken flew up, dropped an egg on the hood and then died! In spite of this sorry occasion, my parents could not help but burst into laughter, because Wilhelm Busch (a German poet and painter who wrote children's books) had drawn and described exactly this scene of the chicken's death in one of his stories: *"Und jedes legt noch schnell ein Ei und dann kam der Tod herbei"* which means: "And each chicken quickly laid an egg and then died."

◆   ◆   ◆

I went to elementary school at the only school in Pernegg, and I was the sole Jewish pupil. Since religious education was compulsory, I was excused from the Catholic class and they hired a Jewish teacher from the city, which was an hour away. He would come once a week, traveling by train from Graz, and teach me to read Hebrew.

I was a very shy and well-behaved little girl, but my parents had one problem with me: I rarely wanted to eat. My mother said that I never even finished a milk bottle when I was a baby. They were worried, but the doctor said "Don't force her, she'll eat when she is hungry." Well, apparently this never happened, and, according to my mother, my stomach shrank. I did not refuse food because I wanted attention. I had enough of that. I just was not hungry and couldn't eat. Every meal was a torture for me as well as for my parents, with everybody sitting around the table saying: "Putzi swallow." (My nickname was Putzi and remained so even into adulthood.) One day I was put to bed for a nap and when I woke up I still had an uneaten plum in my cheek.

In her despair, my mother decided to invite a few of the poorest children in my class to come and eat lunch with me every day. Her thinking was that, aside from feeding these poor children, I would be motivated to eat when I saw how much they appreciated the food. Wrong again! I just sat there watching with great pleasure how much these children liked our cooking. So my parents finally realized they just had to accept my poor eating habits.

One day my mother had to go to a hospital in Graz for minor surgery on her leg, and they brought my older cousin, Grete, to take care of me. She was the daughter of my mother's oldest sister, Irene, and was in her twenties. She was probably a nice young woman but I wasn't particularly thrilled with her; she was too bossy and I missed my mother. When my father came home one noon, he found a very irritated and worried little daughter who kept scratching her head.

"Putzilein, don't scratch yourself so much, what is going on?"

"Oh Daddy," I cried, "I have these little crumbs on my head and the crumbs are moving!"

I was totally ignorant of what had happened, but my father wasn't. He was so shocked that his beloved daughter had lice that he couldn't speak for a moment. He then ordered strict measures to be taken immediately. That afternoon he went to see my mother, who, seeing my father's baleful expression, feared absolute disaster.

"Darling, please tell me what happened!"

"Nothing sweetheart, everything is all right," my father replied.

But after my mother insisted, as only a worried mother can, he finally said,

"Well if you must know, our Putzi has lice!!"

My mother's relieved laughter only offended my father. "How can you laugh at something so serious!" he cried.

In the meantime, back at home I was screaming my head off. My "dear" cousin was adding greatly to my discomfort: she was washing my hair with petroleum, making my poor scratched-up scalp burn like fire.

As there was no secondary school in Pernegg, the plan was to let me finish grade school and then we would all move to the city where I would go to high school. Unfortunately, that was never going to happen.

CHAPTER THREE

Unbeknownst to me the political landscape in Germany was deteriorating rapidly. Through the Treaty of Versailles, at the end of World War I, Germany was faced with the enormous cost of the war reparations demanded by the Allies. Unemployment rose to new heights and inflation was rampant. Large-scale poverty threatened the entire country, breeding fear and civil unrest. The Great Depression hit Germany as hard as it hit the U.S. The value of their currency plummeted. Years later I heard that many children were hungry and lacked even one pair of shoes to wear.

Germany became a battle ground between the political Left and Right. The fear of Socialism and Communism was great and the Right, as ultimately represented by Hitler, gained momentum. The Nazi Party under the leadership of Hitler promised to restore the "honor" of Germany and provide "work and bread" to the German people. After Adolf Hitler was democratically elected in 1933, he suspended civil rights and political freedom. Soon after, Germany became a dictatorship.

As the struggle between Left and Right took place in Germany, it also occurred in Austria. The Austrian Chancellor, Dolfus, was assassinated and there was a civil war primarily in Vienna. The Socialists and Labor parties lost to the Right.

Anti Semitism was always present in Europe and Hitler took advantage of this to put the blame of communism on the Jews. Paradoxically at the same time the Jews were blamed for controlling the banks of the world!

There was an increase in anti Semitism in Germany and many intellectuals left. Unfortunately the majority of Jews did not, because the situation was not yet dire. Most were still able to pursue their business, social and religious lives, and hoped the political situation would improve. After all, the Jews were fully assimilated into German society, much like they are in the United States. In the next few years the intensity of the hate of Jews increased and so did immigration.

Early in the Nazi era in Germany, perhaps in 1936 or 1937, I remember hearing about a bizarre event that occurred at my cousin Heini's school, an event, which was played out in different ways all over the country. Heini's brainless teacher called him, unaware that he was Jewish, to the front of the class to explain about the so-called "pure" Aryan race.

"You see, children," he said, pointing at Heini. "This is the typical Aryan. Look at the shape of his head, the eyes, the coloring!"

Even now, I shudder at the utter insanity that was being presented as the truth.

◆   ◆   ◆

When I was about 7, my mother's older brother, Noldi, married Ilona Kastner. Noldi was a handsome man with black hair and very mischievous brown eyes. He was a big sportsman and consequently had a well-trained physique. His bride called him Puck from the *"Midsummer Night's Dream."* Ilona, a very cultured and pretty lady with blue eyes, long blond hair and a strong fondness for classical music was very much in love with him.

The wedding was held at a vineyard on top of a mountain and in my memory the setting resembled that of a romantic movie. Although my father was out of town on business, it was the last time the whole family came together to celebrate an event.

Noldi and Ilona lived in Slovakia, thinking that they did not have to leave when Hitler invaded Austria. They stayed, and later were sent to a concentration camp with their little son, John. Fortunately, after much suffering they were freed. When the war ended they stayed in Vienna, although all the brothers and sisters who had survived wanted them to join them overseas. I still don't know why they decided against it. Their son, John, studied medicine in Vienna and is now a psychiatrist there. He married an Austrian girl and they have two wonderful sons. We see each other once in a while, but not as much as I would like.

◆   ◆   ◆

In March 1938, Hitler invaded Austria. I was only in third grade. My mother was helping me take a bath, when we heard the goodbye resignation speech of Mr. Schuschnig, the president of Austria. From then on, all hell broke lose and I will never forget the next year as long as I live.

I was nine years old and the world I had known and loved disappeared overnight. The morning after the farewell speech, two Nazis in civil clothing (actually they were young men from our village whom my father knew since they were young boys), pounded on the front door. My mother asked them what they wanted and they replied that they had come to take my father into "protective custody."

"But my husband has never been active in politics," she argued fearfully. "He has been kind and caring to everybody, including you."

"Lady, don't you know there is a revolution going on? Be happy that we are not putting your husband against the wall and shooting him!"

We watched anxiously as my father was taken away. We were terrified, not knowing what they were going to do to him or for how long he would be gone. We finally found out that he had been transported to the next town and put in jail there.

My father was a kind and sensitive man, exceptionally honest and correct in everything and what this did to him is hard to describe. He was demoralized and humiliated, afraid for his life and that of his family, yet still unable, I think, to grasp the full implications of his arrest for being Jewish. My mother was so brave, she went to see him every day, and they allowed her to bring his meals to the jail.

In the meantime, the Nazis enacted a number of oppressive laws and regulations to persecute the Jews. Jews were not only forbidden to work, but their businesses and later their homes were confiscated, and since no Jew was allowed to own a car they took our car away. The next day two Nazis were using our car to drive into the city when a German tank hit them. Our car plus the two Nazi hoodlums were smashed to pieces. Very fast justice, I thought, but it had awful consequences. We, the Jews, were blamed for the entire event. After all, it was our car that produced the first Nazi victims! The funeral procession went by our house and we were filled with fear. We closed all the shutters so that they couldn't throw anything at us through the windows.

A week after they took my father to jail, he was miraculously released. Though my father was only 46 years old, the time he spent in jail made an old man out of him. I saw a man shattered, filled with dread and fear for his family. The distillery had been taken over by the Nazis and my father was thrown out. The family who lived downstairs who had been our neighbors said that they had been given our home and they wanted to move in so we had to move out quickly. It was shocking! How could everybody change so much overnight? We had always been helpful and friendly to this family and now they were kicking us out of our home.

With the help of one of my mother's brothers, Ignaz, a gentle man with the same blue eyes as my aunt Elsa, we began to pack the things that were not too big into wooden crates and had them sent to Vienna to a shipping company, which was going to forward our belongings to wherever we would end up. Our beautiful antique furniture was left behind in the house since we doubted that we would be able to use this wherever we were going.

My parents left for Vienna to see about getting visas to any country that would take us, and I was sent to stay with one of two aunts who lived in the same apartment building in Klagenfurt, the town where my mother was from. I stayed with my mother's oldest sister, Irene Fleischmann, a wonderful, kind woman, who had married at the early age of eighteen. She was not pretty but had such a personality that everybody was drawn to her. She was married to David Fleischman, who, to my recollection was a dandy. They had two daughters, Jenny and Grete, the one who had taken care of me when I had lice. The other aunt on the same floor was my favorite aunt, and my mother's second oldest sister, Mira Salzberger. She was a beautiful woman with a wonderful voice, and she would sing often and with great pleasure. She had two sons, Emerich and Ernest. Emerich, the oldest, I would see again in Mexico, but Ernest ended up dying in a concentration camp. His parents, my aunt Mira and her husband, were able to leave and went to Mexico.

As usual, even though I was nine years old, when I was apart from my parents I felt terribly homesick. With our whole world turned upside down and an unimaginable future, I was definitely beside myself with anxiety. I was very scared and cried often.

Klagenfurt, the capital of Carinthia, was known for its sympathizing with the Nazis. Though my parents had sent me there to be safe, it was a town where everybody knew everybody else and it turned out to be the worst place to be. One afternoon, I was sitting at the dining room table in the Fleischman apartment, doing my English homework, (we were all learning English, thinking that we would emigrate to an English speaking country), when I saw my uncle, who had been standing at the window, rush out of the room and out of the apartment building. Unbeknownst to me he had seen uniformed men approaching the building and was afraid of being arrested. The maid had gone shopping, my aunt was in Vienna; I was home alone! A few minutes later the front doorbell began to ring continuously. Not knowing any better and with shaky legs I went to open the door.

My heart froze when I saw three men dressed in the brown uniform worn by the S.A. *Sturmabteilung* (Stormtroopers). This was a military organization created to instill the Nazi doctrines into the people. They pushed me aside and asked where Mr. Fleischmann was. When I found my voice I said loudly: "They are not here, and you have to leave, please." This had the same effect as if I had not opened my mouth. They pushed their way into the apartment, and seeing where I had been doing my homework, one of them picked up the inkbottle and dumped it on my head, soaking me in black ink. From then on the nightmare only got worse. Things, that as a nine year old I had never heard of or even thought were possible, started to happen. From out of nowhere an axe appeared, and the three men started to hack up the grand piano. Horrified, I yelled: "Please, this belongs to my aunt, you can't do this. Please leave!" The noise was so overwhelming that nobody heard me. And even if they had, it would not have done any good. They went on to destroy everything they could get their hands on, china, crystal and all the furniture. Many of my aunt's belongings were thrown out the windows to crash on the street below. They were so crazed with what they were doing that they did not realize that they were cutting themselves. Blood was flying everywhere covering the walls and remnants of the furniture. The bedroom closets were thrown open so they could shred the dresses and suits with razor blades. I shall never forget that picture of utter evil running wild and the destruction it wrought. I just stood there, too stunned to say a word, too horrified to even try to run away.

Finally, I heard the maid coming home from shopping, and I broke free from my shock. Crying and shouting, I ran into her arms.

"Please help me Frau Duben, please, please help me."

When she saw the violent insanity of what was happening, she began to cry too. She quickly took me into her room, where she hid me under her bed, terrified that they would eventually come after me, and who knew what they would do? Under the bed I continued crying, but at least I did not have to witness the total chaos. Only after the men left did she allow me to come out. However, that was not the end of it. More men arrived to finish off what the first group had not demolished completely. And so it went on all evening.

To my great sorrow, Frau Duben was forced to leave, since Jews were no longer allowed maids and no Gentile could work for a Jew.

A few months earlier (with lots of tears) we had been forced to let our cook go.

Wanting to be with my Aunt Mira, I ran to her apartment, only to witness the whole horror all over again. She was a little more level-headed, and I remember watching her wrap her diamond earrings into newspaper and hide them in the light socket in the bathroom, with the light bulb screwed back in. It is interesting to see what people do when confronted with danger. Those earrings made it all the way to Mexico and were inherited by her daughter-in-law.

When night came, the floors were full of glass and blood, the beds were broken and we did not know where to go or what to do. Where would we sleep? Where would we be safe? Finally my aunt had a thought.

"Putzi, chances are that since you are a child, you won't be bothered, so you must go and get some help from some of our Gentile friends. They will help us clean up enough so that we can at least sleep here tonight."

Oh, I did not want to go! It was dark outside and there were monsters everywhere.

"Please, Auntie Mira, don't make me go. I am afraid!"

"Darling, you are the only one who can help us. You have to be brave."

When she put it that way, I knew I had to do it. After all, I told myself, trying to be courageous, it was only two blocks away. My stomach tight with fear and my mind horribly traumatized, I ran through the dark streets, fleeing from a woman wearing a widow's veil, who was throwing stones at me, shouting, "Jew swine, Jew swine!" I am sure that at some time or another she had been friendly with my aunt! I reached the house of the friends, a younger couple, and fell into the arms of the woman. She was crying when I told her what had happened and she and her husband came with me and helped us clean the apartment. I don't remember how or where we slept, but it was a night full of nightmares.

This was the infamous Kristall Nacht of November 9, 1938.

When I think back to that time I still grapple with the question of how so much evil can exist in human beings. Evil, on the scale that I witnessed, seems so unbelievable that most people now would think that we are too civilized and too sophisticated for such a barbaric situation to occur again. However, anyone who reads the news knows that the evil continues all over the world today. It is clear to me that the only way we can guard against going down the same road as the Nazis, is to remember that it occurred. As individuals and as a nation, we must commit ourselves to ending those conditions that lead to the growth of evil and hate.

◆   ◆   ◆

The next day we found out that many Jewish men had been "arrested" and sent to Dachau, a concentration camp in Germany. Also my Uncle Fleischmann, whom I had seen running away from the window and who could have hidden, turned himself in. He was afraid that hiding would have worse consequences. In those early days everybody tried to behave honorably! Nobody could imagine how things would really end up. He came home a few weeks later, but he and my Aunt Irene eventually died in the gas chamber. Only their two daughters were saved.

Of course my biggest fear was for my parents. How did they fare in Vienna if it was so bad in Klagenfurt? I kept hoping for a message from them, but for a day the phones were out, and my mental condition was grim. I kept praying: "Please let my parents be safe, dear God!" When we finally could speak on the phone I was relieved to hear that it had not been so bad there. I guess in those days, Jews could get lost a little easier in a large city. Thank God, I could breathe again.

I stayed another tense week in Klagenfurt during which a deep bond formed between my aunt Mira and me. We had gone through so much together and she was a wonderful lady, one whom I had always loved. My uncle Nandor, Mira's husband, a little but domineering man, who had been on a trip to Italy, returned home and I helped them pack up their books and papers in their business office. I remember that I had been wearing my favorite Tyrolean hat and when we were ready to go home, my hat had disappeared. It is funny how attached one can get to a silly hat. We looked everywhere but to my consternation, we couldn't find it. Years later, my aunt wrote me that they had found my hat in their boxes when they unpacked them in Mexico!

A few days later I was put on the train to join my parents in Vienna. Although I had always enjoyed Vienna when my parents used to take me, I was frightened and disheartened to see the swastikas everywhere: flags on buildings, in the streets, and on Nazi pins worn by men and women. What had happened to the cultured Austrians? They turned out to be more reactionary and fanatic than the Germans! For when the Germans marched into Vienna they were received with flowers and open arms. It was no "invasion" as they claimed later. The salute *"Heil Hitler"* was on many lips.

My parents had rented a room in the apartment of another Jewish family. It was near where my mother's youngest sister, Franzi, lived with her husband and her daughter Uti, whom I loved dearly. Yet I found no joy or peace there. Our apartment was situated just below some Nazi offices, and I was frightened to death every time I heard the booted steps stomping up and down the stairs. I woke up crying out every night.

◆   ◆   ◆

Recently I watched a documentary about a Polish Jew who had survived the Holocaust. He spoke movingly about how the feeling of anticipating danger had been seared into his consciousness his entire life. His words resonated deeply within me. I, too, have internalized this constant fear that something bad might happen at any time. One of my greatest regrets in life has been my inability to enjoy the present moment without worrying about the future.

CHAPTER FOUR

From then on, all we could think about was getting out of the country. But where would we go? I think the first country we thought of was Australia. Franzi and her family were emigrating there, so of course I was all in favor of going where Uti was going.

As we soon learned, nothing was easy; we were unable to get a visa for Australia. Oddly enough, New Zealand would have given us a visa if my father had been a watchmaker!

The next country to be considered was Mexico; again this was where my aunt and uncle Jawitz, my mother's sister and her husband and their children Heini and Elfi were going. However, it was yet another disappointment. The United States was not an option. I found out later from my mother that my father didn't want to go there because he feared that where there had once been Prohibition there could be Prohibition again. This would not have been good for my father, since he was a distiller by profession. After many difficulties, a friend of a friend was able to obtain some tourist visas to Uruguay. A tourist visa was not what we were looking for. After all, we wanted to stay permanently. But apparently this was the only thing we could get and in their desperation, my parents accepted. Of course with a tourist visa we had to travel like we were wealthy tourists. First of all we had to buy a round trip ticket to show the Uruguayan authorities that we could go back if they didn't accept us as permanent residents. Second, we had to travel first class on a luxury liner to keep up the pretense that we were simply tourists. My parents chose an Italian ship, *"Conte Grande"* and booked two first class cabins. The date of departure from Genoa, Italy, was February 14, 1939.

The time we had left in Vienna was spent in preparation, fear and farewells. Parting from my cousin Uti (Ruth) was very sad for me and we exchanged gifts and cried a lot. We wondered if we would every see each other again.

What would await us in Uruguay, a country so far away from everything we loved and knew? "Is that the country with all the sheep?" Edi Bonyhady, my mother's cousin, asked. It turned out that he ended up with many more sheep, since he went to Australia. Many other family members emigrated there as well.

It was quite unbelievable what this little wallpaper-hanger, Hitler, did to our family, to millions of people. My mother's oldest sister, Irene Fleischman, and her husband were killed in the gas chambers. The youngest son of my mother's sister Mira was killed while trying to escape from a concentration camp. My father's whole family who lived in Slovakia, were killed. The rest of my mother's family were dispersed in Australia, South America, North America and Israel.

It was my mother who said that it was not enough to simply go to another country in Europe. "We should go across the ocean, as far away as possible," she said when the Nazis invaded Austria. In response, Richa Kraus told her, as so many Jews did in Europe, that she should not drive the men crazy: when it was time to leave, everyone would leave. Unfortunately, she and her husband together with their youngest son Fritzl, died in a concentration camp. The other children of the Kraus family managed to get to the United States.

Three days before our departure to Genoa, I became sick with a very bad case of flu. I had a high fever, a bad head cold and congestion. My ears hurt and I coughed constantly. My mother was worried about me and said they did not dare to travel with me in this condition, as I might get pneumonia. The last evening before our departure, I was still running a fever. The doctor, who was also Jewish, told my parents to wrap me up in blankets and take me.

"This could be your only and last chance to escape," he warned.

With great trepidation they took me on the overnight train to Genoa. They were afraid that in Vienna they would not let us on the train if they knew that I was sick, so they made me walk as normally as possible. I was dressed in layers, with a heavy winter coat, hat, and scarf over my mouth. It was snowing and quite cold. When we finally got on the train they put me to bed right away. I was shaking from the fever and the fear.

My parents shared that fear. They still had to pass all the border inspections by the Germans. They were not allowed more than a small amount of money, and any jewelry had to be turned over to the Nazis. Of course we were also traveling with a passport that had a big red J (standing for Jew) stamped in it. My father, who was honest and careful to a fault, had forbidden my mother to keep any jewelry. She, however, didn't want to part with her engagement ring or the diamond pin, which my father had given her. Without telling my father, she took the two pieces and wrapped them tightly into a paper ball, around which she wound knitting yarn. She then started knitting a garment, wrapping it with the needles around the yarn ball. It was a good thing she kept this secret to herself. My father would have died a thousand deaths, waiting to be discovered.

Thank God the inspections went well, and we arrived without any problems in Genoa. We checked into a hotel and I was put to bed again. The next morning we had to embark on our voyage into the unknown. We asked the taxi driver to take us around Genoa on the way to the harbor, so we could see at least a little of the city. After all, we thought, we would never step on European soil again.

The ship was beautiful. The first class accommodations (which we had been forced to buy) were lovely. My mother and I shared a cabin and my father had the other one. When we departed, everybody was on deck looking one more time at what we were leaving behind forever. I looked like a mummy wrapped in all the clothes and scarves with which my mother had dressed me. I was still running a fever. The band played and most of us had tears in our eyes. I stood at the rail holding my parents hands very tightly.

I did not fully understand at that time, but today I consider everybody to be courageous who had to leave everything behind and take off to places unknown. Of course this same experience is still shared today by so many immigrants and refugees who have to leave their country because of political persecution or dreams of financial and cultural improvement.

All in all, in spite of the melancholy and misgivings that enveloped us all, the voyage was a pleasant one. My mother's Italian came in very handy. She was the only one able to speak with the staff on the ship and this was very helpful.

Finally over my flu, I was soon running the decks with other children my age. Most of the passengers were Jewish refugees from Austria and Germany, so we all had something in common. However, my poor mother was seasick most of the time and kept to the cabin.

When we crossed the Equator there was a big party with somebody dressed up as Neptune who then baptized us all. In the evening there was a formal dinner-dance. My father wore his tuxedo (strangely enough he had packed his tuxedo and his tails!) and looked as handsome as ever, in my eyes, like a prince. My mother, fortunately feeling better, wore a lovely long blue gown. I was allowed to attend and I had a new dress that my mother had bought for me in Vienna. It was very pale salmon-colored silk. These were our last good days for a long time to come.

Our first stop in South America was Bahia in Brazil, and Carnival had just started. Carnival in Brazil is a time when people lose all their inhibitions. They go crazy with the desire to have a good time. The masses go into the streets dressed in their fancy costumes, armed with their "*Lanza Perfume*" bottles. These are spray bottles filled with a very strong ether-like perfume, which they try to spray into peoples' eyes and onto their necks. Of course everybody had to wear plastic eye protectors. Later on these spray bottles were strictly forbidden.

It was a shocking experience: Here we were, just off the ship trying to go sightseeing and instead we had to wade through a sea of aggressive merrymakers. My father led us with his arms wrapped around us, trying to keep people from pushing us around. Needless to say, we cut our tour short and were happy to be back in the safety of the ship. Of course we thought that this was the way it was everywhere in South America. Scary thought indeed!

The next port we landed at was Rio de Janeiro, a beautiful city. Approaching it by sea, it seemed like a beautiful dream: the "*Pao de Azucar*" (Sugar Loaf) and the "*Corcovado*" with the big cross on top, standing as sentinels over the city. It was a magnificent view. We went sightseeing and were very impressed with the wonderful beaches, the big avenues, the parks and botanical garden. There were also the very poor sections called *favelas*. These *favelas* were situated on hills with a magnificent view and very near the expensive neighborhoods. This made crime very easy. Even today, the problem has not been solved but has become worse, for there are too many poor people.

The ship that carried us to freedom. In the middle you can
see me, my mother and my father.

PART II
URUGUAY

◆

1939–1966

CHAPTER ONE

On February 28, 1939 we arrived in Montevideo, Uruguay. We were met at the pier by our friends Hanni Lustig and her husband, the Steiners, as well as two brothers of my mother, David and Ignaz Stoessl, all of whom had arrived a month before us. They had been in the new country for four weeks already and were familiar with this foreign place. We were so lucky I thought to myself, they are all going to take care of us. Although my heart had been threatening to jump out from fear of being in a strange place, I was now comforted, that we were not alone in this new adventure. Fortunately, I didn't know that a few days earlier, refugees arriving on a ship to Cuba were not allowed to disembark there because their visas were not in order. Those poor Jews had been forced to return to Europe and a certain death.

Standing at the pier, our friends and my uncles were sick with fear that something like this could happen to our ship in Uruguay. It felt like an eternity passed before the authorities finally allowed us off the ship and we fell into the arms of my uncles and our friends. As we were ready to get into the two cars waiting for us, some men stopped us and said that since we had two cameras, we were not allowed to bring them into the country without paying a high custom duty. So my father decided to leave the two expensive cameras in the customs office and deal with them later.

Everyone with all our luggage got into the taxis and we traveled with pounding hearts through downtown Montevideo, to Pocitos, a lovely suburb by the sea. From the harbor, our route went through the old city with its narrow streets and old buildings until we came to the main square, the "*Plaza de Independencia*." The square, surrounded by palm trees, had a statue of General Jose Gervasio Artigas, one of the independence fighters of Uruguay, sitting on a horse in the center of the square. The buildings around the square housed the *Teatro* Solis, a beautiful old theater, which Darwin was said to have visited on his travels. Amidst the smaller ornate buildings, there was only one high-rise, "The *Palacio* Salvo," which had offices on the first floor, apartments on the others. On the street level there was a big coffee house called Sorocabana, which was always very crowded; Uruguayans love their little espressos. From this square we traveled along the longest and biggest business street, "18 de Julio," to the beautiful *Bulevar* Artigas, a lovely wide boulevard, with big, beautiful homes on both sides. This boulevard was pretty enough to be in Paris. From there, the taxi went down the *Bulevar Espana* down to Pocitos. My first impression of the city was that it held great promise but I think I was the only one looking out the window. My parents and uncles had too much to say to each other to pay attention.

We were taken to a house where our friends had rented a room for us. Our landlords were a Jewish couple from Dresden, Germany, by the name of Jordan. They had three children, a girl two years older than I, and five-year-old identical twin boys. The Jordans were renting out two rooms, one to another Jewish couple who had arrived on the same ship we did. However, we had never seen them because they were traveling second-class. Their name was Neuhaus and they had a daughter two years younger than I, called Trude. I immediately made friends with the Jordan's daughter Uschi and Trude Neuhaus. We all got to bed late that night, as there was so much to talk about. I remember how hot it was and that I could hear music and merrymaking from people in the streets celebrating carnival.

The following days were full of surprises, with so many new impressions. Such a different culture from what I was used to. The people were happy, especially since it was Carnival. We were all worried about the future, yet we still breathed a sigh of relief. We were among friendly people in a peaceful country.

At that time Uruguay was the most peaceful country in Latin America. They had not had a revolution in 100 years, and it was the most democratic of all the Latin-American countries. The population was mainly Spanish and Italian descendants, and as I learned later, there were practically no native Indians left. They had been killed early on as Europeans settled there.

All our friends and my uncles lived in our neighborhood in different rentals, so we met quite often, going to coffeehouses on the beach and taking walks along the *Rambla*, which was the wide street that ran along the beach with houses, hotels and restaurants on the other side.

It was on the *Rambla* that the Carnival celebrants walked and met their friends and made new conquests. This promenade also went on every Sunday after church. If you wanted to meet your friends, you would surely find them there between 11:00 am and 1:00 pm on Sundays.

Carnival was being celebrated all over the city. There were parades along the 18 de Julio, the *Rambla* and other main streets, each day on another street. In *Pocitos* and other suburbs were "*Tabladas*," which were stages erected on the streets where they had shows and dances in the evening. My parents let me go with the other children to the ones nearest to our house. The performers were mainly black people, who had come to Uruguay from Africa or Brazil many years ago and their little children who had a wonderful African rhythm. I thought it was quite impressive how the children beat their drums. What a different life, after the difficult time and horrendous experiences we had just gone through!

As it was summer, the beaches were crowded and very colorful with the different sun umbrellas. Although it looked like the ocean, the water along the beach was really the River Plate, which runs into the Atlantic Ocean further east. The river is so wide at that point that you cannot see anything on the horizon, just like the open ocean. The beaches in Uruguay were beautiful and ran continuously all along the southern coastline.

The climate was subtropical, quite warm and sometimes humid. In the evening people would sit in front of their houses on the steps or on the sidewalks and drink *Mate*, a tea similar to green tea, which was passed from person to person as each drank out of the same hollowed-out gourd. These gourds were lacquered with silver rims and had very fancy figures etched on them. The tea was drunk through a straw-like utensil made out of hammered silver, and I was a little shocked at the fact that not only families but strangers would drink out of the same straw. The hot water would be refilled into the gourd and passed on.

My father started to learn Spanish immediately. After all, he needed to look for a job soon and he needed to speak the language. He would sit for hours in our room and write vocabulary words into a copybook. He was so dedicated, my poor, wonderful father; he would not be without a job for long, and he knew what job he wanted. He was going to work for *Oyama,* the biggest distillery in Uruguay. I think that by now he had regained some of the optimism he had lost entirely during the last year, but maybe he just tried to be brave for us.

For some immigrants it was a difficult battle to secure a job or get back to the career they had in the old country. Physicians, dentists and attorneys were not allowed to practice without passing examinations in their profession, and that would take a long time. In the meantime, they would sell hot dogs on the beach, deliver milk from house to house, sell ice cream on the street and beaches, taking whatever work they could find. What a letdown it must have been after their established lives in Europe, but nevertheless they were all grateful to do this in a free country.

It turned out there were quite a few German/Austrian refugees who, having left in the early '30s, were able to bring all their assets with them. They lived in nice homes and either had a good business or lived off their dividends.

One of the interesting customs of Uruguayan men was that in the summer they would go outside wearing only their pajamas and Chevalier straw hats! I saw them walking on the street and going downtown in buses or cars. It was so strange to me. In winter, you could tell the immigrant from the native since only the immigrant would wear a raincoat! The Uruguayans had umbrellas, but really preferred to stay home when it rained. School children were excused from school when it rained as well. The rains were really not that bad, but those were the customs at that time. I guess with the coming of the foreigners, many things changed, or maybe it was only that times would have changed them anyway. As far as I remember, these particular customs stopped in the early '40s.

As in other Hispanic countries, shops and offices closed from 12:00 p.m. to 2:30 p.m. for siesta and then reopened until 7:00 p.m. Dinner would not be before 8:00 or 8:30 p.m. and in summer the children would be kept up until quite late, just like in Spain.

In March I started school. It was three blocks from where we lived, so I walked with the other children from the Jordan household. Because I didn't know Spanish, they decided to have me repeat a year, and I went back into third grade. There was another German girl in my class, who had arrived six months earlier, and already knew Spanish well enough to be my translator. After three months I spoke Spanish fairly well and was able to fend for myself. What a relief it was to be participating in class instead of just sitting there without knowing what was going on! How elated I was to answer questions and do my homework. I was able to speak to my classmates and laugh at their jokes. I was finally one of the kids. However, internally, I reflected the apprehension of my parents in that I worried constantly about getting established in our new country.

After a few months we moved to a hotel, which had been bought by the Neuhaus family who had been living in the same house as us. The hotel was situated across the street from the beach, a lovely location with a wonderful view. My parents and I shared a large room with a balcony, and I thought things were looking up. We settled into a very pleasant routine. School, homework and play with all the children in the hotel. We really had a wonderful time. What a difference from Pernegg, where I was the only child and forced to be with grownups all the time!

The only bleak times were listening to the news every evening. One of the German Jews living in the hotel had bought radio time and gave us all the international news in German every evening at 7:00 pm. It was always terrible news, scary news. What was happening to the world? Sometimes it seemed as if Hitler and his henchmen would conquer the whole world.

My father was progressing with his Spanish and getting ready for his interview with the people at *Oyama*. Somebody advised him to put his money (the little that we were allowed to take out) into a foreign bank. One day my mother came home and said that she had heard that that bank was having problems.

"Dear, I've heard that people are taking their money out, they don't trust that the bank will remain open."

"Yes, darling," my father said reassuringly. "I shall think about it and see what else to do with our money. Try not to worry."

The next day he went to the *Oyama* interview and showed them how to make Scotch. They were delighted and offered him a job on the spot. He came home very happy and that evening we celebrated his new career. With new prosperity in sight, the next day my parents went out and rented a large, old-Spanish house. We were ready to start a new life. I hadn't felt so secure in some time.

However, before my father was able to start work, he woke up one morning feeling sick. When he tried to get up, he felt dizzy and lethargic. He ran a fever and was so tired he could barely sit up. Over the next day or two, the doctors were unable to diagnose what was wrong and decided that he should go to the hospital to have some tests. My mother tried to hide how worried she was, and I had no idea of the seriousness of my father's condition.

As I was running out to go to school that morning, my mother called me back to tell me that my father was going to the hospital.

"Don't you want to kiss your Daddy goodbye?" she asked.

That was an easy answer: of course I did. I kissed him and gave him a hug, saying, "I'll see you later, Daddy and tell you all about my day."

"Good, *Putzilein*" (this is what he called me) he replied, tenderly. "I shall look forward to it."

I ran out the door, not too worried and anxious to be at school with my friends. I only found out later what happened. My dear, wonderful father suffered a brain embolism on the way to the hospital. He was in serious condition by the time he arrived. Since he was unable to speak or move, my mother kept me away from the hospital, not wanting me to see him in such a bad state. She sent me to stay with Lacy and Clara Steiner, just telling me that my father was going to stay in the hospital for longer than they had thought, but not to worry. I was anxious with the news, but tried to think positively.

Unfortunately, the sanitary conditions in the hospital were substandard which made my poor father very uncomfortable and his condition deteriorated quickly. The doctors decided that he had blood poisoning of unknown origin, and since antibiotics were not yet on the market in 1939 there was no way to treat it. In addition his heart had been weakened by the overwhelming fear and humiliations brought on by the Nazi occupation in Austria.

Two days later, Lacy woke me up and said, "You are not going to school today; your father has gone to heaven and your mother needs you."

I was stunned. I could barely breathe from the shock. The tears started to fall and I must have cried an hour, sobbing uncontrollably. In the background, I overheard Clara admonish Lacy "You should not have told her like that, for God's sake!"

"But," he replied in astonishment, "I had no idea that she would understand it and react this way."

Hearing that made me angry, I was ten years old. What on earth did grown-ups think children couldn't understand? My life felt like it was over. It was exactly six months to the day since our arrival in Uruguay. I was devastated. I could not comprehend what had happened. I had just seen him and kissed him a couple of days ago! In a rush, all my newfound sense of security vanished, leaving me feeling hollow and disconnected.

I ran back to our room at the hotel and found my mother in bed sobbing. I could not help myself, I started to cry again and we lay on the bed together, holding each other tightly, trying to comfort ourselves. We stayed like this for a very long time, and I told my mother not to worry, I would always take care of her. I certainly tried to do this all my life.

Overnight I lost my childhood and shouldered a load of responsibility. I knew with a sinking heart, that things would never be the same again. I already missed my father terribly; he was the best and most loving father and I adored him. The idea of no longer being a normal family bound together by a strong love and respect for each other was staggering. I knew I would soon miss much more. Where would we be without our great protector who had taken care of us and had worked so hard to keep us safe in such a dangerous world? What would I do without the man into whose arms I ran when I was scared or when I was disappointed? I adored my mother, but my relationship with my father was a special one. He had always made me feel so loved and cherished. With his death, I felt that I was not special anymore. I terribly worried that people were going to look down on me because I no longer had a father. My fears were not so farfetched. It turned out, in the years to come, that some people did look down on us because they viewed us as poor and helpless.

Suddenly, my mother found herself in a new country where she did not speak the language and no longer had her loving husband and provider. We soon suffered more heartbreak: The bank in which we had our small bit of money went bankrupt. We were left penniless with little resources. We had a few valuables we had brought from Austria, including the two cameras that we had gotten back from customs. My mother had no choice but to sell them, we were desperate for money. She found a Jewish man who promised to sell them for us quickly, which relieved us a little. Unfortunately, not only did he fail to do so, he ended up in jail! He had taken things from other people as well as from us and had pawned them. The police had all those articles, but demanded that we pay for them if we wanted to have them back. Even the police were taking advantage of a woman and child alone! Of course we did not have the money to buy them back, so we just lost them.

Once again I became fearful and apprehensive about our survival. The world continued to be a scary place, with corruption and degradation not confined to one country or political system. In my short life I had seen and experienced just how dangerous life could be and a bone-deep anxiety settled within me.

CHAPTER TWO

We moved out of the hotel and into the big old house that my parents had rented before my father's death. The two of us lived in the upper floor of a two-story Spanish style house. A Uruguayan family lived on the ground level and we shared a light shaft with them. Most Uruguayan older houses were built with a movable glass roof (*claraboya*). We could crank open the glass roof when we wanted sun and air to come in. The family below us had an awning, which they could open and close in order to keep the sun out or, in case we did not close the roof before it started to rain, to keep the water out. The movable glass roof was over the back hall of our floor. A six-foot wall erected around the opening made it impossible to look down on them, yet we received all the sounds and smells from below. I can't say that there was much privacy. It was certainly not an ideal situation, but it had its advantages. We were fortunate the family below was quite nice. They even promised to watch out for me when I was home alone.

By that time the crates in which we had packed china, silver, books, linen, and our smaller belongings arrived from Austria. My uncles helped us unpack them and having been packed by uncle Ignaz, many pieces of china arrived broken. My uncles, not wanting my mother to know the damage, decided to throw the broken pieces into the garbage. Thus, initially, we had no idea what had happened to them. We also discovered that all the silver flatware was missing. We had packed them, and the only explanation for their loss was that the people of the shipping company in Vienna stole them! It seemed that we suffered one trial after another.

We needed furniture, so my mother went to auctions, where she could buy pieces cheaply. We then hired an immigrant to refinish the pieces that needed it most. I can still remember the strong smell of the varnish permeating the hall for days while he worked.

When my mother finally felt the house was furnished satisfactorily, she decided it was time to take in boarders. She felt that it would be easier to rent out the rooms without board. The renters were mostly refugees like us and were happy to find a place to live. However, it was not ideal. We all had to share one bathroom, so it was important to get along. The only hot water came from a small electric heater installed on the shower. There was not enough warm water to heat a bath, and the sink had only cold water. Luckily I could go to the Steiners, who had since moved to a nice house nearby, to take a bath once a week.

Our refugee boarders soon found their own lives and moved out, thus the character of the people renting our rooms changed completely. Since the house was just two blocks from one of the nice beaches (Pocitos), we attracted vacation people from neighboring Argentina. These vacationers would always be recommended by somebody we knew, but sometimes we encountered unsavory characters, which had to be evicted by my mother.

Of course all this was not enough to ease my mother's worry about the way to support us. All of a sudden, she went from being a well-cared-for and cherished wife and mother to having to agonize about how to put the next meal on the table. She was truly remarkable in her determination, perhaps that same determination which had given her the strength to swim the entire width of the Woerthersee. She ironed men's shirts, did manicures, wrote correspondence for the German-speaking immigrants, and even sold gloves and hosiery from door to door. One day she confessed that she would go around the block four times before getting up the courage to ring a bell! Several times a week she would take the bus and go downtown to the markets where groceries and vegetables were cheaper. I can still see her carrying a heavy bag in each hand, trudging back home. Each night she fell into bed exhausted.

The fear, that I would now lose my mother and stay alone, was all-consuming. The frightening monster would raise its ugly head at any moment and make me weak and depressed. What would I do without my wonderful mother, who so loved me and supported me? She was always available to me in spite of her many worries and responsibilities. I could tell her anything and she would listen, doing her best to advise me in my deliberations. She was a wise woman, who knew what to say and what not to say. Rarely did I so anger her that she would be moved to slap me. One time being when I had spilled ink on a beautiful chair she had just bought. It destroyed the chair and all my mother could think of was the good money she had lost because of my clumsiness. It was horrible for me to be punished like this for an accident and I cried a lot. But as soon as my mother rid herself of her terrible anger, she would feel very sorry and apologize, saying that she was so anxious with all the things she had on her mind. Nonetheless, my mother was my protector, my friend and confidant, and I was never as frank with any of my friends as I was with my mother. One of the greatest gifts she gave me was that she rarely reproached me for my feelings, allowing me to have them and express them without fear of condemnation.

My mother was working hard and I could see she missed my father terribly. I, being the ten year old but going on forty, pushed her to visit with her friends who lived a few blocks from us. So this became our routine every evening after I went to bed:

"Are you sure you will be alright, dear?"

To which I would answer invariably: "Yes mother, I want you to see your friends. You need that. Go, have fun."

However, once she left, I was out of bed in a flash, running down the stairs to make sure that the front door was locked. This I repeated three or four times each night because I was never sure I hadn't accidentally re-opened the lock when I last checked it. Then I would go back to bed and start to pray: "Dear God, please let my mother come home soon!" over and over until I put myself to sleep with the repetition of my prayer. If my dear mother had known!

Those were hard times, although eventually life got better when my mother met a friend from Austria with whom she opened a boutique on a nice street in Pocitos. Though, her partner put up the money, my mother did most of the work. Her partner rarely showed up, leaving my mother alone most of the time. She did the buying, selling, accounting and very often she decorated the showcases and windows. She was constantly busy and tied down to the boutique, so she would run between the store and the house taking care of different chores. Even when my poor mother had the shingles with horrible pain, she could not stay at home. Fortunately the doctor came to the boutique to give her some injections so the pain would be bearable. I am still amazed at my mother's dedication, courage and devotion. She never shirked her responsibilities and became an enduring role model for me.

In the meantime my two uncles set up a leather glove-manufacturing factory and started to do quite well. They bought a car and were able to live in better quarters. The Steiners were able to buy their new house, as Laci was very successful in an import/export business.

Because his mother and Clara's parents, the Brauns, could not get a visa to Uruguay at the time the Steiners did, they remained in Austria waiting for some way to escape. Finally they were forced to go to Shanghai, China, a path many refugees had to take to get out of Europe, and from there they eventually were able to come to Uruguay. We were all so elated to see them and had a big celebration in their honor. They all moved into the Steiner house, which fortunately was large enough to accommodate all six family members!

◆   ◆   ◆

About three years after my father's death, when we were still in our first house, my mother met a wonderful man. It probably was through her correspondence work. He was a very cultured, good-looking Czech Jew, who somehow had been able to get most of his money out in time. Before immigrating he had been an attorney and among his clients was Richard Strauss, the famous composer, for whom he worked in relation with his copyrights.

Alexander Singer was an instant success with me. He was funny and kind, and he adored my mother—and my mother liked him very much. He spent a lot of time with us, once taking us to a symphony concert, which was my first. They played Beethoven's Ninth Symphony and Ravel's Bolero. Afterwards he hummed the most important parts to me and I have remembered them ever since. He often took us to restaurants and we really had a good time. His wife had died of cancer when they first arrived in Uruguay and he was thinking of marrying my mother. My mother started to smile again and I could see she was happy. He certainly had my blessings. However, before this could happen, he died suddenly of a heart attack. It was another devastating blow to my mother and to me as well.

Always worried about my mother's wellbeing, I wished with all my heart for her to meet somebody else who was nice. She was only 42 years of age and deserved a little happiness. I would often say to her "If I only could get you married off!" Sadly, my wishes never came true. She never married again. She could never find another man like my father or Alex Singer. In spite of all this, my mother was a person who laughed easily being pleasant to be with.

After I had been in public school a year, I was 11 years old and my mother decided that it was time that I learned English. So she sent me to a private school, the Anderson Academy, two blocks from our first house, where English was one of the subjects.

This too was a very different experience for me. In public school I had to wear a white apron dress with a blue bow. The Anderson Academy had beautiful blue uniforms with a white blouse and an emblem. I was quite proud to be in that school, but private school was expensive, and we needed my uncles and Laci Steiner to help with the tuition. They would make my mother ask for it every month, which wasn't very nice. Nevertheless I learned English quite fast and enjoyed my schoolmates.

On weekends in the summer we would go to the beach; if my uncles picked us up in their car we would go to Carrasco, a nicer and more exclusive beach. We could also take the bus, but they were always terribly crowded and we had to stand the whole way for 30 minutes. Coming back in the evening it was even worse; people would hang like grapes from the bus. Nevertheless, Montevideo was a city where one could live quite well without a lot of money or a car. The transit system was very good, going from east to west and south to north, but often overloaded. One could stay on the beach all day without paying a penny, and food was not expensive.

My uncle David, who had divorced his first wife with whom he had a son, Ernesto, was dating a very pretty young German refugee by the name of Eva Wasserreich, who had come with her parents from Berlin where her father had been a prosperous businessman. Now her father was selling butter from door to door! My uncle's hobby was horseback riding, and with his factory taking off, he was able to afford a car and to join an equestrian club. He taught Eva to ride also and they went riding every weekend in winter, but in summer they loved to go to the beach. As the club was near Carrasco and the best beach happened to be there as well, we sometimes had the opportunity to get a ride in their car to Carrasco.

David and Eva eventually got married and moved into an apartment near her parents. We often had meals together, especially for the Jewish holy days. My uncle would often say to me, a twelve-year old, "Children should be seen but not heard." Or, "You keep quiet, you are too young to participate in this discussion." Such comments did not encourage me to be outgoing.

On Sundays during the winter, I would take Dorita Steiner, "my little sister" to a movie in our neighborhood, where we would see three movies from 1:00 pm until 6:00 pm. Sometimes my mother and I would go to visit friends who had a farm about an hour from Montevideo. They had a large home and decided to make it into a coffeehouse. In addition, they rented rooms to people who wanted to stay for a weekend or longer on vacation. People enjoyed this lovely country setting and the word got out, so a very nice group of mainly Austrian refugees would be regular guests.

I loved these outings. The owners of the farm, the Ebels, refugees from Germany, had two children, a boy two years younger and a girl, Uschi, of my age. We would run around on the farm and play all kinds of games that we invented. Uschi and I became very good friends for many years, and I visited her in Sao Paulo, where she moved later and got married.

We were friendly with our tenants, the Steins, who had a little girl and a Dachshund. After a while the husband got a job as a head croupier in a casino in *Punta del Este*. This was the most prestigious resort in Uruguay where many wealthy Argentinians and Uruguayans had their summer homes. They invited me to stay with them for a while, and I went to spend the *Carnival* with them. Their house was on the wrong side of the tracks and quite primitive, but I had a grand time.

Punta del Este is a peninsula with a beach on each side and is the point where the river Plate meets the Atlantic Ocean. One beach was called Morning Beach since it was very calm and lovely to swim. The other side, being the ocean side, was the wild beach, which was where people went to see and be seen. In the morning we would go to the calm beach, then go home for lunch and a siesta. Then we'd go back to town and Mr. Stein would smuggle me into the casino. I was twelve or thirteen years old then and the minimum age of admittance in the afternoon was 15. The first time I walked into the casino, I was very excited, yet also afraid of being discovered. Inside, I couldn't believe how beautiful everything was: the elegant rooms with the chandeliers, the fashionable people and the rich atmosphere. It was very different from today's casinos, one of the main differences being that there were no slot machines. I was shocked to see how easily people lost big amounts of money.

Since it was *Carnival* time, there was a costume party to which the Steins took me. My mother had bought me a white Russian hussar outfit with its traditional hat at a second hand store. It was trimmed with red, which, I thought, was very pretty. I insisted that pictures be taken so my mother could see me and I had a wonderful time. It was a great trip and I came home with many stories to tell my mother.

The next summer, when I was 13 years old, mother sent me to a children's camp run by a German woman who was a minister and very good with children. Most of the children were German and Austrian refugees from age 10 to 16. I found this a wonderful place. The girls all slept in one room and the boys in another. We had to obey orders but we also had some freedom. We played volleyball, walked, and swam in the nearby lake. I was allowed to take the horse and buggy to the village to fetch the mail and do some errands. This made me feel very grown-up until the moment I had to stop the buggy. I was supposed to tie the horse's front legs together so he wouldn't take off while I was doing my errands. However, this presented quite a problem because the horse did not want to keep his legs still. Here I was, a young girl squatting in front of a horse saying, "Good horsy nice horsy, please keep still!" I noticed people around me, but I didn't want to ask for help. I guess I was too shy and too proud. After much cajoling, I finally caught him with both legs together! Despite this, I didn't lose my enthusiasm and after a few days things went much better.

The next year when I arrived at this camp, everybody was very excited. There was a German-speaking actress from Buenos Aires, who was producing Shakespeare's Midsummer Night's Dream in German. The young people were the actors, and the roles had already been given out. Because there were more girls than boys, some of the men's roles were going to girls. I was desolate that I had not been there in time to participate, when suddenly the girl who was supposed to play Lysander became ill. There was only one week left before the play and everybody was worried. Hedwig Schlichter, the actress, asked me if I could learn a long role in such a short time and I said yes. I got the part of Lysander and was very happy and excited. I studied the part whenever I could and went to rehearsals already knowing most of it. There was a boy I secretly liked who was playing Demetrius. One day I noticed him looking at me. Oh goody, I thought, he is finally noticing me! He smiled and said:

"Hey, you are really perfect to play a man's role, you are so flat." I was devastated and near tears, but I laughed and through my teeth I said:

"Thank you, you are very handsome too." I lowered my eyes looking for the nearest hole I could crawl into.

Finally the big day arrived and my mother and the other parents came to watch the play, which was done in the open among the trees and bushes. It was a wonderful success, an experience that I still cherish all these years later.

◆   ◆   ◆

The Anderson Academy had only 6 grades, and when I finished them at age thirteen my mother enrolled me in the Crandon Institute. This was an American school where half the subjects were taught in Spanish and half in English. That way I could really learn English well. Again Laci Steiner and my uncles had to help with the tuition, and again my mother had to put aside her pride and ask for the money every month.

I loved my new school, made a lot of new friends, including Hanna Elsbach. We became friendly with her aunt and uncle with whom she lived, and when they suggested that we rent a very nice house together, we were happy to agree. Hanna was a few months younger than I and was just the friend I had always been looking for. She was smart, friendly and very loyal. She was pretty, but was having her teeth straightened. Something I also needed to have done, but we did not have the money for orthodontics.

From then on things got much better. Not only did we move into a better and nicer house, we did not have to rent out so many rooms and I had my friend Hanna in the same house. We became close friends, went to school together each morning, were in the same class and came home together in the afternoon. She had a wonderful talent for writing and after much cajoling she even wrote an essay for me for school. We had so much to talk about that we felt we never had enough time. When we came home we had to do our homework separately; dinner we also ate separately. But whenever it came time to go to bed, it seemed there was always something we still needed to discuss. One night I sneaked downstairs into her room to have an important discussion. Unfortunately her aunt wanted to check on her, and when I heard her coming, I jumped into Hanna's bed to hide. Knowing that it was unlikely that I'd be able to climb back up the stairs unseen, we started to plan how I could make a retreat without being caught. It took quite a while until I felt safe enough to go back up, and then we started to laugh; realizing that I had ended up coming downstairs only to talk about how I would get back upstairs again!

World War II didn't completely by-pass our pleasant little country. When the German warship, the *Graf Spee*, was in our waters and was destroyed by an English warship, we could see the battle from the beach. We saw the *Graf Spee* break out in fire and cheered. There were also American warships, which frequently docked in Montevideo and the city and parks would be crowded with American sailors. When we girls would meet them on the street or in the park we would tell them how proud and grateful we were to the U.S. and to them in particular. It was a good opportunity to practice our English, and some of the sailors were very cute.

Life settled into a pleasant routine; my mother's boutique went quite well, and she became a Uruguayan citizen. I had to wait for citizenship until I was 18 years old, but I was very pleased that we were now officially accepted. I never felt any anti-Semitism; swastikas or Nazi propaganda of any kind was strictly forbidden and Uruguayans really didn't know what a Jew was. The Jews who had arrived earlier, in 1890's or 1900's, were mostly from Turkey and other Mideastern Countries, and were called the Turks. They owned large textile and fashion stores and were completely assimilated as we had been in Austria.

However, the Holocaust was upon us. We heard all kinds of awful, terrifying stories about concentration camps and mass murders. I had nightmares, I was nervous, and when I was 15, the deep-seated anxiety I had carried with me since my father's death increased to such a degree that I started to have trouble sleeping. This insomnia has stayed with me all my life.

In the summer, my mother and I would sometimes go to a resort area called Piriapolis, where some friends of ours managed a hotel. It was a beautiful spot, with the ocean, little hills and woods. It was not as fancy as Punta del Este, but we liked it very much. There were a lot of refugees and we made friends with many of them. For some reason, one of the things I liked most was the sound of horses' hooves in front of our hotel each morning. It was a peaceful sound to me so I decided I wanted to learn how to ride. There was an older German, the father of somebody we knew, who gave riding lessons and my mother agreed to let me take a few lessons. It was wonderful to be on a horse, although I was scared of falling off. The instructor walked next to me giving me instructions, and I started to learn how to trot and gallop. After a few days, he once again showed me that there shouldn't be any space between my pelvis and the saddle. When he put his hand on me to show me that there was too much space, I was so shocked I decided that I would not take any more lessons from him!

One time, coming back on an open bus from Piriapolis, we had a bad accident. My mother was sitting by the window and suffered many injuries. My first thought when I looked at her was: "Oh my God, there is so much blood, she must be badly hurt!" Sitting in the back of the bus was a friend of ours, a Dutch Jew, named Theo Levy; he, his sister and nephew had been our companions many times in Piriapolis and they were good company. Theo, who had jumped out of the bus from the back, was standing at the door and was the first one to come to our aid. We helped my mother out of the bus and he put us into a passing car to take us to a hospital. He promised he would take care of our luggage and take it to his home. At the hospital they found that the blood was coming from a wound on her head, which they said was not serious. However she had suffered a lot of contusions on her arm and a small fracture in her foot. They did all the necessary first aid and sent us home, where she was laid up for a while with a lot of pain. My poor mother; she never drove a car herself but was in so many car accidents! Still, she was very lucky: the passenger sitting in front of her was killed.

My mother, being out of commission for the moment, asked her business partner in the boutique to pick up the luggage from Mr. Levy's house. The meeting between the two turned into a wild romance and a wedding! Who could have guessed we would have turned out to be matchmakers!

The war ended and Montevideo went crazy. Everyone went out on the streets and sang and danced. We all shouted trying to compete with the noise of the car horns. We were all beside ourselves, and we, the refugees, thanked the Lord for the Allies winning and Hitler losing.

CHAPTER THREE

My mother had always suffered a lot of back pain; one day she woke up and could not move. She was in such pain that I had to turn her in bed. I called the doctor, who fortunately made housecalls. He said she should stay in bed for a few days, that it was probably arthritis. After a few days the pain got better, but we decided that she should see a rheumatologist, who sent her for some x-ray studies. A few days later, he called her at the boutique to tell her that he wanted to see her and that she should come with a family member. My mother, fearing the worst, asked her partner to go with her. She didn't want me to hear bad news. The specialist told her that she had a disease of the spine and that she "probably had only one year to live, since one couldn't live with a spine like hers!"

I can only imagine how my mother must have felt in that office. Her partner started to cry and said that I had to be told. However, my mother did not have the courage to tell me. She postponed it from one day to the next until I insisted on knowing what was going on.

My whole body went cold, was this the moment I had so feared all this time? I couldn't and wouldn't believe this horrible verdict, with paralyzing fear in my heart, I sent her to other specialists who, fortunately, did not agree with the first one. However, the horrible threat was now deep in our hearts. I cried myself to sleep every night. I couldn't lose my mother too, dear God! I couldn't live without her! My mother would not believe the second specialist, for she was convinced she would die. For my next birthday she prepared an album with pictures from her whole life, starting with her baby photos. We fell into each other's arms and cried a lot. How can one live with yet another terrible fear? One year went by and she was still alive, thank God. The more time went on, the more optimistic we became, but there was always the fear in the back of our minds.

Then something else dreadful happened. Dorita's mother, Clara, who had traveled a lot after the war ended, committed suicide. We were stunned, but we knew that the main reason was that Dorita had started having deep depressions, blaming the genes she and her mother Clara had inherited from Clara's mother, Zora Braun (who had arrived in Montevideo, via Shanghai). Zora had committed suicide by walking into the ocean to drown in Pocitos. Her suicide was a real shock; she had seemed to be such a balanced woman. She took her life one year after her husband died of lung cancer. They had been so lucky to reach Uruguay finally and fate had again played one of its tricks. Neither of the Brauns survived very long. Clara Steiner, being herself depressed, could not live with Dorita's depression and her feelings of guilt for having "passed down" a genetic predisposition to clinical depression. Also she had never been happy in Uruguay and was always homesick for Austria. She also decided to end her life. After her death, Dorita went further into depression and had to be sent to Buenos Aires, where there were very good psychoanalysts. Fortunately after two years of treatment she was better—and so taken with psychiatry, she studied medicine in order to become a psychiatrist herself!

My 18th birthday came and aside from my coming of age and getting my Uruguayan citizenship, there were two very important things that happened that day. Finally, after many long years, we got our own private telephone! Hallelujah! Montevideo, a city of one million people, didn't have enough telephone lines and therefore the waiting time for a new telephone was "forever." If you paid a lot of money you could get it sooner, but we could not afford that. The other important event was that I received my first real kiss! What a late bloomer! Anyway, I had a lovely birthday party and one of the young men I had invited and whom I really liked a lot, took me aside and kissed me passionately. I almost swooned with the pleasure of my first kiss, and joyfully looked forward to the possibilities. Unfortunately, the relationship did not have a chance to flourish for he died soon after in a car accident.

I had finished high school, and two years of secretarial training. I was so proud and happy. The day had finally come when I could get a job. I could now help my mother financially, taking some of the burden off her shoulders. I felt that after working so hard to support us, she should be able to take it a little easier.

I started looking for a job, and through the father of a girl I knew, I was offered a position in the office of a New York stockbroker firm. I accepted immediately and felt I must surely look different to everybody: Here was a woman with a job!

My first day was the happiest day of my life so far, but I was also filled with a lot of fear; what if I couldn't do my work satisfactorily? What if I made mistakes? I had never shaken my insecurity. Thank God all my fears were unfounded; I had this job for a long time. My duties included being the assistant to the Manager, as well as helping another employee calculate the commissions on the different stock market transactions. It was very interesting and sometimes stressful but I enjoyed the bustling atmosphere. My boss was a middle-aged American, with mischievous blue eyes, always ready to joke and laugh. He had one little problem, however. He enjoyed drinking. Sometimes he would come back from lunch having had a few too many cocktails and get a little sleepy. Yet strangely enough, when he had a little to drink, he would immediately pinpoint a missing comma in my letters. He was very friendly though, and I took good care of him. When I thought he was not in the best condition to see clients, I would suggest that he take a nap, then locking his door, I would tell people he was not in. This never failed to work. He would wake up refreshed and ready to go. I settled very nicely into this job, was appreciated, received salary increases regularly and made good friends with my co-workers. Each month I proudly delivered the money to my mother.

◆   ◆   ◆

I was still underweight for those times and my mother and her friends would tell me how thin I was and that this was not attractive: a good cause for an inferiority complex! Young girls now aspire to look the way I looked then. My mother and I planned that I go to a clinic in Argentina, which specialized in weight gain and loss. The clinic was run by a German doctor who had a very good reputation, and was located near Cordoba, a town in the mountains north of Buenos Aires. It was an idyllic spot with beautiful views of green meadows and rugged mountains. The clinic, a very modern and pleasant building, was situated in the midst of a huge park with lovely trees, flowers and ponds. I was fed several times a day and was told to lie around as much as possible in the comfortable lounge chairs in the park. I took several walks a day and then rested comfortably with a book. After working in a hectic office, this seemed like the good life, but just for a while. A few days later it wasn't so great any more. I had diarrhea and was so sick I could not get out of bed. I couldn't eat anything and the diarrhea did not stop. The nurse came to my room and nonchalantly said to me: "You are not going to kick the bucket, are you?" What comforting words from a nurse!

The clinic was absolutely not prepared for anything like this, and trying to stop diarrhea they brought me chocolates with marzipan! I quickly decided I had to get out of this place as soon as possible. My mother told me on the phone that she had alerted the sister of a friend of hers from Italy, who lived in Buenos Aires. She would meet me at the airport and take me to her home.

Feeling mortally sick, I took the plane in Cordoba and flew two hours to Buenos Aires. When I found the woman who was waiting for me at the airport I collapsed in her arms. Luckily she took over from there on. She put me to bed and spoon-fed me some tea, which helped me fall asleep. The next day she took me to her doctor, who after some tests diagnosed that I had an amoebic dysentery. This is caused by a very bad parasite, an amoeba, that ran rampant in the area of that clinic, and which one gets from eating salad or other raw vegetables. I still wonder why if it was so rampant, they were not prepared? The doctor prescribed a very strong medication, which was supposed to get rid of these bugs. By now of course, I had lost so much weight, and was so weak, I could barely walk. Yet I was determined to go home. So my friend put me on a plane and I breathed a sigh of relief when I was finally in my mother's arms. It took me another two weeks before I could go back to work. Aside from having wasted hard earned money, I now was thinner than before.

◆   ◆   ◆

I had a suitor, who would have been considered good looking by many, but to me he was a bit of a milquetoast. He came from a nice, well-off Jewish family, who had a large wholesale hardware company. We would go to the Philharmonic concerts every Saturday evening and afterwards join other friends for dinner. It was a pleasant friendship, but he wanted to see more and more of me, for he had fallen in love.

Unfortunately, I did not return his feelings and told him so. Nevertheless, he proposed marriage and I had to refuse. In his despair he went to my mother and begged her to use her influence on me to accept him. Although my mother liked him and probably would have been happy to have him for a son-in-law, her answer was that she couldn't, and wouldn't, influence me. He cried a lot and said he couldn't live without me, but though I felt sorry for him, I didn't change my mind. I liked him somewhat, but did not find it possible to fall in love with him. Very soon after, he married a Hungarian girl named Eva!

I must say I had a lot of admirers. I went out with many of them, but I didn't fall in love and I wouldn't settle for less for marriage. By now I was 21 and people (other than my mother) would ask me:

"So when are we going to dance at your wedding, my dear?"

Thankfully, even though my mother wanted me to be happily married, she never put pressure on me.

Although the Uruguayans were very nice to us, somehow the refugees tended to interact mostly among themselves. So I only went out with young Jewish men, who were all very respectful and nice, but I kept wondering where the Prince Charming was who would one day carry me off. Many of my school friends were getting married, but I decided to wait for love.

By now I had the reputation of being very choosey and I found out that our circle of friends were always gossiping about me. I have never been able to understand what made me so interesting. Whatever I did, I felt I couldn't do it right, which bothered my mother, for she cared about what other people would say. After a while I realized that no matter what I did, I couldn't please everybody. So I came to the conclusion that from then on, I would stop caring about other people's opinion, which of course was not so easy. Somehow one always wants to make a good impression and rather have people speak well. But I stopped worrying so much about appearances, or what people would say. My mother and I were very close and spent many weekends together, and I simply shut my ears when I heard the comment: "The Madarasz girl is tied to her mother's apron strings." The truth was that we really enjoyed each other.

One day we got bad news from Mexico where my aunt and uncle Jawitz with their two children, Elfi and Heini, had immigrated. Much to our sorrow, my Aunt Elsa wrote that Elfi had come down with Hodgkins disease! They were going from one doctor to another and doing all the treatments recommended, and were hoping for a miracle. We all prayed for such a miracle!

Sometimes, when I had a week off from work, I would go to Piriapolis by myself, since my mother had to stay at the boutique. I always went to the hotel owned by our friends, the Neuhaus. They had sold the hotel in Pocitos and now had a new one in Piriapolis. This way I was not alone and I could eat with them. But during the day, my time was my own. And I tried to take good advantage of it and get a good rest. In the morning I would go to the beach, which was across the street from the hotel. The water was unbelievably blue and clean, and swimming in the ocean was like healing medicine for me. Lying in the sun was not considered a taboo yet, so I did this with a lot of pleasure and got a nice tan. In the afternoon I would take a blanket and walk in the eucalyptus woods and sit under a tree and read. I have always been very shy; it was very hard for me to be the first to start a conversation with strangers, so I kept very much to myself. I would always come back home feeling, and looking fit and ready to go to work.

◆   ◆   ◆

After graduation, my friend, Hanna Elsbach, with whom we had shared the house, had gone to Rio de Janeiro to live with her grandmother. She invited me to come visit her and I was thrilled to accept her invitation. Hanna's grandmother was very wealthy; her husband had started a brewery in Brazil and she was still a stockholder. She lived in a hotel on the Avenida Atlantica in Copacabana. Of course Hanna had her rooms there too and since I was her guest I stayed with her. In those days Copacabana was still a fairly safe and beautiful place. I felt that I was in paradise: the wonderful beach, the warm climate, music, and the people all contributed to make me feel as if I was tipsy on champagne. Hanna had a job in some office, so I was pretty much left to myself until she returned in the evening. I went to the beach, walked along the Avenida Atlantica and was surprised when cars would stop and invite me to take a ride or to take me back to my hotel. I always refused, but was even more surprised when I was told that this was a custom many girls from good families accepted. Hanna took a few days off and showed me many interesting sites of Rio. What a beautiful and exciting city. We went up to both the *Pao de Azucar* and the *Corcovado*, which I had only seen from a distance from the ship in 1939. It was a breathtaking experience. The view from both mountains was unbelievable. On one of them, we stayed until the sun went down and when the lights went on, there was a carpet of millions of lights spread below us. Hanna's friends took us to a nightclub with a great show and I was carried away with all the music and colors. Although I'd only had a small drink, I felt completely drunk with all the impressions.

After a week in Rio I went to Sao Paulo, where I visited Uschi Ebel my friend from the farm. She was living in Sao Paulo with her aunt and uncle for a while. Sao Paulo is a gigantic metropolis where new buildings mushroom overnight, and is buzzing with activity. My friends told me about a resort in the mountains called Campos de Jordao that I should visit. When they offered to take me there, I was thrilled with the idea, and we stayed at a beautiful hotel located in the middle of the mountains, surrounded by meadows and gardens. I was enchanted, as I was not used to being in the mountains. (Uruguay is quite flat, with a few hills. One special hill, the Cerro, is in Montevideo and towers over the city. It is near the harbor, and the story goes, that when Magellan's ship was nearing land, one sailor shouted "*Monte-Vid-Eo*" which means: "I see a mountain." This is how the capital of Uruguay got its name.)

Campos was a wonderful place to spend a day or two. At dinner a gentleman came to our table and introduced himself, since he had heard us speaking German. His name was Hans Bierman and he said that he was originally from Graz, Austria. When I heard this, I started to get excited. What a coincidence to meet somebody from the area in which I spent my childhood. However, I was not quite comfortable with him. He didn't look Jewish and I was afraid he had been a Nazi supporter. He started to ask me about myself and I was very short with him. Then he said something unbelievable. He asked me whether I knew the Bonyhady family. My eyes and ears opened; how could this be happening, the Bonyhadys were my family! He said he had been very good friends with Martha, but that he also knew Mira. Speak of "six degrees of separation!" Mira was my mother's beloved cousin who visited us in Pernegg, and Martha was her sister! After my astonishment faded and I regained my speech, we embraced and started talking. We became friends and he sometimes wrote to me in Montevideo.

CHAPTER FOUR

By now most of my friends were married and I really felt that I was missing the boat. However, the young men I had met so far were not what I was looking for. There were a few I liked, but I suspected they wanted somebody with money! Many of the refugees were very well settled, with successful businesses, but we were not one of them. Had my father lived, it would certainly have been different!

In 1955, at the age of 26, I finally decided to quit my first job, where I had been working for seven years. It was still a good job, and I had gotten raises throughout the years, but I needed a change. I was immediately offered a very good job at a Dutch bank. However, since I thought I needed an opportunity to meet more young men, we decided that it would be a good idea for me to go to Buenos Aires for a few months. There were more eligible young men in the bigger city and I had already met two of them. I would go there, look for a temporary job, and see what happened next. In Buenos Aires I also had a third cousin of my mother as well as a couple of friends who had lived in Montevideo and moved there. Hanni Lustig lived there as well, so I would not be alone.

Buenos Aires was a beautiful city. Larger and more sophisticated than Montevideo, it had the widest boulevards, great buildings, big and luxurious hotels, wonderful shops and boutiques, and was rightfully called the Paris of South America. People dressed well, and men were especially well groomed. An exciting city, it was also a very important cultural center, where the *Teatro Colon* produced great operas with first-class singers. I had been there previously on short trips and was always fascinated by this pulsating metropolis. Argentina, itself, originally one of the wealthiest economies of the world, had many different climates and therefore all the natural resources needed to thrive. It was a country of contrasts, both economic and political, which sparked tumultuous civil upheavals from time to time. However, the current government, headed by the dictator, Juan Peron and his late wife, Evita, had been in power for some time, and in spite of his greed, he had done well for the working class.

As planned, I immediately found a job through a young woman I had met, who had a temporary office service. The job was in an office in the old city where my relatives lived, and I found a room to rent nearby in the apartment of friends of my cousins. My cousins invited me to come for lunch every day. What a kind and wonderful offer. It was all so convenient and my only regret was that I was not with my mother. We talked on the phone quite often, but we worried about each other, never feeling quite comfortable being apart.

Work progressed well and I was enjoying my stay there when one morning there was an announcement on the radio that a *coup d'etat* was in progress! I could not believe it. Apparently, Argentina was finally tired of the long-lasting dictatorship and was trying to oust Peron. I could hear people running and shouting in the streets. There were blasts of bombs and shots ringing out close enough to be heard. I was frightened and I quickly called the airlines to see if I could get a flight out. No luck: all flights and ships to Uruguay had been cancelled. The borders were closed, and Buenos Aires was in a state of siege. To my mounting alarm, I heard the radio announcer saying that thousands of people were gathering on the Plaza de Mayo in front of the Casa Rosada, the official residence of Peron. Peron and his cohorts were trying to defend themselves, and the remaining military under his command were throwing bombs into the crowds.

Without considering how foolish I was, I ran to the office where I was working and quit my job. On the street the noise was deafening, people were running around yelling and screaming. It was very frightening and I hurried back to my room. When I got there, I heard that the government forces were planning to have warships bomb the city in an effort to regain control. I was now really terri-fied. The building I was living in was very near the waterfront! I thought, oh my God, what should I do now? I can't go home and once again I am in a revolution. Memories of Austria spun in the back of my mind, adding to my dread. I knew just how dangerous political revolutions could be, although I was very much in favor of getting rid of Peron. The phones weren't working well, but I was finally able to get through to some friends who lived in Belgrano, a suburb outside the city. I asked them whether I could come there and they immediately invited me to stay as long as I wanted. Their apartment was a small one and they had a baby, but if they were will-ing to take me, I was willing to go. I hurriedly packed my things and managed to find a taxi to take me to their apartment. From there I started to make telephone calls, trying to get through to my mother. Communication with the outside world was cut off completely. I called my mother's cousins and told them where I was so they would not worry about me. They, as everybody else, were quite anxious about the outcome of the revolution. We had no idea as to who would win or what the country would be like after hostilities ended. The next day we were horrified to hear that two thousand people had been killed on the Plaza de Mayo and the streets. I shook with the knowledge that I had not been far from the center of the fighting. Later I learned that the husband of an acquaintance of mine was killed in his parked car on Plaza de Mayo. He had saved himself from the Nazis only to be killed on the streets of Buenos Aires! What tragedy!

My friends and I stayed in their little apartment without going out, except to the corner store to buy the daily necessities. After a week we were all a little claustrophobic, but only when it seemed that things were almost back to normal did we dare to move around a little more. Peron was sent into exile and almost everybody gave a sigh of relief. (Little did we know that he was to return again with his second wife, Isabel, and when he died she would become President of Argentina for a short time.) A few days earlier I had been able to reach my mother who was sick with fear for me and I was able to assure her that I was safe. I was so anxious to go home, I think I took the first flight out. I could not believe that after so many years of Peron ruling the country, I happened to be in Buenos Aires at the exact time of his overthrow! How bizarre was that?

Coming back home I promptly started to look for a new job. There were two ads in the paper and both of them looked like they were tailored just for me. One was executive assistant to the President of Shell Oil, the other was assistant to the Chief of Mission of the Food and Agricultural Organization, (FAO) of the United Nations. I had an interview with both of them, was accepted by both of them, and didn't know which to choose! What a dilemma! Talking to my friends about it, one woman said: "That's an easy decision, you take the one that is nearest to a bus station!" I wish I could be as simple as that lady! So I started to rationalize: I remembered that at Shell Oil they had told me that I would not be allowed to socialize with other employees, because being the right hand of the president I would have very much proprietory information. I decided that I didn't like this condition, and accepted the job at the FAO of the United Nations. I never regretted it.

Since Uruguay was an agricultural country, which had to compete with Argentina and Australia, they asked for advice from the United Nations.

This was not a third world country asking for aid, but a country contracting with the U.N. for consultation so of course Uruguay was going to pay for their services. For this reason the FAO sent several experts in a variety of fields, and the Uruguay mission was created. The Chief of Mission was Carrol Deyoe, a pasture expert from Seattle, Washington. There was a soil expert from England, a parasitologist from Italy and a sheep expert from Australia. My title was "Administrative Assistant" but I had a number of jobs. I took care of the welfare of our experts and was in charge of getting their reports out in time. I was also the accountant as well as an interpreter. Working with us was a Uruguayan agricultural engineer, who would go on field trips with our people and was the interpreter in technical matters. I also accompanied the Chief of Mission to governmental meetings, to serve as interpreter. None of our experts knew enough Spanish, so it was up to me to help get the messages across. Sometimes, when I felt that the tone was a little too sharp, I would try to soften the discussion in the way I interpreted. I must say it worked well. I also was hostess at their receptions and took care of planning events.

To prepare for the job, I needed new clothes, especially because I would be attending many receptions and parties. My mother had wonderful taste so I asked her to go shopping with me. In Montevideo there were young ladies from good families who set up stores to sell the clothes they no longer wanted. So we went to these stores to find elegant apparel at good prices.

I was very busy at my job, but I enjoyed it tremendously. Every day brought new experiences and challenges. The mission even had sheep shearers come in from Australia. There were three of them, and I was astounded when one came into the office one morning and spoke in the worst dialect I had ever heard:

"Our *myd* didn't come this morning because of the *ryn*."

I had to make an effort not to laugh. This was the first time I had heard this language. However, when it came to shearing they were like magicians. They could shear a sheep with one stroke!

My mother was busy with her boutique and I was busy with my work, but I still would worry about her health and pray to God that he would not take her from me. She on the other hand worried about me and wanted me to have the best of everything, whereas she never bought herself a new winter coat or a nice dress. It was I who had to force her to have a nice suit made by a tailor.

◆   ◆   ◆

When it was time again for my vacation, my mother called one of her many cousins, this one in Santiago, Chile, and asked whether they would mind if I came for a little visit. My mother's cousin, Klema Stoessl, who with her husband had immigrated to Chile, had always loved my mother, so she immediately said yes. Klema was married to a very interesting and cultured man, Fritz Groetzinger, her second husband, a German Jew, who was an avid collector of art and had wonderful original paintings and sculptures. He and Klema were very much in love and lived in an apartment, which was beautiful but not very big. It was only when I was there that I found out that they had really been anxious about my visit. After all they had never met me as an adult. Would I be demanding and intrusive into their peaceful lives? An unwanted stranger in this loving home would be a problem.

The flight over the Andes was spectacular. It was 1956 and planes at that time were not pressurized yet so we had to wear masks at that altitude. This made the passengers look like voyagers from outer space. Looking down on the snow-covered mountain chain was impressive. What a world! What beauty! This was all virgin country and not many people had seen this view from the air. I get very emotional with the beauty of nature and that time was no exception.

Klema met me at the airport and we measured each other up, deciding immediately that we liked each other. She was dressed in red (her favorite color and one she wore a lot); she was rather tall for those days with a very interesting face; it was pretty in spite of a slightly aquiline nose. Her hair was black and made a nice contrast to her red outfit. We drove to their apartment building and I was introduced to her husband. He was tall, slightly bent and had a shock of white hair with a white mustache. He was very kind and soft-spoken and I made up my mind that I would get along well with these two newfound relatives. They showed me around their apartment with all their magnificent art, and took me into the library, where a bed had been made up for me. I felt at home very quickly.

Later, during dinner there were a number of phone calls and all I could hear was "Yes, imagine our luck, she is a lovely young woman. So pretty and so pleasant!"

I didn't know what to say and got quite embarrassed, but then they explained to me that, as they had never seen me before they didn't know what to expect. They had expressed their fear to their friends, and now their friends wanted to know how we were getting along.

Chile was a totally new country and Santiago was so different from Montevideo and Buenos Aires. The whole panorama of the city was colorful and I saw Indians there for the first time. I saw big markets where they displayed a large variety of fruits and vegetables as well as colorful folk art. There was an appealing hustle and bustle of people shopping and bargaining. The climate was warm but not too hot because of the altitude and the air was invigorating in the morning. I liked this new country.

Friends of the Groetzingers had a son who was introduced to me and who seemed very pleasant. He took me out in the evening and also asked me if I wanted to join him and his friends for a New Year's party at the Hotel Carrera, the nicest and most elegant hotel in Santiago. Of course I was thrilled to go with them at the end of the week. In the meantime he took me sightseeing in the city and to afternoon tea at the Hotel Carrera. The next day he drove me down to Vina del Mar, a resort on the Pacific coast. In spite of it being summer, it was freezing cold and windy. Being used to the Atlantic beaches in Uruguay, which are located at nearly the same latitude as this coast, I was astonished at the weather and the temperature of the Pacific Ocean.

I also wanted to get to see something of the interior of Chile, but not too far away from Santiago. Distances are very big in that long and narrow country. People recommended a very popular place in the mountains, Panimavida, a little south of Santiago. I made reservations to go there on the 1st of January and stay for a few days. In the meantime I got to know my relatives better and we became good friends in a short time. I met many of their friends, all refugees from Austria and Germany.

One morning I awoke to noisy clattering, and shaking of my bed. For a moment I didn't know what was happening, but soon realized that this must be an earthquake. My very first one! I put on my dressing gown and hurried outside to see what was going on. Nobody seemed to be particularly excited, as this was a frequent occurrence.

On New Year's Eve I packed my suitcase because I was leaving for Panimavida the next morning. I only left out the dress, which I was going to wear to the party in the evening. My cousins were going to stay home and gave me a key to the apartment, knowing that I would return very late. The dinner-dance at the Hotel Carrera was magnificent: lovely food, nice music and great company. We danced until quite late, and my friends asked me to join them for breakfast. However, I excused myself because I had to get up very early to catch a train. So my escort took me home and we said goodbye at the elevator.

Afterwards I regretted that I didn't let him see me to the door of the apartment. I came upstairs, took out my key and tried to open the apartment door. The key turned, but the door didn't open. I tried again and again until it finally dawned on me that my cousins must have forgotten and locked the top bolt. Well, I couldn't help it, I had to wake them up. I rang the bell. No answer. I rang again and only realized then that their bedroom was far away from the entrance. If they were good sleepers they wouldn't hear me! What to do? I only had a few hours to sleep and get ready for my trip! I took my shoe off and started banging on the door. The only result was that our maid who had her quarters on the top floor of the building heard me and came rushing down. She also had a key but there was no way to get into the apartment. Finally she decided to take me to the next floor, where another maid was standing in front of an apartment door. After a hurried conversation, they told me that the gentleman this other maid was working for was asleep, but she could let me into his apartment and let me sleep on his sofa in the living room if I promised to get out in the morning before he got up. She assured me that she would wake me in time. Shaking with apprehension and frustration I accepted. They gave me a blanket and I lay down without taking off my dress. Although I was dead tired, I couldn't fall asleep. I was too busy thinking that I was alone with a strange man in an apartment. What if he got up and saw me? He might get angry with his maid, or he might try to seduce me. When she finally came to wake me up I was already out of bed. I quietly left the apartment and prayed that I would finally be able to wake my cousins.

Again I started to bang the door. Again there was no answer. They were fast asleep. This time the banging woke up the neighbors across the hall. They were very kind and invited me to stay with them until my relatives got up. They served me breakfast and finally I heard the door of my cousins' apartment open. I ran out and when I told them my story, Klema was beside herself. They had forgotten, and bolted the door from inside as they did every evening. I just had time to grab my suitcase and call a taxi to take me to the train station.

The train ride was wonderful. We went through beautiful dark green woods, lovely fields, and little villages. The mountains were not large in that area, but you could see some major mountain chains in the distance. The weather was lovely and my spirits began to rise. Gone was the frustration of the previous night and I was starting to look forward to spending a few peaceful days.

Panimavida was as pretty as they had described. The hotel was old and lovely, in the middle of a large park. There was a fountain near the hotel and the whole setting was very peaceful. Again here, the mountains were not too large, but the gentle hills around the hotel and the woods everywhere made it a wonderful place. I took long walks to see the surroundings. In the evening dinner was served around long tables so that people could talk to each other, and I was very happy that I didn't have to sit by myself. The guests were of all ages. Big families had come to spend their Christmas and New Year holidays, and there were even a few young men who belonged to these families.

When I got back to Santiago, the maid told me that the young man had been very upset when he heard that a young lady had slept in his living room and that nobody had awakened him. He was very anxious to meet me now, better late than never. She also told me that he worked for the United Nations. What a coincidence! Of course I wanted to meet him, but there was no time; I was leaving the next morning. Speaking of two ships passing in the night! I boarded the plane still smiling about this funny adventure.

Back home I heard that my cousin, Elfi Jawitz, had died of the Hodgkins disease that she had been sick with for six years. Also a week earlier, my mother's sister Mira, with whom I had experienced the Kristall Nacht, died in Mexico of ovarian cancer. My mother and I were devastated, even though we had been prepared for this. But I was so sad that I had not seen my aunt Mira again before her death. I was also thinking of my poor aunt and uncle who had lost a daughter. It must be horrible to lose a child.

The next day I went back to work and really enjoyed having my duties as usual. I got along well with all the men. I was the only woman working in this office, but they never made me feel awkward. There was a pleasant comradeship among us. The Chief of Mission and the expert from Australia had both brought their wives with them. They were very friendly, and we often went shopping together and I was invited to their homes.

Everything went well until the Uruguayan government had to pay for the services of the FAO. Each time I would have to call them and remind them that they were behind in their payments. Sometimes it worked, but generally they were in arrears. Our experts' advice to them was of great importance and would have been of great help, but it turned out that Uruguay had so much bureaucracy that they were not able to implement our suggestions. There were too many government employees spending most of the time drinking "*Cortados*" (little coffees with a drop of milk in them). It was a shame. So much work and money invested in this project, and so little good came of it.

When we were told that Uruguay could not implement the good suggestions the FAO had been giving them during the last five years, it was finally decided to close the Mission. It was sad to see all the work go down the drain! It was also sad to say goodbye to my friends.

About the same time, my mother's partner decided that she did not want to have the boutique any more; and so in spite of the protests of the faithful customers, the store was closed. My mother also felt sorry, but at least she would be free to do things she wanted to do and could rest more. I was happy; maybe now she would travel more with me, and take better care of herself.

With no job to hold me back, I decided to return to Buenos Aires and asked my mother to go with me. She was not ready to go, but promised to join me later. Peron had left, so everything was at peace. This time I went to live with the mother of a friend of mine. Her apartment was in Belgrano, where I had lived during the siege. My mother was happy that I would be in a safe place. I called my friend who had the temporary secretarial service and told her that I was available for a while. She had very good private clients who always called her when they needed something, and she sent me to some places that were unbelievable. I met interesting people most of whom worked from their homes. It was great to work in the luxurious surroundings of these elegant villas and apartments. The employers were very friendly and treated me with a lot of respect, always praising my work, and their wives would often invite me to have lunch with them. It was a pleasant atmosphere to work in.

It was fall and the weather started to get very bad. It was raining a lot, and as I stood at bus stops the wind would blow right through me. I came down with the flu and was confined to bed with a bad cough and a fever. I was so miserable and felt so lonely for my mother! I tried to sleep most of the time but couldn't and things didn't seem to improve. But one day, I awakened suddenly to find my mother standing in the room! I couldn't believe my eyes. I hadn't even told her that I was sick. Out of kindness, my friend, with whom I was staying, had called my mother and told her how sick I was. My dear, beloved mother was there, and settling into the room with me, she began to take care of me. Almost immediately, I felt much better, so protected and loved. I only hoped that she wouldn't get my flu! Thank God I recovered quickly and she escaped the illness. We were so happy to be together and I convinced her to stay a while. This was also a good opportunity for her to get a check-up with a good doctor. There was one who was well recommended, who had been taking care of all our friends for years. He found her quite run-down and recommended a series of injections. Goody, I thought, this way she has to stay longer with me in Buenos Aires!

We had a lot of fun and when I wasn't working we would go window-shopping and sightseeing. The daughter-in-law of a friend of my mother's in Montevideo had a very fashionable boutique on the most elegant shopping avenue in Buenos Aires. She was a beautiful and elegant woman with a perfect figure. We went into the boutique to say hello and she received us with enthusiasm. When I admired her dress and said I wished I could afford to dress that way, she told us that she had dresses that she had not worn very much and would I be interested in buying them at a good price. I was delighted and asked her to bring them to the store where I could try them on. It was a great success. We were the same size and her clothes fit me perfectly. Thus I acquired very nice outfits for a low price.

After one month, my mother wanted to go back home. Reluctantly I took her to the airport, promising her I wouldn't stay too much longer. I had planned to get my friend, who owned the temporary service, to teach me the ropes of that business. I thought it would be a good idea to start my own business.

One Saturday morning my landlady told me that there was a man on the phone who wanted to speak to me. When I answered the phone, there was a very nice male voice asking:

"Is this Miss Eva Madarasz?"

"Yes," I said, "who is this?"

"I am Mr. Casseres and I am here from Chile; I am sure you know who I am, and I would like to speak with you. Could you meet me for lunch?"

I had to sit down. Of course I knew who he was. He was the regional director of the FAO of the United Nations, and though I'd never met him, I had addressed a lot of reports and communications to him. My God, I thought, what can he want from me? I must have done something wrong and they just found out. I was shaking all over and had to make an effort to keep my voice steady when I finally answered him:

"Of course, Mr. Casseres, I will be happy to have lunch with you; but how did you find me here?"

He told me that he called our house in Montevideo and that my mother had given him my number. He gave me the address of the restaurant and told me to meet him there. After I hung up I had difficulty breathing. What on earth does he want? I knew I would soon find out. I dressed very carefully and took a taxi to the restaurant. It was a famous and good restaurant, I was pleased to note. I went in, not even knowing whether I would recognize him. I had never even seen a picture of him. However, it was easy, for when I came in, a man stood up and gestured to me to come and sit down. We shook hands, and I thought he looked nice, well dressed and pleasant. We ordered and he made some suggestions about what I should have. After some small talk, he finally broached the subject that had brought him all the way from Santiago to Buenos Aires.

"Well, Miss Madarasz, you are probably wondering why I asked you to meet me here. What I wanted to say to you is that we were so very impressed with your work at the Mission in Montevideo, we want to offer you a job at the FAO headquarters at *Terme di Caracalla"* in Rome. It would be a very good job and the salary would be excellent. We want you to think about it and hope that you will decide in favor of this offer. We need somebody like you and it is not so easy to find an exceptional person like you with your high intelligence, excellent personality and great charm."

I was so astonished that for a moment I couldn't utter a word. Finally I said.

"Thank you so much for saying such nice things and for offering me such a wonderful position. I appreciate it very much, but I could never move to Italy and leave my mother behind. It would be too hard to move us both."

I couldn't even think of dragging my mother to a country where she didn't know anybody and where I would be working and leaving her alone all day. But I was so proud! I would go up the ladder in a big way. I was also thinking that it would be interesting and fun. But would I want to be back in Europe? Mr. Caseres seemed to be disappointed in my turning down his offer and asked me to reconsider it.

"You can think it over some more and talk it over with your mother. Please let me know in a month what you decided."

When we finished the meal we said goodbye and I thanked him again a thousand times. My goodness, what a boost to my ego! Walking to the bus station I felt as though I had grown wings and was floating! I couldn't wait to tell my mother, and as soon as I got home I called her. She was as proud as I was and told me that if I decided that I did want to go, it would be all right with her. What an understanding and supportive mother I had! No wonder I loved her so much.

◆   ◆   ◆

As far as romance was concerned in Buenos Aires, there was nothing new. I had been going out with a couple of nice men, but I still had not found my soul mate. There was one young man, Bill Cohn, whom I had met through friends. He had an important job in the company owned by these friends, and this young man was a very valued part of the enterprise. I liked him very much, and when he finally invited me on a date I was delighted. He was interested in music and he took me to concerts and operas. He happened to have a weekend house in Tigre, a place near Buenos Aires, with canals leading from rivers, which made boating the favorite sport. Each house was situated along the water and had its own dock. He often invited me to a party there on a Sunday, and a group of friends would gather. We would go boating, then have a picnic and hang out until evening, when everybody went home. Among those young people also was a young man visiting from the U.S. He was delightful and we talked a lot. The next weekend he told me that he had come to like me very much and was very interested in me. I told him that I couldn't return his feelings because I had fallen in love with Bill. He was very disappointed but did not give up. He wrote me several letters always in the hope that I might have changed my mind. My relationship with Bill didn't pan out. He never got married and I have a funny feeling that he might not have liked women. That thought had never occurred to me before. I guess I was a little bit sorry that I had turned his friend down. But it would have been too difficult, with him living in the States and me in Uruguay.

Every day it got colder and more unpleasant and I was getting anxious to get home. I had learned everything important about how to go into the temporary secretarial service business, and I was ready to give it a try. Of course there would be a lot of work to be done to get ready for this endeavor. I packed my suitcase and went back to Montevideo.

It was wonderful to be home again, seeing all my friends and being re-united with my mother. I felt that it was time to start my business. I had all the necessary material printed, and put ads in the paper looking for temporary help. I would run the business from home. But what if I didn't get enough business? What if I didn't find the right help? Trying not to invest too much money, I went ahead with the preparations. Soon I had a few answers to my ads. Now came the moment when I had to start letting businesses know how I could help them. Big hotels also were on the list, as out of town businessmen always needed somebody to help them with their correspondence.

In the meantime I met a very nice young man from Switzerland. He was a journalist who had recently come to Uruguay. I found him quite interesting; he was cultured and intelligent and had a good sense of humor. He was also handsome, and I was quite attracted to him. We went out together and had a good time, going to movies, concerts and the theater. When the weather got better we would go to the countryside and have a picnic. He was very nice to my mother and invited her to join us whenever possible. The fact that we could speak German together helped a lot. We got close to each other and, I think, were falling in love. I had forgotten the impossible Bill, and was thinking that I had at last found the man I could love and marry.

One night as we sat in his car, he took me in his arms and told me that he had a wife and children in Switzerland and that they would join him in a few months. I was so shocked that I couldn't see straight.

"Why didn't you tell me when we met?" I shouted at him and slapped him in the face.

He tried to calm me down and told me he never thought that we would fall in love. It had taken him by surprise and he was considering divorcing his wife.

"Impossible" I shouted. I would never break up a family, especially with small children. "I don't want to ever see you again!" I declared, jumping out of the car to run home, shattered and furious.

I was heartbroken. It had never occurred to me that he was married. I was crying my eyes out, when my mother took me into her arms and told me that he was not worth my tears.

I tried to put the whole messy affair behind me, but it was difficult. I felt cheated and cried for days.

A few weeks earlier, our landlord, who also owned the house next door in which he lived, had given us notice. He said that in a year both houses would be torn down, and a high rise would be built in their place. Since Hanna and her family had left a few years ago, we now had the whole house to ourselves and had rented out a few more rooms. We were looking around for another house and couldn't make up our minds which one to take, when a letter came from my aunt in Mexico, saying that as long as we had to move, why didn't we move to Mexico? Now that Elfi was dead they had a house that was too large and they were very lonely. We were quite ambivalent about this, but when I suffered that disappointment with my friend, my mother and I decided that it would be the best thing to go to Mexico; I wanted to get away from Montevideo, and mother also had been wishing to join her sister.

Again we made up our minds to emigrate! We felt like the Flying Dutchman, condemned to sail around the world forever. Once again we began to pack our personal belongings. Looking for a place to stay until our departure, we found a nice pension (which offered room and board) on the same street where we were living. Then we sold all our furniture, and stored our big ship trunks containing things that we did not need for the present in my uncles' factory. It sounds so fast and easy, but this whole process went on for months and we were tired and, understandably, quite sad. Actually I was unhappier than my mother, since I was coping with the grief caused by the ending of my relationship. Also my mother had a different temperament than I. She didn't mind change, whereas I feared it, and under these circumstances all the more so.

We had to get a visa to enter Mexico, but of course we knew that once again we could only get a tourist visa. So we went to the Mexican consulate, and the consul, a fairly old man, interviewed us and kept looking at me all the time. Then, taking my mother's passport and with his eyes still focused on me, he began to write in her passport. It made me very nervous because I was afraid he would make a mistake in what he was writing. I was happy to get out of there, but I was relieved that we finally had our visas.

Our friends were shocked to hear that we were leaving, and poor Dorita was devastated. She loved my mother so much, that her stepmother (her father had married again after poor Clari died) was extremely jealous. The truth be told, she wasn't a very nice stepmother and should not have expected Dorita to fall into her arms.

Now came the question of logistics. How could we possibly take our luggage on the plane to Mexico? We were leaving the big trunks at my uncle's factory, but we had a lot of personal belongings, which we wanted to take. It would be a fortune to pay overweight for this, and shipping them by boat, would have taken much too long, and we were afraid of losing things. We had booked the flight on Canadian Pacific Airlines, which left from Buenos Aires. After a lot of discussion it was settled that I should fly to Buenos Aires and talk to the manager of Canadian Pacific and ask what could be done. I was going to take a morning flight to Buenos Aires and come back in the evening. Fortunately, the manager was very helpful and I was able to get a special rate for our luggage. He suggested that we ship the luggage ahead of time to their office in Buenos Aires and they would make sure that it was loaded on the plane that we were traveling on. This was a great achievement. One less worry!

We stayed at the pension for two months and enjoyed the fact that we had everything organized. I had stopped my efforts with my business venture since we were leaving and we were able to take it easy and say goodbye to our friends. My married friend did not believe my threats that I did not want to see him ever again and somehow found out where we were staying. He came almost every day and after a while I consented to see him, strictly as friends or acquaintances. His wife had not arrived yet, but I told myself I didn't care about him anymore.

Finally the day of our departure came. My uncles, with eyes red from crying, took us to the airport. The Steiners also came and we were able to fit all our hand luggage into the two cars. Saying good-bye at the airport, we all started to cry. Would we ever see each other again? This was the second time that we had to change our lives. Would it be for the best? We were leaving our friends and the country that had been so good to us when we most needed it to save our lives.

We spent the night at the Claridge Hotel in Buenos Aires and were going to leave for Mexico the next morning. We called all our friends in Buenos Aires to say goodbye and the Stoessls, my mother's cousins, and other friends came to the hotel to see us. Everybody was sad to say goodbye.

During the night my poor mother had her hands full; I kept crying and couldn't go to sleep. The next morning we went to the airport, made sure the luggage that we had shipped was on our flight, and boarded the plane. This was going to be an eighteen-hour flight as there were no jets yet, and we had never taken such a long flight before. My mother would always get seasick on a ship so I was worried about this trip. We had been given some pills, but would they work? This was not a nonstop flight; we would stop in Santiago and Lima before landing in Mexico. In Santiago, Fritz Groetzinger came to the airport to see us. Poor Klema had died in the meantime of lung cancer and he was very sad. He had loved her so much and now he was alone and missed her. We cried on each other's shoulder, and he told me not to go if I was so sad. Later I found out that he would have liked to marry me. He could have been my grandfather, but he was nice.

Finally we were on our way. My mother was doing very well; she did not get sick, but I, who had never been seasick or airsick before, got deathly sick after dinner. Fortunately, it didn't last long because we soon landed in Lima, Peru. I was so happy to be on firm land, I almost kissed the ground. After a two-hour stop, we took off again. I was praying fervently that I wouldn't get sick again, and luckily I was all right for the rest of the flight.

On the morning of April 1, 1960, we landed in Mexico City. Full of trepidation we stepped off the plane and were received by my aunt Elsa, uncle Emil and their son Heini as well as my cousin Emerich, (the surviving son of my dear aunt Mira). What a welcoming party! We were so surprised at the wonderful reception that I started to cry again. So much nice family, I thought to myself, we are blessed. At the age of 30, again I was starting a new life.

PART III

MEXICO

✦

1960–1966

CHAPTER ONE

After a very emotional reunion with the family it was time to go to my uncle's home. While mother went in the car with my aunt, uncle and Heini (Henry), Emerich took me by the hand and led me to his car. He wanted to spend some time with me and I was happy to have an opportunity to re-acquaint myself with him. When I had last seen him I was only seven years old and he was eighteen. We had both changed a lot, not only in appearance but also because we both had gone through very painful experiences. He seemed excited to see me and I liked him immediately.

While we were driving through the congested streets of Mexico City we exchanged a little information, but we knew that this was not the best time to have a serious conversation; so I started to look out the window to get my first impression of this very big and crowded city. By this time, we had reached Avenida Insurgentes, a very long avenue with businesses on both sides mixed with office and apartment buildings. It was a busy street and not one of the nicer ones. Then we drove onto the Paseo de la Reforma, the most beautiful avenue I have ever seen in any city, with its broad divide filled with trees and colorful plants. On each side of the avenue were large hotels, luxurious buildings, which housed embassies, private homes and various office buildings. Beautiful monuments and splendid water fountains graced almost every major cross street. Soon we came to Chapultepec Park, a large and fertile park dotted with small lakes and possessing a great variety of trees and plants. The flowers alone were spectacular. When I noticed a magnificent castle on a hill, Emerich explained that it had once belonged to the Emperor Maximilian, who had inhabited it during his reign in Mexico in the 19th century. It had since been made into a museum and had become a tourist attraction with all the furniture exactly as it was during Maximilian's time.

Maximilian was a brother of Emperor Franz Joseph of Austria, who did not want to have Maximilian in the Austrian Government. In 1864 Napoleon III offered Maximilian the crown of Mexico. However, the empire was a failure. Mexico was hostile to him, and his liberal tendencies alienated the conservatives who had brought him over. With the exception of Napoleon III, even the European monarchs were not too fond of him, and the United States was frankly hostile, prevented from interfering only by its own Civil War. When the French troops were withdrawn from Mexico, the Empire fell apart. In 1866 Carlota went to Europe to seek help from Napoleon and the Pope. Maximilian was driven out of the capital and went to Queretaro. There he was captured and shot.

I was told that he had had the beautiful Paseo de la Reforma built so he could watch his Carlota's carriage drive home from the Cathedral which was located on the Zocalo, several miles away from the Castle.

Finally we arrived in Lomas de Chapultepec, one of the nicest suburbs in Mexico City, where my aunt and uncle lived. Unfortunately, one could not see the beautiful houses because every one was afraid of burglars and therefore enclosed their property with high walls, sometimes even with glass spikes on top.

My uncle Jawitz, (upon arriving in Mexico they converted their name to Jarvis), who had been in the lumber business in Germany, had started another lumber business when he arrived in Mexico. He often went to the jungles himself to show his employees which trees to fell. Sometimes he stayed away for weeks at a time, leaving my aunt alone to take care of the children. Fortunately, the business went well and he was soon able to diversify. Since they had done well financially, they were able to buy their house in Lomas in 1945. In the ensuing years and before we came to Mexico he and his son became partners in a formica business. However, since my uncle had suffered a stroke a year after their daughter, Elfie, died of Hodgkins disease, he was now semi-retired. Fortunately, the stroke was not too severe, but it did leave his left leg and arm paralyzed. He walked with a cane, dragging his left leg, managing his left arm as well as he could.

The house was a lovely Spanish-style home, built by Jorge Del Rio, one of the best-known Mexican architects of the time. The property, like all the others in the area, was surrounded by a high wall and had a gated entrance. We had to ring the bell before the gate was opened, and our car followed the driveway as it led to their carport. From this area, we went up some tiled steps to the main entrance of the split-level house. The entrance door was made out of very dark and heavy wood with black iron trimmings, and when we entered the hall it felt pleasantly cool after the heat outside. As they showed my mother and me around the house, I thought that it was so large it would take me days to find my way around! The large foyer was also tiled but covered with oriental carpets and from there I could see many doors that led to different rooms. The first door on the left led to the breakfast room, from which we could go into the kitchen. To the right of the door to the breakfast room was an open arch leading to the grand dining room. I could tell that the walls were very thick, for the arch was wide and also inlaid with color tiles. The furniture in the dining room was made of elegantly carved dark wood. Across the hall was a double door that led to the garden room, which, in turn led into a lovely garden. To the right of this room was a double door opening into a spacious living room, which had many windows facing the garden, a large fireplace and very comfortable seating arrangements. I was particularly impressed with the magnificent library, which was down the hall. It had dark wood paneling and built-in bookshelves. Near a window was a big, antique, very imposing desk. With the large easy chair, elegant sofa and other seating, the whole room was cozy and inviting. Every room in the house had oriental carpets covering the hardwood floors. Our rooms, which were downstairs in a half-basement, were private and included a bathroom. The windows looked out into the garden, from which there was a separate entrance to our rooms. My aunt explained that these rooms had originally been Heini's. The servants' quarters were on the other side of the kitchen.

It took a while until we got settled and we only unpacked the most necessary things to begin with. Then we were called to lunch, which was served in the garden. The table was beautifully set under an umbrella and we were served a wonderful lunch by the maid. (My aunt had a cook as well.) Sitting in the lush garden, I felt very spoiled and loved, every minute of it!

After lunch my aunt suggested that we should lie down since the high altitude (7400 feet) was hard to take the first few days. We were surprised to realize that it really did have an effect on us, as we were quite exhausted. I think we stayed in bed most of the afternoon, recuperating. Before we knew it, it was already time for dinner. That night was Friday, which always brought the family together for Shabbat dinner. Henry as he was now called, was married to an American girl from Dallas. They had two small children, a boy three years old and a baby girl, two months old. Since Henry's wife was currently visiting her mother to show her the new baby, that night we had Henry all to ourselves, which I was not too unhappy about! The table was beautifully set with good silver, porcelain and crystal. My aunt lit the two Shabbat candles, everything looked very festive and we were all in a convivial mood. To be together again after so many years was wonderful! We laughed often and talked until late in the night. I went to bed thinking that our decision to come to Mexico was certainly the right one. When I thought about Elfi's death, I felt so sorry for my aunt and uncle losing their 28-year-old daughter after a 4-year sickness. My aunt's sad eyes broke my heart, and I hoped that perhaps our being here with them would in some way make their terrible loneliness a little easier to bear.

My aunt had established a tradition of having an open house on Saturday afternoons for her friends to visit and usually a fairly large number of people would gather for high tea and gossip. One of the ladies talked and gossiped so much, that my uncle called her "the Daily News." This afternoon there were more people than usual, since everybody wanted to meet my mother and me. After an enjoyable afternoon, the guests left and my mother and I were exhausted. The new people we had met and the altitude had taken their toll and we fell into bed at 8 p.m.

The next day was beautiful and exciting. We spent the morning lounging in the lovely garden. The weather was wonderful, but we still had a little trouble breathing, for in addition to the high altitude we could smell the bad traffic fumes which blew into the garden over the wall. Mexico had no pollution control, and the cars were using a low quality gasoline. To me it smelled like ozone combined with a foul smelling gasoline. The people living there were used to it, but we felt the discomfort of the odor very strongly. Even in the suburbs there was no escape from the pollution. Unfortunately for Mexico, this pollution would get much worse before things improved.

In the late afternoon my dear cousin Henry came and offered to show me Mexico City at night. Of course I jumped at the invitation and we embarked on what seemed to me to be the most spectacular and impressive sightseeing tour I ever took. We drove down Paseo de la Reforma with all its monuments lit up and when we reached the park, Henry pointed out the castle, which you could see in the distance, ablaze with light. Disney could not have done a better job! It looked like it belonged in a fairy tale. It was the custom that on weekends all monuments and important buildings in the city were lit up with thousands of tiny bulbs. When we arrived at the Zocalo, the main square where all the government buildings and the cathedral were located, I thought I was in a dream. The spectacle was absolutely breathtaking. Every building around the square was lit up. In my 30 years, I had never seen anything like this and I decided that Mexico City had to be the most exciting and beautiful city in the world! I could not thank Henry enough for his kindness in bringing me to see this. It was such a romantic moment; here I was with my handsome Henry, with whom I had been in love as a child, and we were in the middle of a fairy tale setting! Henry had turned into a stunning young man, six foot five with curly blond hair and very blue eyes. He had a strong nose, which I thought fit beautifully with his long well shaped face and square chin. However, I reminded myself that not only was he my first cousin but there was the "little" fact that he was married and had two children! Nevertheless we had a beautiful evening. He took me to dinner at a very popular restaurant in the Zona Rosa, which was the area of the city in which the luxury hotels, restaurants and boutiques were located. It was a favorite place for tourists and Mexicans alike. I tried to order some food, which was not so spicy, since I was used to Uruguayan food, which is not hot at all. Finding something without hot peppers was difficult, but I managed. (During the six years that I ended up living there, I never ate anything too spicy, or drank the water or ate anything that couldn't be cooked or peeled.) On our drive home, I realized that I had fallen in love with this great and exciting city!

When my aunt first arrived in Mexico, a friend who was helping her unpack her trunks noticed a glove pattern and asked her what it was for. My aunt explained that before leaving Austria she had taken a course in glove making. Intrigued, her friend asked my aunt to make her a pair of leather gloves, which she needed as a gift. This pair of gloves was so well made that everybody wanted a pair—and thus a new business was established. As my uncle was out of town a lot, it was good for my aunt to have something to do when he was gone, and she decided to run her new business from her home. However, at the time we arrived my uncle was semi-retired and was unhappy not having my aunt's full attention when he was home, so he really wanted to get rid of the business. The answer came naturally to have my mother and me take over and everyone was happy with this solution.

Monday morning seemed as good a time as any to acquaint ourselves with the workings of my aunt's business. My aunt bought her leather from a German tanner who provided the finest kidskin available, in the preferred colors of black, beige, white, navy and brown. The tanned skins were then cut to different sizes of gloves. The cutter's name was Pachita and she was quite chubby with a ready smile on her lips; being Indian she could speak several Indian dialects. She would sit in the breakfast room at the big table, where she worked with scissors and patterns. After they were cut they would be given to piece workers who picked up the work and brought the finished glove back. These workers were all Indians and very talented. They would hand-embroider, bead and hand-sew the gloves and return the finished product quickly. Then the gloves would be ironed on an electrically heated flat metal with five fingers to make the leather smooth. The women embroidered the gloves according to specific orders or sometimes they would invent a design on their own which was usually very pretty and well done. I couldn't get over the dexterity and imagination of these Indian women. They had a hard life most of them had many children without being married. Often, the money the women made from their work would end up in the men's pockets for alcohol. Sometimes in their drunken stupor they would mistreat their women, occasionally even when the women were pregnant. It was a very sad state of affairs. During the years I worked with these women I came to know them well, liking and appreciating them greatly. The experience gave me insight into the Mexican working class. Unfortunately, Mexico was, and still is, one of those countries where the class differences are enormous, with barely any middle class. The poverty was terrible and it was a disturbing part of Mexico that I found difficult to accept.

My aunt had designated one room in the house as the workshop, where customers could come and choose which gloves they wanted. Many of the customers were American tourists who came back every year with a list of gloves they needed since they had spread my aunt's name amongst their friends. Sometimes a tourist guide would bring a group of ladies and my aunt would give him a little commission. In addition she had a lot of fashionable stores and boutiques in Mexico who were repeat customers.

Very soon my mother and I learned the business and although my aunt still helped and was there for advice, we could manage it quite well by ourselves. We really enjoyed it very much. We did not have to try to sell at all; the merchandise was taken out of our hands with so much enthusiasm that I was really surprised at how easy it was. Almost every day ladies would come to the house to shop. On other occasions we had long letters from American customers who sent their orders ahead of time, so that they would be ready when they arrived in Mexico. Often I had to deliver orders to the different boutiques using my uncle's car and driver. I would sit comfortably in the back and let myself be driven to the different places, having the opportunity of seeing more of the colorful city.

One time when I went with my aunt to deliver gloves to a boutique in the middle of the city center, I met the owner, Nanette Oleskovsky a beautiful, sophisticated young woman full of life. She was born in Belgium, fled with her parents from the Nazis, had lived in Brazil and was now married to a Russian named Benny Oleskovsky. She and her husband owned a leather store called Alligator. They had two children, a girl and a boy, and I soon became close friends with them, with Nanette ultimately becoming my closest friend in Mexico. Eventually she divorced her husband and after a while she married my cousin Emerich Salzberger.

Speaking of Emerich, at the time we came to Mexico he was divorced from his first wife and was living with his father half a block from my aunt's house. His mother had died of ovarian cancer the same week Elfie died. I was so sorry that she was gone for I had loved her dearly. I saw Emerich quite often. He took me out to dinner and showed me a lot of the city. And he told me his story.

In 1938 and 1939 he was in Turin, Italy, where he studied aeronautical engineering. While he was in Italy, his mother and I went through the Kristall Nacht together. Later, his younger brother Ernst, whom I had adored, (I don't know where he was when his mother and I went through the Crystal Night) was taken to a concentration camp where later he was shot while trying to escape. This was a horrible blow for Emerich; he felt guilty for having left Austria and not having taken his brother with him. He felt that he had failed to protect him and was terribly angry and full of hatred. In Italy, Emerich was put into a concentration camp. Having learned to fly in his early youth, after his release he went to England and joined the R.A.F. (Royal Air Force). He was soon promoted to wing commander and led a lot of missions for the British.

The King bestowed the Distinguished Flying Cross on him for his heroic and loyal services to the country. After much travel, he joined his parents in Mexico and established an aerial photography and survey company. I had not known all of this, and I was amazed and proud of him. However, I could tell that he was still suffering from losing his brother, and I ached for his grief. He was such a gentleman and I enjoyed his company. When I started to date young men, it was to him I told my feelings and my frustrations. Many a time I would cry on his shoulder and he would try to give me hope and advice. A year later he married a young Czech painter, Tanya Kohn.

A few days after our arrival in Mexico, Henry's wife Jean and the children Robby and Betsy returned home, and I was delighted to meet them. Jean was a beautiful young woman and the children were adorable. They were such a lovely family! We saw them often on weekends, and sometimes Robby would spend the night at my aunt's home and slept in his grandparents' room.

I had found out that one of the partners of the New York brokerage firm, Swan, Culbertson and Fritz, for whom I had worked in Montevideo (my first job), had a house in Cuernavaca. It was one hour south of Mexico City, located in a valley and therefore not as high an altitude and with a better climate. There were a lot of retired Americans living in the area, and Mr. Culbertson and his wife spent their winters there. His permanent home however, was in San Mateo, California. I had never met him before since he had never come to Montevideo during my time at the firm. I was very curious to meet this man so I called him in Cuernavaca. He was very receptive on the phone and immediately invited me to have lunch with him and his wife. My uncle allowed me to take the car and driver and I went to Cuernavaca. It was a very nice little town, typical of all other small Mexican towns with a *Zocalo*, the main square in the center. The flowers and trees bloomed with colors I had never seen before. The color of the bougainvillea ranged from a delicate light pink to a rich dark red, and there were wonderful jacaranda blossoms in blue and orange. The homes had deceptively ordinary facades, but when the Culbertson's maid opened the door and asked me to come in, my eyes and mouth stayed open as I absorbed the beauty in front of me. I felt that I was walking into another world, or perhaps into paradise. A huge garden with marvelous plants and thousands of glorious colors surrounded a round swimming pool. My hosts received me very graciously, even though they had never met me before. We sat by the pool and I was offered drinks or juices of every possible tropical fruit. It seemed that we talked about everything and I was especially interested to hear what had become of the firm, and how the Culbertsons spent their time in Cuernavaca and in California. Apparently they only went back to San Mateo in order to enjoy the concerts and opera performances in San Francisco, but they loved their home in Cuernavaca, with its lovely climate, helpful servants and natural beauty.

After lunch Mr. Culbertson asked me what I was doing in Mexico and how I was spending my time. After I explained my situation, he asked me if I would be interested in helping him with his correspondence. I told him that I was working quite a bit with the glove business and that I could not drive down to Cuernavaca, but he said he would be willing to drive to Mexico City once a week. We agreed that he would come to my house and dictate his letters to me. I would type them, sign for him and mail them. On the next visit he would take home the copies. This arrangement worked for a long time and we both enjoyed it.

By now my mother and I were practically taking care of the glove business by ourselves, and my aunt offered to share the profit fifty-fifty with us. This was a wonderful offer and we accepted it gratefully. However, my aunt did not tell my uncle about the arrangement because she thought he would probably be against it. She knew her husband's unpredictability. Nevertheless, we had a good time with the business, our income was not bad, and we were able to save a fair amount of money. The only problem was that not knowing the arrangement, my uncle kept telling me that it was time that I looked for a job. This put me in a very unpleasant predicament, as I was not free to tell him the truth. There were times when he was terribly unpleasant and I really hated the whole situation.

CHAPTER TWO

After six months in Mexico, we had to leave the country in order to get a new visa, which would then be good for another six months. So my mother and I decided to go to San Antonio, Texas. When we came to the emigration officer at the airport we gave him our passports. He looked at them for a long time and finally he said:

"Where is the baby?"

We couldn't understand what he was talking about, so I said:

"I am the daughter, sir."

"That is not possible," he said. "In this passport it says that Mrs. Madarasz is traveling with her daughter, and that is only written when it is an infant, so you cannot leave without the baby!"

I was remembering the old, stupid consul in Montevideo, who instead of paying attention to his job was gawking at me and I got mad.

"Sir, I am afraid you will have to let us leave right now because it will take me nine months to produce a baby and I am afraid we cannot wait that long!"

"Miss Madarasz, I understand your problem and I am trying to help you, but this is against the law. However, I will see what I can do for you."

At this point I knew that he was waiting for a bribe. Every government employee was bribable, and the corruption was so great bribing was an unwritten law. I, however, did not want to contribute to this problem so I ignored his insinuation and played dumb. My mother was getting very worried, but I, in an impassive, firm voice told him:

"You are not only holding up the people in the line behind us, you are losing time because I assure you that I will take the plane waiting outside. Please give us back our passports right now!"

"But of course, young lady," he finally conceded, handing us our passports. "I do not want you to miss your plane. Have a good flight."

We had to run to board our plane and were exhausted from this experience. This was my first, but unfortunately not last, encounter with corruption.

San Antonio was our first introduction to the U.S., but because it had such a big Mexican population it didn't seem very different. However, we were very impressed with the pretty canals running through the city and the nice department stores. We were happy to be able to drink the water and eat lettuce, which we had not done since arriving in Mexico. Little did we know that they imported their lettuce from Mexico!

Of course we did a lot of shopping, which was much better than in Mexico or Montevideo. We received our new visas, which would be good for another six months. This time I made sure everything was in order and that no infant showed up in my mother's passport when we returned to Mexico.

♦   ♦   ♦

With fresh energy we dedicated ourselves to our new glove business. We really enjoyed it and my mother would often stay in the workroom very late in the evening. I made friends with the workers and pretty soon they confided in me and asked me for advice. They told me their heartrending stories and I was upset and frustrated

because there was not that much I could do. One of the big problems in Mexico with the poor classes was that they were very religious and superstitious at the same time. This meant that they took
their last cent and gave it to the church because they were afraid of
being punished if they didn't. Another problem was, that they did
not know about contraception nor would they dare to do anything
about it. So one child was born after the other, with the women having to take care of them. Only one of our workers was married, to a
very decent man, a carpenter. Even she came to me one day:

"Ay Miss Eva, I am thinking of getting a divorce."

"Coty, for heavens sakes, why? You are the only one with a good
husband; what happened?"

"I will be very frank with you, Miss Eva, I don't want to have any
more children."

"But you don't have to divorce your husband to stop having children. Please go see your doctor and ask what you should do. There
are several methods and he or she will tell you."

"You don't know the Mexican macho, my husband would never
agree to anything like that. He would feel that he is not man
enough."

I was terribly upset and I really had no idea what I, as an individual, could do about the extreme poverty and ignorance of these wonderful people. I would talk about it constantly until finally somebody
asked me what I was planning to do. When I answered that I could
not think of anything, the person told me to forget it. This was no
solution, but unfortunately, with time I started to get used to seeing
the poverty.

It turned out that Coty didn't have to get a divorce; her husband
died of a heart attack. As far as our workers were concerned, we paid
them more than they would ordinarily make, but I had the feeling

that this would only provide more drink for the men who liked their *copa* a little too much and would come home drunk sometimes.

We enjoyed meeting our different customers and sometimes we would make friends with them. The Americans who came were all very interested in talking to us. When they heard that we had to leave the country every six months, they would invite me to come and visit them in the U.S. and I did accept some invitations over the years.

◆   ◆   ◆

One day my aunt's friend, "The Daily News," invited my mother and me to spend a week with her at her children's condominium in Acapulco. I was so excited. I had heard so much about Acapulco, even when I was in South America.

It was the winter of 1961 and Acapulco was still like a paradise. There were just the right amount of hotels and the beaches were clean. I couldn't believe my eyes when I saw the beauty of the mountains, ocean, beaches and the tropical vegetation everywhere. I had never seen anything so lush and vibrant. The condominium was situated near the ocean, and was surrounded by a garden with a swimming pool in the middle. There were many glorious palm trees full of coconuts, banana trees, and other tropical fruit trees. Subtropical Uruguay had a few palm trees but that was all whereas this was very tropical in climate and vegetation. It was exceedingly hot, but I loved it. Since there was no glass in the windows, the condominium had no air conditioning, but was surrounded by wooden shutters, which you could open and close. From every window you could see the greenery and the blue ocean. Unfortunately the good swimming beaches were a little removed, but buses or taxis came by every few minutes so it was no problem to go to the beach, which we did with great pleasure. Every morning at 10 a.m. we would go to one or another beach. There were so many and most of them were very good for swimming. The shore of the Pacific Ocean was warm and clean and it felt like swimming in champagne. At 1 p.m. we would go home and have a little lunch and then take a siesta. Sometimes we would stay on the beach and have lunch at a place, which was very popular and always crowded. There was great music and people were often singing and dancing. The waiters were wearing shirts that said "Another shitty day in paradise." A monkey dressed in finery walked from table to table visiting with customers. What a fun place!

After the afternoon siesta we would go sightseeing. There were some nice hotels where they had music and afternoon tea. There was a place called "El Mirador" which had a show where young men would jump into the water from very high cliffs. This was very exciting and scary. I wondered if many got hurt, but it was a big tourist attraction. For me, Acapulco was the most romantic and intoxicating resort I had been to and when the week was gone I was sad to have to return home.

My mother in Acapulco

CHAPTER THREE

One day a family named Green came to our house. They were from Chicago, and brought a letter of introduction from one of my aunt's old customers, a friend of theirs. They happened to be from the same synagogue as this friend. They had been sightseeing and came with their son, David, who was tall, six feet three inches, with black, wavy hair, combed back, and light blue eyes. He had big white teeth and smiled a lot. His mother, Betty, was a pretty and charming woman with the same blue eyes as her son. Harry, the father, was not very tall with a little paunch. He seemed to be easy going. They stayed quite a while and ended up inviting me for dinner that evening. It didn't end with just one dinner, it turned out to be a series of invitations and a lot of compliments both from David as well as from his parents. They came back to the house and, after a lot of conversation, invited my mother and me to visit them in Chicago the next time we had to leave the country. David kissed me when we parted and said that he had fallen head over heels in love with me. I was really quite overwhelmed by all this attention, and wasn't quite sure how I felt about his sudden declaration of love. I guess I was flattered and intrigued and I promised that we would come and see them in Chicago. This was followed by some correspondence before we needed to leave the country again in November.

This was not the best time of the year to visit Chicago and I told them so in my letter. However they insisted we come so we packed our warmest clothes. I even pulled out an old fur coat while my mother brought her very warm winter coat. We had heard how cold and windy it was in Chicago, so we even packed warm underwear. I guess one has to try everything once, but I hadn't been in a cold climate since I was a child in Austria.

We arrived in what was nearly a blizzard and Betty Green, her husband Harry and their son, David were standing at the gate. After we went through customs we were finally allowed to join our friends and the first thing Betty did was hand me a very warm hat with a fur trim. She was happy when she saw that I was wearing a fur coat, but she was worried that my head would be cold. What a kind and caring soul; I was practically moved to tears and my mother was very impressed by their warm and welcoming reception. We piled into David's car, a white Lincoln Continental. I wasn't used to elegant cars like this. Cars in Uruguay and Mexico were very expensive and everybody drove small cars and kept them until they fell apart. They took us to their lovely apartment in the north end of Chicago and we had drinks and dinner. It was a very good dinner and I was so surprised that Betty did not have any help. She did everything by herself, which I was not used to either. In South America and Mexico everybody had maids. I didn't realize how expensive this would be here in the States. After the lovely dinner they said that they were going to take us to their club where they had reserved a room for us, as we surely were tired and wanted to call it a night.

The Standard Club was located in downtown Chicago, so on our way there we got a great look at the lake and the lit up homes surrounding it. There were many very impressive apartment buildings facing the lake. As we went up Michigan Avenue, we saw beautiful stores and interesting buildings. By now it had stopped snowing so we could see everything pretty well. After introducing us to the receptionist of the club, they said goodnight and left us in the lobby. They would pick us up next morning at 10 a.m.

The bellboy took our luggage and showed us to the room. He opened the door and both my mother and I stood there with our mouths open. When I regained my speech I told the bellboy that there must be a mistake that this could not be our room. However, he insisted that this was the room, which the Green family had reserved for us and left. My mother looked at me and I looked at my mother still not believing what we saw. The room looked like a flower shop plus a gift shop. There was a huge flower arrangement for my mother and me with a welcoming card. Both beds were covered with gift-wrapped boxes and the floors were filled with bigger boxes. There was a complete set of Lark luggage for me standing by my bed, and there were boxes with all kinds of gifts for my mother and me. There was a beautiful white evening gown, a nightgown and robe for me, and many more gifts than I can remember. There were tickets to the opera and reservations to all kinds of shows as well.

What on earth does this mean we asked each other. This was a simple trip to Chicago where we were going to see our new friends. We had asked them to make a reservation at a hotel, which we of course were going to pay for. Here we were staying at their club at their expense and on top of that, they were showering us with gifts as they might do for a bride. Oh, my God, this was not what I had in mind! I ran to the phone and told them that under no circumstances could we accept all these gifts and that I was afraid that maybe there had been a misunderstanding. David and I were new friends, I said, we didn't know each other very well. They didn't allow me to finish with my litany. Betty came to the phone and begged us to accept these gifts that were from their heart and not to read anything further into them. They would be deeply hurt if we wouldn't accept what was only their hospitality, and they hoped that we would have a wonderful time in their city.

My mother and I barely slept that night we were so worried. At the same time it was like a dream or a fairy tale. We felt loved and cherished, but also it seemed that we were being bribed into making a decision that I was not ready to make. I barely knew David and cupid hadn't shot me in the heart as he apparently had David.

What is the protocol for such a situation? Should we leave the gifts behind and move out of the club? But we could not hurt these nice people in such a way. We knew that the Green family was financially secure. Harry Green was retired, Betty was a saleslady at Saks Fifth Avenue only because she would be bored at home, and David was a toy representative with a very good income. Yet, was it fair to take all these expensive gifts, when I didn't know if I would accept him if he proposed?

When we got together the next day I tried to be very frank, and we had a long talk. I told them that although I liked David, I didn't know him well enough to make any commitments. They agreed and suggested that when my mother left in a few days, I should stay with them for as long as I wanted. I could stay in their apartment. David could sleep on the living room couch and I could have his room.

Not knowing what to do, I accepted. I guess one doesn't run away from such kindness and love. We still had a few lovely days before my mother left. She enjoyed the opera and the concert, as well as the lovely restaurants they took us to. Of course we took them out to dinner too. When it was time for my mother to leave, we all took her to the airport and I moved into the Green apartment.

I must say I had a great time. Betty was a lovely lady and I thought she would make a wonderful mother-in-law. David was very kind and went out of his way to show me a good time. We were invited to visit some of their friends, who all wanted to show me what a great life I would have in Chicago. I was impressed with the American women. They had careers, took care of their families and had no help. I thought they were superwomen, and I have to admit that I got frightened at the thought of having to do all this myself. Would I be able to handle all my responsibilities? There were still a lot of questions in my mind.

After two weeks I decided that I needed to go home before I could make such an important decision, but I promised that I would meet them again at Christmas in New York. Although I had grown very fond of David I was getting too uncomfortable. Every morning there was a picture of a new car or some jewelry or a mink coat with a little note from Betty: "Wouldn't this be nice for you?"

On my last day, David brought an engagement ring. It was a three-carat pear shaped diamond and it was gorgeous. I had to be very strong in order to tell him I couldn't accept it. After renewing my promise of returning for Christmas they let me go.

I was one confused person when I came back home! What was I to do? It was really time to get married; I was already 32 years old, but did I love him enough, or at all? I talked it over with my mother many times but she just said that it was my decision. However, if I didn't feel that I was sure, I shouldn't do it. I went out with my cousin Emerich; he had just gotten engaged to a young painter. He concurred with my mother. My uncle of course thought that it was high time that I settled down, and had done his best to introduce me to sons of his acquaintances. So far, none of them had been of interest to me. But this situation was different; in the real sense of the word, David and his parents had swept me off my feet with their kindness and generosity. After all, don't they say that love comes later?

There were only three weeks before I had to go back and make up my mind. Although no ultimatum had been given, it was practically understood that we might get engaged the next time I saw him. I was a nervous wreck. I was also thinking about having to move to the U.S. and on top of that to a climate that was cold and windy. If I could worry about the climate so much, didn't that mean that I didn't care for him enough? I had never been very good at making decisions; would I make the right one? Had fate brought David to my doorstep?

With all these questions in my mind I couldn't function very well. I had sleepless nights and by the time I had to leave for New York, I was exhausted.

This was supposed to be a fun trip with my friends. We were meeting in New York where we would stay for Christmas, and then drive to Chicago in David's car to celebrate New Year's. My beautiful white party dress was waiting for me in Chicago, where Betty had had it altered for me. My aunt presented me with a white fox stole which had been Elfi's. I had also had a fashionable cobalt blue velvet dress made by a very good dressmaker friend of my aunt. It was a formfitting strapless dress with a little bolero jacket. The dress was so tight that when I went to the ladies room I could not lift the skirt. I had to take the whole dress off to use the facilities!

I had bought nice gifts for David and his parents. For Betty I had a beautiful gold pendant, which opened like an accordion and accommodated many photographs; for Harry, a lovely silver letter opener inlaid with all kinds of interesting stones. For David I was bringing a tie pin that had been my father's. It had a pearl and a little diamond. I had all this gift-wrapped. Big mistake! I should just have put them in with my personal jewelry because Customs in New York kept me for a long time, making me unwrap each package, and I ended up having to pay duty.

The Greens, who had been waiting at Customs, were frantic with worry when I finally appeared. "What on earth could have taken you so long? Are you alright?"

After I assured them that I was fine and we had hugged each other, we finally were able to get to the car. On our way to the hotel I told them the whole story and they were so sorry that I had gone through all that trouble for them. This was my first trip to New York and when we arrived in Manhattan, I was completely overwhelmed by the huge skyscrapers and the crowds. I had heard about New York, and I had seen movies of New York, but seeing it "for real" was impressive. The sun was shining, although it was extremely cold and there was snow on the streets. When we stepped out of the hotel I couldn't catch my breath because of the cold.

"Never mind," they assured me, "we are not going to be on the street that much. We have such a huge program planned and it will all be inside."

They had tickets to just about every show in town. We went to the Jack Benny hour and other TV shows where audiences were allowed. They even took me to Radio City. What a show before the movies! Everything seemed unreal to me. They had tickets for the Copacabana nightclub, and because we had tickets we were allowed to stand in line on the sidewalk! After waiting half an hour in the cold snow, we were finally admitted and shown to our table behind a column from where we could barely see the show. I guess New York should be avoided around Christmas. Nevertheless, I had a wonderful time. Everything was new to me, and my friends did their best to show me as much as possible. They had done a wonderful job organizing everything ahead of time.

Shortly after Christmas we set out for Chicago. We drove over the Pennsylvania Turnpike, stopped at many Howard Johnson restaurants for our meals and spent the night in one of them. At one point we ran out of gas because Harry didn't want to listen to David when he said that we needed to fill up. Well, I thought to myself, here we are in the middle of nowhere, and there is no car in sight. It will take hours and I am freezing to death. However, I did not open my mouth. Much to my amazement, a police patrol came within 15 minutes and gave us enough gasoline to get to the next station. I was told that the police patrol the freeway constantly and that one never has to wait very long. Well, this was America! We were all very happy and started to joke around. The two men sat in front sharing the driving and Betty and I sat in the back. We had very nice talks, but often she would fall asleep and I just sat there thinking or listening to the men's conversation. It was snowing again but the driving was easy because they were constantly clearing the freeway.

Finally we arrived back at their apartment in Chicago and getting out of the car was not easy. We had all gotten stiff from sitting so long in one position, but we managed to get ourselves up the stairs. We barely ate anything before going to bed. We needed a good night's sleep and tomorrow was another day.

Cold but lovely days followed. The Greens kept spoiling me and I still had not made up my mind what to do or say. However, I think that by my behavior they must have guessed that I wasn't head over heels in love. I noticed it by the way they looked at me, and one time when Betty and I were alone, she said: "You know, Eva, when I was a bride I felt that Harry was the most handsome and wonderful man alive. If you don't feel that way, you shouldn't force yourself to do anything."

With tears in her eyes, she embraced me and told me: "David is madly in love with you and we, now that we have come to know you, are crazy about you. You are so pretty and petite, that we call you our Dresden china doll. I would do anything if I could make you love my son, but forced love is not good for anyone."

I couldn't help crying as I said: "Betty dear, you are the most wonderful mother-in-law any girl could wish for and I love you dearly. My feelings towards your son are very mixed and I am afraid I can't make up my mind yet. I am so sorry."

The next evening was New Year's Eve and David and I were going to the most elegant ball in Chicago. Dressed in the beautiful white gown with the bodice beaded in white and pink beads, my white satin slippers and the white fox, I looked fantastic. I believe we were the handsomest couple on the dance floor, but also the unhappiest. At midnight we kissed and went home. The next day we spent relaxing and talking. We talked and talked but nothing positive came from it. David gave me his college ring, which I put on a chain around my neck. We were exhausted. The next morning after hugging Harry and Betty, David took me to the airport. We cried in each other's arms and promised to write and to talk on the phone. The flight back was a sad one. Already I felt that I had made the wrong decision.

The next few days at home were not good. I was depressed, I felt that I had failed my friends and let myself down, too. Everybody tried to comfort me, and when I sat in Emerich's car I went through everything and cried my heart out.

With the tears running down my cheeks I said: "I will never find a man who loves me as much again, and he had such a lovely caaar!" At this display of regression to childhood we both broke into laughter.

When I had to leave the country again, this time to Los Angeles and San Francisco, I mailed the ring back to David from San Francisco. He in turn mailed back my father's tie pin. A year later David married someone else.

Reflecting on my decision not to marry him, I can only come to the conclusion that I was not attracted to him.

CHAPTER FOUR

I started going out with some men introduced to me by my uncle; they were Jewish engineers and businessmen. Although I wanted to stay in Mexico, and the only way was for me to marry a Mexican, I just wasn't attracted to any of them. According to my uncle I was spoiled and too choosy; after all what was I waiting for? The bachelors he had introduced to me were good marriage candidates, well established and financially secure, and very interested in me. Once in a while I would go out with one or the other. However, I still had my dream of marrying for love. Also I was starting to get very irritated with being offered in marriage.

My "little sister," Dorita Steiner, wrote that she wanted to come and visit, so my aunt and uncle graciously invited her. She could stay in my room on the day bed. She had her medical degree and was now working as a psychiatrist. I told one of my admirers that she was coming to visit and if he had a friend with whom she could go out I would appreciate it if he would arrange something. When I told him that she was a psychiatrist he was very enthusiastic and told me that he had a friend who was also a psychiatrist. So far so good! I also asked the children of "The Daily News" whether we could rent their condominium in Acapulco for a week, so I could take Dorita to their lovely place. They were very kind and told me we could have it but they would not accept any rent. Everything seemed to be in place and I was looking forward to a nice visit with her.

We hadn't seen each other in two years, and I found her looking good. She was attractive, had a wonderful figure and quite a pretty face, and with her auburn hair falling almost to her shoulders, she looked very young. It was hard to imagine that she was a physician and a psychiatrist! Although she said she was tired from the trip, she couldn't stop talking she had so much to say about her life. The reunion with my mother was heartwarming, for Dorita still had great love for her, the kind a child had for her mother. Poor Dorita; not only had she lost her mother when she needed her most, but it had occurred in such a tragic way. Now she had to deal with a step-mother who was selfish and had no compassion for what Dorita had gone through. Added to this were her recurring depressions.

When Dorita was five, the situation in Austria had become dangerous for Jews. Dorita's parents wanted to protect her so they decided to get her baptized before leaving the country. Dorita was too young to understand any of this. All she knew was that she was no longer Jewish, which resulted in her growing up without any beliefs. During her big depression before and after her mother died, Dorita needed something to hold on to so she fervently embraced the Roman Catholic religion. Before Dorita's arrival in Mexico I pre-pared my aunt who was the only one of all the siblings who still had a kosher household and was very religious. She knew most of Dorita's history and assured me that there was nothing to worry about.

Everybody was very nice to Dorita, except my uncle, who had become a grumpy old man. There were days where I tried to stay away from him he was so unpleasant. But my friend did not seem to notice or to mind, she was so happy to be with my mother and me and looked forward to exploring Mexico. My young man arranged for him and his friend to come and meet Dorita at my aunt's house, from where we would go on a little tour of Mexico City and then to dinner. We were waiting for them in the living room when the maid showed them in. My first impression of his friend Dr. Ricardo Weber was that he seemed like a nice guy but was nothing special to look at. He was 5 feet 9 inches tall, had brown hair and brown eyes, a pleasant face with irregular features and a nice smile. We got into my friend's car, Ricky (as his friends called him) and Dorita in the back and I in the front passenger seat. We drove around the park and all the interesting sites of the city, eventually going to a restaurant in the Zona Rosa. Dorita liked everything she saw and seemed to be having a good time, so I was content. Over dinner, I found myself incredibly attracted to Ricky, and we exchanged a number of intrigued glances with each other. He had such a wonderful smile, such a sense of humor I couldn't help but smile back. He was great company and to my big surprise, I felt my heart pounding. What was going on? I couldn't believe how attracted I was to this man whom I had just met a few hours ago. All of a sudden he seemed terribly sexy and full of charisma. I hadn't felt like this in a very long time and I enjoyed it! When they drove us home they offered to take us on a one-day tour to San Miguel de Allende, a famous artists' colony, and to nearby Guanajuato, the capital of the State of Guanajuato, which was a little over 100 miles north of Mexico CIty. This was a wonderful offer; I had wanted to go there for a long time, and I was sure that Dorita would enjoy it.

During Dorita's visit we went out several times, always as a foursome. One evening we went dancing at a beautiful nightclub in the Zona Rosa, called "Jacaranda." Mexican architects and interior designers were unbelievably good in those days and many Americans came to Mexico City to get ideas of how to build and design. The nightclub had a magnificent waterfall, an open roof, and the lighting was pleasant and conducive to romance. We danced to a wonderful band, and of course exchanged partners once in a while. I could have danced all night with Ricky!

When the time came for Dorita to go back home she was in tears and she promised that she would come back to Mexico. There were still so many things to see and do. I was happy that I was able to show her such a good time and to give her so many new experiences.

After she left, much to my surprise and joy, I had a phone call from Ricky.

"Eva, come out with me dancing. We can go to Jacaranda again, just the two of us."

Well of course I was not going to decline! I had not been able to stop thinking about him since Dorita had left. We had a wonderful time that night and began seeing each other regularly. Our dating soon turned into a passionate romance and we found ourselves deeply in love. He was exciting, and cultured and charming yet there was one problem: I was 32 and he was only 27. I worried about this a lot afraid the difference in our ages would eventually cause our separation. Ricky didn't agree and wooed me with ardor and tenacity.

Since we didn't want to be gossiped about we had to be very circumspect about our relationship. Only three people knew how intimate it had become: my mother, my aunt and my friend, Nanette.

"Eva, darling, let's go to Acapulco for a few days," Ricky suggested one day. "I know a lovely hotel, in a good but discrete location. We should have all the privacy we will need."

It sounded heavenly to me and I quickly consented. Dear Nanette loaned me a couple of attractive beach outfits to take with me, apparel she was certain Ricky would enjoy.

We set out on a glorious day, driving with the top down on his yellow convertible. We arrived at the hotel and registered as husband

and wife. I was so excited to be there in Acapulco. I remembered how romantic I thought this place was. This time I was there with my "dream-lover," and I thought nothing could be better.

Since I was anxious that no one should know that we were there together, I constantly cautioned him to keep a low profile. One morning, however, we were downstairs in the restaurant and I was displeased with the condition of the eggs I had ordered. Frustrated at having my order misunderstood, I got up from the table and confronted the waiter.

"Do you not see how bad these are?" I asked, my voice loud with my irritation. The waiter apologized and promised to bring a new order. When I got back to the table, Ricky was almost doubled over in laughter.

"This is how you keep a low profile?" he questioned. "The whole hotel could probably hear you!"

I was mortified. I had completely forgotten my worry over being discovered. Things did not end there however. Mexico may be a large country, but its society is small. Somehow Ricky's aunt who lived in Acapulco heard he was in town. Apparently she tried calling the room, but when she didn't receive an answer, she had the hotel bellman take her up. Imagine both our surprise when I answered the door! It was not my finest hour.

Nevertheless, our relationship continued to grow and when Ricky went to Houston for his residency, I went to visit him. While I was there, he begged me to stay there and live with him.

"Please, Eva, I love you and I want to be with you. I miss you too much."

"I miss you too, but I can't live with you without being married," I replied. "It is really too much."

"You know why I can't marry you now. I am still in school, I have no money, no way to support a wife."

We argued about it but came to no resolution. I loved him but I was not willing to live with him. It was 1964 and respectable couples did not live together without marriage. If he really wanted to marry me his parents, who were very wealthy would have helped. I told myself that he really was not ready to get married and then I started to think about our age difference. Ultimately we broke up and I was heartbroken. He was one of the great loves of my life and it took me a long time to get over him. Was it something in me that only made me fall in love with the wrong person?

CHAPTER FIVE

Dorita did come back and we visited Acapulco again. However, I was not prepared for the disaster that would happen. On the beach we met two young, good-looking men who started talking to us. It turned out that one of them was of Hungarian origin, the same as Dorita's father, and they soon found a lot in common. We accepted an invitation to go out with them in the evening, met them again the next day and spent the whole week with them, only coming home to the condo to sleep. Dorita, who was so keen on getting married, fell in love with the Hungarian who led us to believe he was a count, and encouraged her infatuation. His friend, who was my partner, sometimes made comments like: "She should be careful," but when I asked him what he meant he gave evasive replies. When I warned Dorita she paid absolutely no heed. By now she was completely carried away. When it was time to go back to Mexico City she had convinced herself that she was practically engaged to the count!

When we came home, she embraced my mother telling her about the encounter and said: "Tante Paula, don't you think I am engaged?" My mother fearing the worst looked at me and told her that things were going too fast. Before leaving Acapulco Dorita told the young man that he should call her in Mexico City, and since she was leaving three days later he should come to take her to the airport. Her big wish, she told him, would be if he would bring her a bracelet with his name engraved inside.

There was no call and he did not show up on her departure day. Dorita left with a broken heart and I felt that I shouldn't have let it get this far. A few days later, a woman who happened to know his family told me that he was married and had children. The bastards! I condemned them both, because his friend should have told me when he saw what was happening, but he did not want to spoil his friend's fun! As much as it hurt me to do so, I had to write to Dorita and tell her. I knew how devastating this news had to be.

◆　　　◆　　　◆

Through some friends in Mexico I had met the Froehlichs from Los Angeles, who after a while invited me to spend some time with them in Pacific Palisades, where they had a beautiful house on top of a hill. The house was full of modern art, which they had collected through the years. They had added a second floor to their ranch house and my room was upstairs. In back of the house was a large patio with a nice size swimming pool and an absolutely gorgeous view down to the ocean. On a clear night with all the lights on in Santa Monica, it was like a magic kingdom. From my room I had the same view and many an evening instead of going to bed right away I stood on the balcony looking out on this great world.

Harry and Anne Froehlich had two very nice teenage children, Marion and Clyde. Anne, a good-looking, very bright woman, was working as a CPA at a corporation. She was also very interested in politics and was active in the Democratic Party at the Pacific Palisades for many years. Harry was a tall and quite handsome man. He had a bras factory, which he had inherited from his father, and which was doing very well. Everybody treated me as family; they had known my late cousin Elfi very well, so I was no stranger to them, and they insisted that I stay a while because they enjoyed company.

They showed me around and one day took me to the Hollywood Bowl to a fabulous concert.

When they went to work I sometimes stayed home and swam in the pool. One day I decided that this was so private that I wanted to find out how it felt to skinny dip, and I fully enjoyed swimming in my birthday suit. When I confessed what I had done, they laughed and told me that I had been very lucky that the man who cleans the pool hadn't shown up. They said that many women did this in order to invite him to a little fun together. Well, I said, no more skinny dipping. After a wonderful couple of weeks I was sad to go home. The Froehlichs are still some of my best friends.

◆   ◆   ◆

Life with my uncle was getting more and more trying. He was still asking me when I would be looking for a job. I was taking driving lessons because I wanted a car and had to get a driver's license in Mexico. When he heard that, he said that I didn't have a car and therefore didn't need to drive. My reply was that everybody should know how to drive and reminded him that his daughter also had been driving.

"Yes," he said, "but she knew how to drive."

"Well, she wasn't born knowing how to drive, uncle, she had to learn it and that is what I want to do."

"Well, I certainly will never drive with you!" he shouted and stalked out of the room.

Finally I was ready to buy my first car! I was ecstatic. I could afford this because our savings from the income of the factory had been increasing and we did not have too many expenses while we were living at my aunt's house. Emerich had recommended a second-hand car dealer where I found a cute little car, a German Ford, light blue with white seats. It was in good condition and the man gave me a very good deal.

When I took my driver's test I was confronted again with the corruption. The inspector sat next to me in the car and asked me to drive him around. He gave me directions to where he wanted to go, where I should stop and start again, where I should turn. It is terrible to drive in downtown Mexico City. People don't respect traffic rules and whoever has the stronger car is out to win. However, the inspector complimented me on my driving and asked me to park the car so he could give me an oral test. After many questions, which I answered satisfactorily, he asked me which vehicles had the right of way. I listed all the obvious ones, but he said that I had forgotten one. When I asked him what it was, he said:

"A military convoy, of course." He then declared, "My dear lady; since you did not know the answer I will have to flunk you." He waited a moment. "So what will you do about it?"

"Well, if you really want to flunk me, I guess I will have to repeat the test as soon as possible."

"But that would be so embarrassing, don't you think? What will you tell your relatives and friends! Believe me I am really trying to help you so you don't have to repeat your test."

I knew full well what that meant, and I was determined not to bribe him. I wanted to get my driver's license on my own merits without having to buy it. The official cost of the license was high enough. So I just sat there and looked at him.

"Well," he finally said, "I guess I will make an exception this time and let you pass because you are such a good driver."

"That is very kind of you, sir, I really appreciate it," I managed to grit out of clenched teeth.

The first day I had my car and my driver's license, my uncle asked me to drive him to his friend's house for lunch. Consistency was not one of his strong points.

The first few times I had to venture into the center of the city I was absolutely petrified. I had to overcome the desire to close my eyes and pray, especially when at an intersection with a roundabout and six cars looked like they were coming at me from all directions. However, practice does make perfect and soon I became quite confident. Here I was 34 years old and only starting to drive!

◆   ◆   ◆

By this time I was becoming more worried about our future. My mother and I did not have a home or a country. To stay in Mexico permanently I would have to get married to a Mexican citizen, and although many young men I had met, except Ricky, wanted to marry me, I did not have the necessary attraction to them. I still wanted love, the kind of love my parents had. My worries about the future started to intensify, old fears of financial instability and lack of safety bubbling to the surface. What was to become of us? Would I really have to marry for convenience? I just couldn't see myself doing that.

One day Nanette had a wonderful idea. Knowing that my mother and I could not officially take over the business because we were not citizens, she offered to go into partnership with me. We would buy the business from my aunt and then establish it in Nanette's home or business. My aunt was happy with the idea and it would have worked out very well, if my disagreeable uncle hadn't vetoed this categorically. I was devastated. First he wanted to get rid of the business, and then he didn't want my aunt to sell it! We had some words and I decided that I had had enough. I convinced my mother that we should move out and get our own place.

Although my aunt hated to see us leave, we started looking for something suitable to rent. It should be near enough to my aunt's house so that if I was not available my mother could walk to the business. It was an expensive area yet we needed to find something affordable. Fortunately, through an ad in a paper, we found the perfect place. It was the upper floor of an old villa owned by a widow. She had had the upper floor converted into a one-room studio apartment, with a little kitchen, a bathroom and two rooms separated by an archway with a curtain. One room was furnished as a bedroom with a full size bed. The other room was a living room with a fireplace and a narrow day bed, which served as the sofa during the day. There was a balcony facing the street, and from the kitchen there was a door that led to a terrace, which was the roof of the lower part of the house. There was a separate entrance to our apartment from the driveway and stairs that led to our entrance door. The furniture, the kitchen and the bathroom were simple, but all we needed. As a matter of fact we thought this was the perfect place for us and the rent was reasonable. I was even allowed to park my car inside the gates in the driveway. Both my mother and I were ecstatic and wanted to move in as soon as possible. Before we moved in, however, I had to clean the place from top to bottom, and my good friend Nanette came to help me. It took us two days to get the apartment the way it should be.

Finally we were ready to move in and I was so excited! This was the first time since Austria, that we had a place of our own without having to share the bathroom with other people or accept hospitality. We had our privacy and we were free to do what we wanted when we wanted. The time we lived there was one of the happiest we'd had in quite a while. In the morning after making our break-fast, we would get into my car and I would drive us to my aunt's house to work. Lunch usually had to be eaten with them, but our evenings were free to make any kind of meal we wanted at whatever time we felt like eating. Our dinners were usually smaller, since in Mexico the main meal of the day was eaten at lunch.

One morning I woke up sick. I had a fever with a bad headache and I was terribly nauseated. On my chest I saw one red spot. We called our doctor who made housecalls. He came quickly and I told him that I suspected I had a children's disease. He laughed and said he doubted that at my age I would have anything like that, especially since I had not been in contact with any sick children.

"When you are covered with red spots, call me," he said, "in the meantime I think it is a flu. I recommend aspirins and bed-rest until you have no fever."

Sure enough, the next morning I woke up with a multitude of red spots and felt much worse. My dear doctor had to revise his diagno-sis; I did indeed have the chickenpox, which I had never had as a child. I was feeling miserable and aghast at all the "firsts" at my age. Clearly, I was a late bloomer in more than one way! Eventually I recovered, and life continued on in a comfortable way.

With our large family all around the world, every once in awhile, someone would come to visit us in Mexico. Among them was Eric, the son of my mother's cousin, Eddie Bonyhady, who had immi-grated to Australia. Eric was divorced and came to visit his relatives in Mexico on his way back home to Australia from Boston. We were very happy to see him and hear all about his parents. He had two sons, but didn't see much of them since the divorce. He was a delightful young man and the two of us hit it off right away. I took him around in my car and showed him the sights in Mexico City, including the pyramids of Tehotihuacan, and later the museums where all the great Mexican painters like Diego Rivera, Siqueiros and Orozco were exhibited. By the time he went back to Australia, we had become good friends and have remained so since then.

One day a man whom I had heard much about from his aunt in Switzerland, arrived in Mexico City. His name was Hans Kronberger, a famous physicist from Great Britain who was working for the United Kingdom Atomic Energy Authority. He was a third or fourth cousin of mine and his aunt, who had visited us in Mexico City recently, had told us that he was a widower. She worried about him being alone, although he had two daughters. Each time she said this, she would cast a meaningful look at me, describing in detail his achievements and emphasizing what a "catch" he was. Not surprisingly, I became curious about him. When he called to say that he was in Mexico and could he come to visit, I was excited. Apparently he was on a mission to review a water desalination project. When he came to my aunt's house and we were sitting in the living room, I finally had an opportunity to observe him. He was in his early forties, of medium height, quite slim, with blue eyes and a ruddy face. He was a sportsman and I learned that he was an avid mountaineer, as well as being a great swimmer and sailor. He had a ready smile and was full of wit and humor. Great, I thought to myself: an "ideal" man for an "ideal" woman. Not only was I not a sportswoman, I was concerned about measuring up to him intellectually.

I guess I was so buried in my thoughts, I didn't realize he was ready to leave. When he embraced me to say goodbye, he asked me if I would be willing to show him around Mexico the next day. I was delighted to do so and quickly promised him I would be his tourist guide.

The next day I picked him up at his hotel and gave him the grand tour. He was full of enthusiasm and curiosity, which I enjoyed very much. It made me feel proud to be living in Mexico and able to show off the marvelous sights. From then on we were together almost every day, except for the hours he had to work with the people from the university. As we were driving together he told me about his life, which had been fascinating.

During the Nazi era he had been put on a children's transport to England. Since he was only 14 years old he was temporarily put into a home with a family and told that he had two choices: go to a temporary camp for aliens or go to Australia. This, as was pointed out, presented great danger; there were threats of torpedoes everywhere and nobody could guarantee the safety of the transport. Despite this, my cousin opted for the latter and went to Australia for a while. Later he returned to Great Britain where he completed his studies and became a renowned nuclear physicist. His career took him to the top; he was awarded a title and medal from the Queen, attached to the British Atomic Energy Authority, and promised a knighthood in the near future. Aside from his professional achievements he also was a very accomplished pianist. I was terribly impressed by all this; but as I was soon to learn, he had also had a very sad life. His wife, whom he had loved dearly, died of a brain tumor after a long sickness and left him with two children. We both cried when he told me this. Why did one have to pay so dearly for every good thing that was received? Life wasn't fair, but I had discovered that a long time ago.

One day he introduced me to his host, Professor Nabor Carrillo, also a physicist and Dean of Science of the University of Mexico. Nabor Carrillo was a Mexican Indian, and as he told me, the only Indian who had reached such a high position in academia. Though he was not good looking, he was a very interesting man, full of great ideas and a drive to do good things for his country. His ambitions and ideas were so similar to my cousin's that they got along famously. Nabor Carrillo took an immediate liking to me and invited me to a dinner with all the scientists involved with Hans. He said he hoped I would not be intimidated by the fact that I was going to be the only woman. I assured him that I would be honored. Secretly, however I did have my doubts: I didn't mind being the only woman but I did feel out of my element as the only non-scientist. It turned out that I had nothing to fear, I was seated between Nabor and Hans, and everybody treated me with respect and admiration. The conversation was very general and we laughed a lot. Everybody was in a good mood and I had a wonderful time. When we said goodbye, Nabor invited me to a garden party he was giving at his house in a few days to honor Hans.

"Not bad, not bad at all," I told my mirror image later that week as I was dressing for the party. The white Dior sleeveless linen dress, which we had bought in a second-hand shop in Montevideo, looked very elegant and I was pleased. My mother sweetly said I looked like a fashion model. I had a tan and the white was very becoming. When Hans picked me up he complimented me on the beautiful dress. When we arrived at Nabor Carrillo's house the men looked at me admiringly and the ladies asked me where I had bought my lovely dress. Nabor Carillo's house was in Pedregal, a suburb near the university where all the natural lava stones of the area had been left to enhance the gardens. The garden was magnificent and there were many tables elegantly set on a well-cared lawn. For a while we stood around with drinks and I got to meet many interesting people with different professions and careers. Finally we sat down to a very late lunch. The waiters were serving and squeezing through tables and then it happened: A waiter carrying a large platter tripped behind my chair, spilling red, sticky sauce all over my dress! Aghast, everyone jumped up. I was almost in tears and Mrs. Carrillo quickly showed me to the powder room. We valiantly tried to wash the huge red stain out, but were not successful. My beautiful, new dress was sopping wet and the big stain only slightly washed out. There was no alternative; I had to go back to my table and make light of what had happened. During the whole party I felt very self-conscious yet was determined to have a good time anyway. The Carrillos offered to buy me a new dress but of course I refused. The drycleaners never got the stain out so I ended up having to throw the dress away. Nevertheless, I didn't care. The party was an experience that I wouldn't have wanted to miss.

When it was time for Hans to leave I drove him to the airport, and after a lot of hugs and kisses we parted. He assured me he would be back soon and that he would miss me. Of course I missed him too and I was totally confused about my feelings. However, I was very proud of the latest developments and needless to say, so was my mother.

Me and Hans Kronberger

Life went back to normal, we worked in the factory, and followed our old routine. I went out with couples and different friends, went to parties and worried about the future. Looking back I feel that instead of enjoying my interesting life, I worried too much. The fears and insecurities of my childhood had never really gone away. Unfortunately this was a trait that has accompanied me all my life.

At a cocktail party I happened to meet the Austrian ambassador, who asked me:

"How come we never see such a lovely young woman at our parties?"

"That, Mr. Ambassador, is because I would not dream of attending a party given by a country that threw me out."

"You have to forgive and forget, young lady!"

"No I don't!" I declared, and turned around and walked out.

That was the way I felt at the time, although in the end, those sentiments would return to haunt me. Life has the power to change one's perspective and outlook in so many ways. I had only to look at my own life to know this. I learned one thing however: never say "never." With maturity, beliefs, which are black and white, often mute into grey.

When Hans came back to Mexico, he brought me a nice cashmere sweater twin-set, and we continued where we had left off. We talked a lot, went on short day trips and he declared that he was interested in a serious relationship with me. He asked me to come visit him in Manchester, which was near his home. He told me that he was about to be knighted by the Queen, which would make me Lady Eva. Well, I don't think he could have put it any clearer that he wanted to marry me, but first I had to see where and how he lived. I promised to visit him very soon.

My mother had always talked about visiting her brother Noldi and his family, who had stayed in Vienna. Actually we had never been able to afford such a trip, but now that we had some money saved, it was not so far out of reach. In view of my mother's seventieth birthday coming up, I thought that if we didn't make this trip now, when would we? She wasn't getting any younger nor was the family in Vienna, and who knew how long I would be able to travel with her? If I married, it would not be so easy any more. So we planned to go to Europe for her birthday, and on the way go to Great Britain to visit Hans.

CHAPTER SIX

It seems like life is either feast or famine! A couple of weeks after Hans left, I had a call from a man who said he was Dr. Jay Miller from Seattle, and that he was a friend of someone I knew in Los Angeles. He said he was on a trip to South America, and our mutual friend had told him that I had been living there and could give him advice for his trip. He wanted to know if it would be possible to take me to dinner? I told him I would be happy to meet him at his hotel. I pulled up at the hotel entrance and standing there was a very tall man with brown hair and glasses and a big smile. He approached my car, which I had described to him, and he introduced himself. He seemed a little shy, but he told me how this meeting was only due to a strange coincidence. Jay had gone through Los Angeles where he was visiting relatives and had called Bart Stern, our mutual friend, several times without finding him. As he was leaving the hotel to go to the airport he heard the phone ring in his room and returned to answer. It was Bart, who apologized for not having returned his calls sooner, but he had been out of town. After hearing about Jay's trip, he told him that he knew a nice girl in Mexico who would surely be happy to show him around and give him some pointers about visiting Uruguay and Argentina. Who would have known that this last minute phone call would yield such heavy consequences!

I took Jay on my now "standard" sightseeing tour. The evening ended with an enjoyable dinner before I took him back to his hotel. The next day I drove him to Cuernavaca. He was tired and slept the whole way. I thought to myself that he trusted my driving but he was bored with my company! Well, I decided, this will be the end of my tour guide services for you, Dr. Miller. However, when we arrived in Cuernavaca he was awake and apologized profusely. He did not know what had happened to him, and I remembered the altitude and what it had done to us the first days in Mexico. I showed him the lovely *Zocalo* (there is a *Zocalo in every town and village*) and then took him to a hotel that had a large swimming pool. It was very hot and I had told him to bring a bathing suit. When I met him by the pool clad in my bathing suit and without shoes, he looked me up and down and declared:

"You have flat feet."

I had to laugh; what a weird guy, I thought, is that all he has to say about me? Thanks a lot! His comment reminded me of the boy I'd had a crush on when we were in the same play. He had told me I was perfect for playing a boy since my chest was so flat. Well, I decided, at least that part of my anatomy had improved greatly. Now all I had to worry about were my feet!

However, the rest of the day was pleasant and he was quite forthcoming about himself. He was born of Jewish Russian parents who had come to the U.S. in the early 1900s. He had two sisters and they were both married with children. His father had had a meat packing plant and when he died a few years after Jay's mother, the three children inherited it. Although Jay was a veterinarian, he wanted to be the sole owner of the plant and had therefore bought out his sisters. All this had not contributed to a good relationship among the siblings, and unfortunately, he was not on speaking terms with them at the time.

I felt rather inundated by the amount of personal information Jay shared with me at this outing, but I managed to make the right comments at the right time. I supposed Jay just needed to get it off his chest, and I felt very sorry thinking how lonely he must be. On our way back to Mexico City he apologized for talking so much and asked me if he could spend the next day with me. I promised I would show him around some of the museums and agreed to have dinner with him at a place of his choice.

The next day when I picked Jay up from his hotel, I explained that I had one errand to run before going to the museums. I had to deliver an order of gloves to the boutique in the Hotel Maria Isabel. Jay came with me and made a big deal over how efficient I was. I thought it was a bit overdone: All I did was add up the prices of each glove the owner of the boutique picked, and write out an invoice. Yet his warm regard was enjoyable and created a comfortable atmosphere between us.

After that, we went sightseeing and he especially appreciated the new *Museo de Antropologia*. It had just been built and both the architecture and the exhibits were absolutely stunning. There were examples of Mayan and Aztec cultures as well as other Indian tribes in every aspect. The art was breathtaking and although I had been in the museum many times I could never get enough of it, seeing something new every time I went.

Filled with all these wonderful impressions, and in a very good mood, we went to a restaurant that had music and dancing. Jay had brought a tape recorder, which in those days was rather large, and a movie camera. He was so impressed with the restaurant that he used them both. He taped the music and I translated the words of the Spanish songs, most of which were love songs, by softly singing them in his ear. We danced late into the night, ending with a slow dance that engendered considerable warmth between us. All in all it was a lovely evening and I must say surprisingly romantic. I had not thought to be attracted to another man so quickly after seeing Hans. I felt confused and unsure, yet despite that intrigued and a little sorry that he would soon be leaving.

When I left Jay at his hotel that night we said our farewells since he was departing the next morning to go to Argentina. I never thought I would see him again. He was visiting relatives in Buenos Aires, and being in the meat packing business, wanted to see the cattle that Argentina was famous for. Putting him out of my mind, I went back to life as usual.

A week later I unexpectedly received a long distance call from Jay in Montevideo, Uruguay. He had gone there specifically because it was where I had grown up and therefore he felt the urge to call me. What a nice gesture, I thought to myself. I was flattered by his interest. He then told me that he was on his way to Brazil, but that he had changed his return ticket so he could come through Mexico again on his way back to the States. I was pleasantly surprised by his new schedule, as I hadn't expected him to return to Mexico. This opened up a whole new situation and I wondered how I would feel when I saw him again. Would I still feel an attraction to him? Or had it simply been the romantic nature of the night we had spent dancing?

His next call came from his hotel in Mexico. He was back and looking forward to seeing me. When I picked him up he was so excited to see me that he hugged me and told me how much he had missed me. He had brought me a beautiful yellow topaz ring, which he had bought at H. Stern in Rio de Janeiro, one of the most expensive and exclusive gem jewelers. I was overwhelmed and didn't know what to say. Then I told him that although it was a beautiful ring, I couldn't possibly accept such a costly gift from him. He responded that it was solely a thank you gift for my having been such an enjoyable guide. After some discussion I decided to accept it. Rings usually were too big on my small fingers, but this one, to my amazement, fit perfectly. He smiled and told me he had brought a picture of me to show the jeweler! Once again I was flattered, yet also a little wary. Despite his words to the contrary, I felt like I was being wooed, and I wasn't sure what I thought about that.

I took him home for lunch at my aunt's house. Aunt Elsa was curious to meet him after having heard about him and his phone calls. My mother had already met him once on his previous visit when I had stopped home to change for dinner. So we had lunch with the whole family, whom he enjoyed meeting, being very impressed by my relatives' lovely home.

He insisted that we go dancing that evening and he was in such a great mood he swept me up in his excitement. While dancing he told me how much he liked me and declared that I was the only woman whom he would ever consider marrying. I was astonished to hear his sentiments. Though I knew we both had felt an attraction to each other, it had never occurred to me that he would feel so strongly so quickly.

He went on to say that he was 46 years old and had never been married. He had once been madly in love with a Gentile girl, but his parents had made him promise that he'd only marry a Jewish woman. He had practically given up on that until he met me. What could I say, except that I liked him too, but that we didn't really know each other?

"Well," he said, "that can be remedied very easily. Why don't you and your mother visit me in Seattle? That way we can get to know each other better and you can see Seattle and my business."

I thanked him for his invitation but replied: "Unfortunately it won't be possible right now because we have planned a trip to

Europe next month. We won't be able to go to Seattle until later in the year."

"Why don't you come to Seattle first and then go from there to Europe?" he suggested. "Please say yes, I promise to make it worth your while." He was very sweet and charming, almost like a child, as he enumerated all the enjoyable activities we would experience in Seattle. I felt the tug of possibilities and wondered if it would be a mistake not to explore them.

So, although it was a roundabout way to travel to Europe, my mother and I accepted the invitation. We also decided that we should visit more places than just England and Vienna. After all she had two brothers in Israel, and cousins and friends all over Europe. So we arranged to take a long trip, stay in pensions and do a little sightseeing. Since we did not know how long we would be gone, we gave up our apartment and I sold my car. I could always replace it. Our excitement grew as we planned our trip and we couldn't wait to get started.

When we arrived in Seattle, Jay met us at the airport. He drove us to a very nice hotel downtown. It was spring and the weather was gorgeous. The azaleas and rhododendrons were in full bloom and the majestic mountains surrounding Seattle were clearly visible. We were awed when we saw the rugged mountains and verdant hills. Jay took us all around Seattle to show us the deep blue Puget Sound and harbor as well as Lake Washington, which was very impressive. Lovely villas were built along the shores of the lake and there was a floating bridge crossing from Seattle to Mercer Island. It was a stunning city.

The next morning Jay picked us up to take us to his business, the Miller Packing Plant. It was located about 15 miles south of Seattle in Renton. It was a large establishment, which included a small private house where Jay had made his home since he didn't want to be too far from the business. It was quite cozy, but Jay hurriedly explained that this was only his bachelor pad.

Then he took us on a tour of his plant. As we entered, my mother and I had to hold our breaths at the awful smell that assaulted us. What we saw was even worse: Hanging from big hooks along the walls were dozens of bloody carcasses, with blood slowly dripping down to the ground. I realized that a packing plant was really just another name for a slaughterhouse, with the meat sold to different butcher stores. Despite the gory scene, neither my mother nor I fainted or ran out of the place, apparently passing Jay's test of our stomachs and endurance. Though daunting, we thought it was an impressive enterprise, but were we relieved when we finally walked out of there.

We got in the car and the fresh air did much to revive our energy as Jay took us back to Lake Washington. He drove us to a house that was situated right on the edge of the lake. The two-story home was beautifully located, and just needed a little tender loving care. He explained that the house had belonged to his parents. They had lived there many years and he had inherited it. At the moment, a cousin of his was staying there with his family, but he planned to move all three of us into the house. He turned to my mother and said,

"Mutti, I have lost my mother, so I would be so happy to have you as my mother. You could live in the apartment on the ground level, and we would live upstairs."

This touched my mother and me very much. Without having told Jay, he had somehow realized how much I wanted to be able to have my mother near me. We had been through so much, she and I. Living in separate countries would have been terribly arduous. We thanked him profusely for his kind understanding.

More sightseeing followed with him taking us to the marketplace in the city. Pike Place is a wonderful market where vegetables, meats, fish, spices and other wares are displayed. It also has a spectacular flower market. Jay gallantly bought some flowers for our room, being quite the attentive gentleman squiring us about town. After a few days, it was time to continue our trip and Jay wanted to know all the places we were going to and when we would be there. I gave him our itinerary and schedule. With a sad face he took us to the airport and we said our goodbyes. Despite the success of the visit, I felt strongly that we still didn't know each other well enough for any commitment.

When we arrived in New York we checked into the Sheraton Hotel on Sixth Avenue. Since this was my mother's first time in this exciting and bustling city, I tried to show her as much as I could. I wanted her to have at least a whiff of this amazing place. One of our activities was buying my mother a beautiful mink stole (which was a birthday gift from my aunt). We went to see a furrier we had met in Mexico who had promised to give us a good price whenever we needed a fur piece. My mother was thrilled and, since she was always cold, she really enjoyed the warmth and elegance of it. We also called Martha Reuss, my mother's cousin, who lived in New York with her husband Dr. Erich Reuss. They invited us to their apartment and we had a memorable meeting. I had never met them before. They had lived in Berlin, but my mother of course knew Martha, who was the sister of our beloved cousin Mira Hafner. We talked a lot and one of the subjects was why I was not married yet. We explained the strange dilemma I was in, having received a marriage proposal from two men at the same time! Martha knew of Hans Kronberger, and she certainly knew his aunt, Grete Arnthal. After all Martha was also related to them. When we finally returned to our hotel we promised to let them know my decision when we came back to New York on the way back from our trip.

After a few interesting days we took off for Europe, our first stop to be England. My feelings were very mixed; when my mother had first mentioned that she wanted to go back to Vienna for a visit with her brother, I was shocked. I couldn't imagine going back to the country that had been so hateful and where I had been so afraid. Would I see a murderer in every person I would meet? Would the word "monster" be written all over their faces? I only agreed to go to Austria to please my mother and to see our family. I reassured myself that it would be a short trip. I would try to make the best of it and then leave. However, I was looking forward to visiting London, where we would meet not only Hans but also Wilma Wolff, a very good friend of my mother and my aunt.

Wilma was a very lively, charming lady. Although a little on the heavy side, she carried herself very elegantly, especially dressed in the most expensive designer clothes. She was the mother of some good friends in Mexico, where she had also once lived. However, after the war she and her husband went back to Europe where they were able to reclaim all their businesses so they had become quite wealthy. They later moved to Switzerland and had been living there since. Wilma's husband had died early on, but her son carried on the business in Switzerland. Although Wilma was living in Geneva, she made it a point to be in London at the same time we were. She even promised that she would meet us at the airport. We thought it was a lovely sentiment, but we certainly did not expect her, especially as our flight arrived at seven o'clock in the morning.

It was a wonderful surprise though, when we saw her standing outside Customs. Bless her heart this was more than just a friendly gesture! This was real friendship.

Outside a Rolls Royce was waiting and the chauffeur put our luggage in the trunk and then took us to our hotel. Wilma said she would pick us up again later for lunch, so we went up to our room to unpack. Another big surprise was in store for us. There was a gorgeous flower arrangement standing on one of the tables. Mother immediately said that it must surely be from Hans for me. Delighted, I hurried over to open the card. As I read it, my mouth dropped open. "To Mutti, for Mother's Day with best wishes and love, Jay." I was astounded. This man really knew how to get to me! Once again I felt the threads of his wooing, stretching all they way to Europe.

We went to lunch with Wilma and she promised to show us around London the next day. In the meantime I had to meet Hans, who was coming to our hotel that afternoon.

By the time Hans arrived at the hotel, it had started to rain. He apologized for being a bit late; he had had trouble getting a taxi. He hugged and kissed me and told me how he had missed me and how happy he was that we were finally here. He said hello to my mother and asked me to come with him so he could show me his favorite places and sights in London. It was raining quite a bit when we stepped on the street but he said, "This is London, you have to get used to the weather!"

We walked to one museum and then took a bus to another, eventually walking by the guards in front of Buckingham Palace. By this time I was drenched, so I asked him if we could have some tea or something where we would be indoors. He was quite willing to do so, and finally took us to a dry place. He wanted to talk about our future, telling me that when I came back from our extended tour to the Continent, he wanted me to come to his hometown near Manchester so I could see whether I could live there. He told me that he loved me and wanted to marry me, but that there was one problem: Where would my mother live? She could not live with us in Manchester as my mother would not know anybody, and her English was not very good. He felt that she should stay in Mexico with our relatives. This issue had not occurred to me. I had always thought that wherever I went, so would my mother. But Hans was right, what would she do in Manchester? I suddenly felt very cold and it wasn't because I was wet from the rain. I was finally forced to face reality, and I didn't like it—as a matter of fact, I hated it.

I had very tender feelings towards Hans and was very proud that he wanted to marry me. Why couldn't things be different? Why does one have to give up one's life in order to start another? When I told my mother about our conversation, she was quick to assure me that I should not worry about her. Nevertheless I did. Had my father been alive all of this would not have been a problem. I thought about Jay and how willing he was to include my mother in his plans, despite her lack of English. But I knew that was not enough of a reason to marry him and I struggled with my conflicting emotions.

I told Hans that I really cared for him very much, but that at the moment I couldn't give him an answer. He was disappointed but understanding. He told me he had to go back to Manchester, where he had a meeting in the morning, but he would come back the day of our departure to see us off. Perhaps by then, I would have arrived at a decision.

The next day Wilma Wolff took us around in her Rolls Royce; we met her son, who happened to be in London also. Although Wilma only shopped at the most expensive designer shops, she gave us the names of stores where we could get fine clothes for lower prices and I was able to buy a lovely coat at Marks and Spencer, a much less expensive department store. When we parted, she warmly invited us to visit her in Geneva.

The day we were going to leave London, Hans came early to see us off. I must admit we had quite a bit of luggage. After all, we were going to be gone for months. Hans, however, was shocked to see how we were traveling. Of course he was right, we had so many stops that the luggage would become a burden, but we did not want to leave anything behind. I realized that the heavy traveling iron I had packed would be ridiculous to take with me. So I took it out of my bag and handed it to him saying:

"Please keep this for me and I will collect it on my way back when I come to see you in Manchester."

I wasn't sure I meant it, but at that moment I felt sorry for him and, when it came right down to it, I wasn't sure what I wanted. We hugged and kissed and went to the gate.

◆　　　◆　　　◆

We were flying non-stop to Tel Aviv, Israel, where two of my mother's brothers lived. One was the youngest of my mother's nine siblings, named Emil, and the other was the second oldest,—a physician named Sylvio Stoessl. I hadn't seen the youngest since I was a child. Being a Zionist he went to Israel in the early 1930s. The physician, however, had visited us in Montevideo, and to my chagrin at the time, stayed with us for a while before going on to Mexico. He still happened to be there when we arrived in Mexico in 1960. He was a strange individual who couldn't get along with anybody, had his own ideas and wouldn't change them if it cost him his life. He certainly had not endeared himself to me, but I was hoping that I would be able to tolerate him. However, I was looking forward to seeing my younger uncle and was very excited about visiting Israel for the first time.

When the United Nations was voting whether to declare Israel a nation, Uruguay had been one of the first countries to recognize Israel as a State. I had been so very proud of Uruguay, my adopted country. Now we would see what had become of all the difficult work and heartbreaking hardships that the Jewish settlers had suffered.

We landed in Tel Aviv, and with my heart pounding my mother and I embraced each other in excitement. What an exhilarating moment! To be in the country every Jewish person in the world revered and longed for. We wanted to run right out and hug my uncles and the whole country in delight. But we had to be patient, there was a long line and the custom officers were very thorough. Everything had to be opened and inspected as part of their security efforts. When we finally came out and saw my two uncles, we were so full of joy I even forgot my antagonistic feelings toward Sylvio. We hugged and looked at each other and laughed and talked. Finally we took a *sherut* (a taxi) to the pension where my uncles had reserved a room for us. We drove through Tel Aviv and I was amazed by the size of the city. There were many high-rises, which housed offices and apartments, and on the oceanfront, there were a few large hotels. The traffic was amazingly heavy and reminded me of Mexico. The pension they had picked was only two blocks from the ocean and although it was an old house, our rooms were pleasant and clean. We left our things in the room and went out to a restaurant located on a side street, which was quite busy with traffic and pedestrians. Lunch was served in the garden on a communal table, which my uncles, my mother and I shared with other people. Some of them spoke German, some spoke Yiddish, but the younger ones spoke only Hebrew.

Sylvio was a bachelor and lived in an apartment by himself. He had a little car and when a patient was sick on *Shabbat* he would make a house call. Unfortunately, the strict Orthodox sect in Tel Aviv did not want cars to be driven on *Shabbat*, because driving a car was considered work, so they threw stones at him. The conflicts between the Orthodox and the more liberal Jews were ongoing and divisive. Sadly they continue to be problematic.

My mother's younger brother, Emil, was married to a German widow, and was an actor in a German-speaking theater in Tel Aviv. We went to one play while we were there and were quite impressed. Many years later, Austria decided to award my uncle with a medal of merit for having been an ambassador for German culture. Emil drove a Moped and went everywhere on it. When he went out with his wife they took a taxi, but I had the pleasure of riding on the back of the scooter. Pleasure is perhaps exaggerated, since I held on tightly to his back and was scared stiff by the crazy traffic in Tel Aviv!

My mother and I booked several tours and visited Haifa, Jerusalem, Lake Kenerit (also known as the Sea of Galilee), the towns of Galilee, Nazareth and many of the important monuments and memorials.

On the roads to Jerusalem and Haifa, we saw the remains of destroyed tanks which were left as memorials of the 1948 war. Seeing them we could feel the agony and hope simultaneously that the Israelis must have experienced during those days of that decisive war. All through our stay in Israel I felt the presence of an ideal in the society: one of building a Jewish homeland, of fulfilling the dream of returning to the land of our ancestors, and of amassing the strength to defend a fledgling country. This found expression particularly in the *kibbutzim* that we visited where the members lived and worked together as a commune, committed to a common cause. The people worked hard without the desire to enrich their own pockets. It was idealism in the truest sense of the word.

Another issue that became evident was that the Israeli youth were absolutely shocked and enraged by the fact that the European Jews had allowed themselves to be killed by the Nazis in concentration camps without fighting back. They were so outraged that they could not even feel sorry for the victims. They were absolutely certain that this was something that would never have happened to them. While I admired their self-sufficiency and determination to be free from persecution, I realized they didn't understand how unprepared and incredulous the European Jews were about the Nazis. Their families had lived there for generations, fully assimilated into society, and they could not imagine the extremes to which the Nazis would go in committing genocide.

Sadly, whenever I listened to the news on the radio, I would hear President Nassar of Egypt raving against Israel and threatening the country. "We will push Israel into the sea," he kept shouting. This was something that sent tremors of fear down my spine and I admired the brave, young people who were not afraid.

After two weeks of sightseeing in Israel, we said goodbye to a country, which had been so interesting and inspiring to us, and went to Rome, Italy.

We had booked a room in a hotel near a park, and were happy to see that we had a wonderful view of the green trees and flowers. Rome was very impressive and beautiful. We didn't know where to go first, so we took the tours that had been recommended and saw the glorious monuments, churches and of course the Vatican with St. Peter's Cathedral. We were admiring this Cathedral, when all of a sudden there was silence, people stood up and I could hear them murmuring: "The Pope is coming, the Pope is coming." My mother and I stood in awe as the Pope was carried in on his chaise. He lifted his hand and blessed us all. Then he was gone. We were amazed that we just happened to be there at that particular moment. We were sure it couldn't hurt to be blessed by the Pope!

In Rome we met friends from Mexico, Dr. and Mrs. Kratzmar and decided to travel together as long as possible. Dr. Kratzmar was a gynecologist, he was short and bald, but with a wonderful personality. His wife was a lovely woman who adored her husband and was kind to everybody. Mother had made an appointment to get together in Venice with her childhood friend, Edith Segre, who now lived in Milan with her husband. Since we still had a week before we were to meet her, we decided to go to Florence for a week with the Kratzmars. At a very good travel agency we were able to make a reservation at a lovely pension in the center of town in Florence, which had reasonable rates. We also booked seats on the train to Florence and from there to Venice.

How can one city contain so much beauty and art as Florence did! At that time, in 1966, the floods that destroyed so much art in the Uffizi Galleries had not happened yet, so we were able to see everything. We went there twice and still saw only a part of what we wanted. With seeing these galleries, the other museums and all the beautiful sculptures, we were saturated and could barely remember what we saw and where. It was asking too much to assimilate all that beauty in such a short time.

One afternoon it was very sunny so I bought myself a lovely white hat with a navy trim. It was very becoming indeed and I was walking quite proudly, when a dove decided to do her business right on top of my new hat! Our friend, the doctor, broke out in laughter; he was so happy that it had dropped on me and not on his bald head! How mean; I thought he could have wiped his head off with a handkerchief, whereas I had a new hat that could never be clean again. Of course the stain never came out and the hat had the same ending as my white dress in Mexico. Oh, well, as my "little sister" Dorita used to say: "More has been lost in war."

All four of us took a train to Venice; however, the Kratzmars were going to a spa at some lake, so they had to get off before us and we were sorry to see them go.

Venice was lovely and my mother's reunion with the friend that she hadn't seen in almost 30 years was wonderful to see. Edith Segre was a charming person and very good company. She was the sister of the kind lady in Buenos Aires, who had rescued me when I was so sick from Cordoba. Together we visited parts of Venice including the Doges Palace and St. Mark's Cathedral. We took a few gondola rides and I loved the singing of the gondoliers. Unfortunately, after a few days we had to say goodbye to Edith and to Italy and to continue with our trip to Austria.

On the plane to Vienna I was very anxious. How would I feel coming back to the country that we had sworn never to set foot in again? 27 years after our dramatic departure we were returning to Vienna; I was filled with trepidation. But then I thought about my uncle and his family who had been in a concentration camp and were still living in Austria, as well as my cousin Jenny Fleischmann, whose parents had perished in the gas chamber. Jenny, having survived a concentration camp herself, was also back in Vienna with her husband Laci. Since the camp she had been in was not a death camp, she was saved when the Allies came and liberated her. Jenny was the older sister of my cousin Grete, who had been with me when I had the lice. All these relatives were now living in Vienna, so I swallowed all my fears and promised myself that I would look at things in a more positive way.

My uncle Noldi met us at the airport and tearfully we hugged each other. His hair had turned completely white, but he was still quite good-looking. Noldi was a few years older than my mother, but he had always been a big sportsman and had kept himself physically fit. We took a taxi and went to the pension at which they had reserved a room for us. Driving through the somewhat familiar streets I couldn't help remembering the swastikas flying from the buildings the way I had last seen it. However, the joy of my mother seeing her brother again and their happy chatter soon made me change my mood. I finally was able to participate in the banter and the, sometimes serious conversation.

We had dinner at Noldi and Ilona's apartment and we met John, their son, who was studying medicine, though he would have rather become a music conductor. He loved classical music and could recognize the conductor just by listening to the piece. John had not even been born when we left Austria, and he was a baby when they were put in a concentration camp. How they all must have suffered!

Although John still carried the experience around with him, he was a very nice young man and we felt close immediately. During our two months stay in Vienna we often spent time together and talked about everything, including Hans Kronberger, who he said, had suffered bouts of depression, which he had inherited from his father. I was surprised to hear this and somewhat disconcerted. I knew that he was very sad about losing his wife to such a lingering and terrible disease, but this put a new light on our relationship and the possibility of marriage.

Next morning, my mother and I took a streetcar to the boutique owned by Jenny Fleischmann. We hadn't seen her yet and were going to take her out to lunch. We asked the streetcar conductor where we had to get off to go to a certain street and he told us he would let us know. However, there was a passenger who said that he was going the same way and we could get off with him.

"But please, sir, take good care of these ladies, I am very particular about my passengers!" said the conductor in typical Viennese dialect, and we all had to laugh. I think this moment was the turning point; after all, most of the people now were too young to have been Nazis, I thought. From then on I looked at things with different eyes and a more open mind.

Jenny was ecstatic to see us, but she couldn't help the bitterness that surfaced in almost all conversations. During lunch she told us all about her past and present life and we were happy to see that she had done fairly well for herself. She was a very resolute woman and knew what she wanted. She lived in a delightful, small apartment near the Stephan's Cathedral, and owned a comfortable apartment at a nearby mountain resort called Semmering. She had a successful boutique and a loving husband. Life should be so good for everyone! She invited us to Semmering the following weekend. It was a beautiful resort in the mountains, which I remembered as a child. During the two months of our stay in Vienna we went there several times and enjoyed it immensely, although it was quite cold even in the middle of summer. Other times we went to Baden with Noldi and Ilona where she was "taking the cure." Baden was a lovely little town near Vienna and there were mineral baths offered in various hotels as part of the "cure." The air was clear and fresh; there were many trees and parks, and people from Vienna enjoyed going there for weekends or vacation.

Our time in Vienna was spent in part going to the opera, where we saw "The Magic Flute," and to plays and concerts. We took advantage of many of the cultural events and sometimes went to a performance every evening. We also revisited old familiar places, and I must admit that we enjoyed our stay.

Unexpectedly, Jay telephoned me in Vienna. He had gotten our phone number from my uncle Noldi, where he had called first. He told me that he missed me and begged me to meet him in New York. During the whole trip I had been thinking about Hans and Jay and it slowly dawned on me that I had given up the idea of marrying Hans, especially with what my cousin John had said about him. I wrote him that I would not be able to come to Manchester, which was my way of letting him know that I would not marry him. He understood right away and was furious. I was sorry to let him down like that, but I had to do it. I was not prepared to make the sacrifices needed to live in Manchester without my mother and I had become concerned about his mental health. Three years later I heard that he had committed suicide, and I was devastated. I mourned the loss of such a brilliant man whom I was very fond of, and struggled with lingering guilt feelings for having turned down his proposal. Perhaps he would have been a happier man, married, although I knew that depression was not so easily cured. Yet a part of me could only be relieved that I had not married him.

The three-months trip had been lovely and a wonderful experience. Both my mother and I enjoyed seeing all the new and familiar places together, and we had relished the time we spent with our relatives. However, now, as we returned from Europe, a more difficult time arrived. I had to make up my mind about what to do with my life. I was 36 years old, unmarried and with no permanent home.

We arrived in New York at the end of August. The first person I saw when we came out of Customs was Jay with flowers in his hands. I had mixed feelings when we hugged: He was a very good-looking person but I did not feel a serious attraction to this near stranger; yet

I was happy to see him. He was so obviously delighted to have me back. There still remained one problem: my mother's English wasn't good and their communication was very difficult. We spent a week with Jay in New York, where he introduced me to his uncle who lived there, and the two of them took me around the jewelry district in search of an engagement ring for me. My protestations that I could not and would not accept a ring right now, fell onto deaf ears. Jay was resolved and I once again felt the strength of his determination to marry me. Only after looking at a number of very ornate rings was I finally able to get my message across. It was not the right time for us to make this decision. I had not spent more than 21 days with Jay since I had met him, and this week in New York was crucial to form an opinion about what this man was like. Even then, I felt that only a total of one month was not sufficient to get to know him, and I told him that we needed more time. Nevertheless, he was charming, attentive, and presented his most gracious side. He was disappointed that I couldn't make a commitment, but he understood and agreed to confine our relationship strictly to the telephone for a while.

CHAPTER SEVEN

Back in Mexico, at my aunt and uncle's house we were received by the servants who informed us that Mr. and Mrs. Jarvis were on a trip and wouldn't be back for three weeks. In the meantime we should occupy the master bedroom. It was strange to come back to this large empty house, but we needed rest. A few days later I was in bed with a kidney infection, had high fever and felt miserable. My poor mother worried a lot, but with the right antibiotic I was soon recovering. In the meantime Jay called from Seattle every other day.

So as I recuperated, I asked myself, where do we go from here? We would have to look for another apartment when my aunt and uncle came back, the glove business was not something that I could count on, and we would have to leave the country every six months. The young men I had met in Mexico were not sufficiently attractive and did not appeal to me. I started to think of the cute house on the lake in Seattle where my mother was welcome to stay and have her own quarters, and Jay's kindness so far; with time, his marriage proposal became appealing. A few weeks later, I told him that I would be happy to be his wife. He was so excited that he said the wedding should take place as soon as possible. We set the date for a day in October. I asked myself whether I was doing what I never wanted to do: marry for convenience?

My aunt and uncle were not happy that I was getting married and leaving Mexico. I asked my uncle whether my mother could stay with them for a few months, so that Jay and I would have some time alone as a couple; with my mother joining us later. Everything seemed to fall into place, and I was relieved that I had finally made a decision. In retrospect I did not know him long enough or well enough; but time was growing short and I felt compelled to make a decision.

Three weeks before the wedding Jay called me to say that business was deteriorating in the packing plant. Hides, which had a large profit margin compared to the meat which had a very small one, had gone down in price, and his business was failing. Did I want to back out of the marriage? From the way he said it I knew that he was very scared that I might decide in favor of his suggestion. Of course my decision to marry him was not based on financial considerations, so I told him that this development had nothing to do with our getting married. After all, he could be a veterinarian again and I could always find a job. His relief and joy were heartwarming, and we decided to keep everything as it was.

Jay had sent me a list of people to invite to the wedding and I sent out the invitations. I had forgotten his sister's last names so I didn't know that their names were included on the list. They became upset that I had not written a few personal lines on their invitation and they and their husbands had decided not to come to their brother's wedding in Mexico. I was disappointed, especially for Jay. It seemed amazing to me that they wouldn't attend their only brother's wedding. It appeared that relations with his siblings were still rocky. However, his uncle, whom I had never met before, accepted the invitation. I was relieved that poor Jay would at least have one family member at his wedding.

To enter the U.S. I had to show the consul that I was married to an American, and then it would take two weeks before a visa was issued. In order to comply with this, we decided to get married by a judge two days before our religious wedding. This way we could get the paperwork started, and by the time we were ready to go Seattle I would have my visa.

My uncle magnanimously offered to pay for the wedding, which was planned to take place in an orthodox synagogue with a banquet hall on the premises. Through the six years of our stay in Mexico we had made many friends, all of which were invited. We planned the menu, which had to be kosher, and everything was organized by the time Jay arrived three days before the religious ceremony.

When I picked him up at the airport he had disappointing news: The house by the lake was no longer available, he had given it to his cousin because he felt the neighborhood was deteriorating. In addition, some of his friends had advised him not to live with his mother-in-law, so that was no longer an option. I was very unhappy with his unilateral decision and asked him why he hadn't told me this before he arrived. It took me a while to get over this initial shock, and I think, some bitterness remained which as much as I tried, I could not shake. However, he brought me a very lovely solitaire diamond ring that he had picked out in Seattle.

The next day we went to the judge for our civil ceremony and my whole family was there: Of course my mother, my aunt and uncle, cousin Henry and his wife, and my cousin Emerich. After the ceremony Henry took us to a nice restaurant for lunch and I enjoyed being with my relatives. In the afternoon we went to the American Embassy to initiate my visa procedure.

When we picked up Jay's uncle at the airport and told him that we were already married by civil law, he seemed shocked. I had the feeling that his uncle had come to warn me or inform me of something that I should have known, but he kept quiet. We took him to the house, and he was impressed with my relatives and their nice home.

He stayed at the same hotel where Jay was staying and I finally took Jay and his uncle back there for the night. The next time we would see each other would be in front of the rabbi.

That night I couldn't sleep. I was worried that I had made the wrong decision. Would I be able to make a go of this marriage? Was I jumping into something prematurely? I had never met his sisters, and the fact that they were not even coming to our wedding bothered me. How would I get along with them? Talk about cold feet, mine were icicles! Where were all the dreams that a bride was supposed to have?

My wedding dress was long white silk with a shorter veil. After the wedding, as we were saying goodbye to the family, my mother told Jay that I needed a lot of love because I had lost my father so early. This is something that Jay would never forgive her for.

"What does your mother want from me?" he growled, "I am not your father."

I thought this was an unnatural reaction and as we got in the car, all my apprehensions came rushing back. We went to the Hotel Presidente, the nicest hotel in the Zona Rosa, where we spent the wedding night. Next morning we went to Acapulco, where we had a pleasant stay, in spite of the fact that after a couple of days I got sick for two days. I had a fever and finally passed a kidney stone that had been bothering me all through Europe. The timing could not have been worse.

When we came back from Acapulco we checked into a hotel and had a disagreement, which to me seemed very banal and silly. He exploded however, and after a long diatribe, shouted:

"I think we both made a mistake!" He then stomped out of the hotel room.

I was crushed. I ran to the phone to call my mother. I told her that I thought that this was not working and that I would like to come home and forget the whole thing. My mother was shocked at this news and of course told me to come home. However, she thought it was better to consult with the other family members, who were having *Shabbat* dinner. When she came back to the phone she told me that my cousin Henry had said that I had made my bed and now had to lie in it. But she was so worried. After half an hour, Jay came back, apologized a thousand times and hugged and kissed me, telling me how much he loved me. Unfortunately my marriage started out badly, these early events heralding many difficult and debilitating episodes that I had no way of avoiding.

Fortunately, it seemed that Jay's uncle, who had been the family's ambassador at the wedding, now became my ambassador. He had been so taken by my family and me that he called Jay's sisters and told them to change their attitude, that Jay had married a wonderful woman from a great family and they should welcome me. When we were on our way to the airport in Mexico to go to Los Angeles, from where we were to take a plane to Seattle, we received a phone call from Jay's sisters saying that we should stop in Los Angeles. They would come down from San Francisco where they lived and meet us in L.A.

Jay's oldest sister, Arlene, was at the airport with her husband Herb Bell, and I couldn't believe it when I saw these two handsome and sophisticated people. What a gorgeous looking couple! Arlene was tall with big blue eyes and brown hair and looked very much like Greer Garson. Herb was also tall with very white hair combed back. His face had a tan, which made a nice contrast with his white hair.

We hugged and I was thrilled to have a new sister- and brother-in-law. We all took a taxi to the hotel where we were to meet the younger sister, Francey, and her husband Sol Capper. When I saw them standing in front of the hotel, I couldn't help marveling at these good looking, elegant people. Francey was pretty in a different way. She was more slender and petite than Arlene, but also had blue eyes and blond hair. She was very vivacious and laughed a lot. Sol on the other hand was quiet but friendly. He was almost bald and had a large nose, but a very nice smile.

We had a couple of wonderful days in Los Angeles, and then they invited us to come to San Francisco for a while so we could get better acquainted. Arlene invited us to stay at their home and we were happy to accept. Forgotten was the animosity among the siblings. Everybody was on his best behavior, and the charm was comforting. Sol had a ladies apparel factory and he invited me to come and pick out a few dresses. I was delighted when I saw the lovely styles they showed me and couldn't believe my luck when he said that I could pick any number I liked. Every time we visited San Francisco I was urged to pick a wardrobe! They were most generous.

After a very well spent week where I met the rest of the family, Janis, Arlene's eighteen-year-old daughter, a very pretty young woman, and Francey's three sons, Norman, Steven and David, we had to think about going on to Seattle.

This was another beginning for me; I was starting a new life again and it was all unknown and a little scary. Again a new country, new friends, new customs and a newly acquired husband!

PART IV
SEATTLE

◆

1966–1977

CHAPTER ONE

It was pouring when we arrived in Seattle at the end of October, 1966. Little did I know, that I would not see the sun again until March 1967. The gloomy weather seemed to underscore the disappointment I had felt in Mexico upon learning about the changes Jay had made for the beginning of our married life. Fortunately, we were met at the airport by Jay's accountant Harry and his wife Alice, who had been so very kind to invite us to stay in their home until we found an apartment to rent. I had never met them before, but they were absolutely wonderful. They were very fond of Jay and treated me like a family member, which soothed much of the anxiety I felt beginning this new stage of my life. They had prepared their guest room especially for us, which made us feel at home right away.

The next day Alice accompanied me to look for apartments. After showing me a map and explaining the layout of the city and surrounding communities, we decided to concentrate on two areas. One was near Renton, where they lived and where the plant was located, and the other was Mercer Island, which is a beautiful residential area on Lake Washington across from Seattle. We finally ended up choosing a two-bedroom apartment in a small building on Mercer Island. Since it was located on top of a little hill we had a lovely view of the lake. Jay liked the place especially because it had a reasonable rent. All we had to do then was furnish it. We were able to use some of the furniture from Jay's little house near the plant, but had to buy everything for the bedroom. Since the plant was not doing well at that time, we decided to buy inexpensive furniture to start with. I was amazed at how cheap the dressers and other items were that we purchased through a friend of his. I had never seen furniture or household goods made so cheaply and in such quantities like these before. All I wanted to do was get everything organized so we could move in. I didn't want to take advantage of these kind people's hospitality longer than absolutely necessary.

Before we moved into the apartment Jay and I set out to buy a car for me, which we did at the first car dealer we saw, as Jay was anxious for me to be able to get around independently. We found a nice Plymouth Barracuda, light yellow with a black vinyl top, which I fell in love with right away. It happened to be a demonstration car, had 1500 miles on it and was only $3,000. Much to my surprise we didn't pay cash for it, but made arrangements to pay monthly. This, I figured out, would make the car much more expensive, but Jay assured me that this was the way to buy a car. Nevertheless, it seemed a strange way to me to go about it.

There were many things I didn't know prior to our marriage, one being we had no cash, which was, I later realized, why we had to buy the car on credit. Unfortunately, the plant was having real difficulties. Jay had wanted to own the Packing Plant so badly, specially when the hides were selling at a premium price and the plant showed a wonderful profit, but I think now he was sorry he'd bought it. When business was good, and everything went smoothly, he wanted to show everybody that he could be as successful as his father. However, when conditions went downhill as they had at that time, it took a smart businessman with experience in this field to stay afloat. Jay, being a veterinarian by profession, had no expertise in business. He had told his sisters that I was such a good businesswoman (basing this point of view solely on the time he saw me delivering gloves and writing out an invoice at a boutique in the hotel), that with my help he could manage the plant very well. Hearing this I was speechless and shocked. Did Jay expect me to save the packing plant for him? I couldn't believe that he could be so naïve. Not to mention that we had never discussed the possibility of me working at the packing plant. Although I had not fainted the first time I saw the bloody carcasses, I certainly did not have the stomach to work there!

After we moved into the apartment and I made it into a livable place, I had one more problem. Although I had watched my aunt cook and had taken a few classes with an Austrian lady in Mexico, I was still woefully inexperienced in the kitchen. I had never cooked much. In Uruguay, because my mother was so busy working, we ate lunch at the house of a Czech lady, who made her living cooking for people. How in the world would I bring an edible meal to the table? Fortunately Jay was able to show me a few tricks and short cuts, and I knew a few meals that I could make. One benefit of owning the plant was that our freezer was always full of choice meats, which Jay brought home once a week.

One day Jay came home and told me two physicians had come to the packing plant looking for cows' blood. They were doing research on hemophilia and needed it for their experiments. Since one of them, Dr. Gottfried Schmer, was also an Austrian, they struck up a conversation. We became good friends with him and his wife, Elizabeth. They were from Vienna and he was currently working as a chemist in the field of hemophilia.

Despite my doubts, Jay asked me if I would come to the plant to see if I could collect the accounts receivable. Fortunately, the office was upstairs and quite removed from the stench and noise. I discovered that the meat markets owed him a fortune, and the accounts were considerably past due. My mornings were spent on the phone calling and cajoling them to please pay their bills, always with the same result:

"We will pay as soon as we can."

Part of the problem was that we could not stop providing them with meat because there were not many independent meat markets around to buy our products. If we stopped shipping we would be left without customers. The plant would have to close and Jay was not ready for that to happen. One of his reasons was that hides might go up in price again, bringing in profits. The other was he wanted to be able to sell the plant while it was running. He was sure that one of the big meat packers would come along and be interested.

All these issues created a lot of stress for Jay, and he had terrible temper tantrums on a regular basis for the smallest reasons, just as he had had in the hotel in Mexico City. I kept telling myself that things would get better I just needed to be patient. Surely, once he got rid of the business, things would improve. I would focus on the future and try to look towards better days.

To improve our income I decided to look for a job and found one working for a Washington lobbyist. I was the only employee and had to run the office when he went on his frequent trips. This went well for a while until I got sick and had to stay home for a week. When I came back he said that he had hired another person because the office could not stay open without anyone to staff it. So I lost my job.

◆   ◆   ◆

When my mother had to leave Mexico again to receive a new visa, she went back to Uruguay to check on the things that we had stored at my uncles' factory. She unpacked the whole big trunk, gave away things she thought I would never need or want, and had the rest shipped to me in Seattle. I was so happy to receive all the familiar things that we had managed to bring from Austria, such as crystal, silver, paintings and other art objects.

After visiting friends and relatives in Uruguay, my mother came to Seattle. I rented an apartment in our building and furnished it with some of the furniture that was still in Jay's parents' house. There was also a French provincial dining room set, for which, at that time, we did not have enough room. What a joy to see her again and be with her! Even Jay was glad to see her and for a few days we were a happy family. It was spring and I wanted my mother to stay for the summer. Seattle in the spring and summer is absolutely gorgeous. It makes up for the long and gloomy winter.

I took my mother to a luncheon given at one of the synagogues, and when we were walking out I saw a woman whose face looked very familiar to me. I knew that I had not met her in Seattle, yet I could not remember where I had seen her. All of a sudden it dawned on me that she was somebody from my past. I had not seen her in at least 25 years, but I realized that she was little Lucy's mother, Friedl Sondland. I approached her and asked her whether she had lived in Montevideo and whether she had a little daughter called Lucy. She was so moved that she started to cry and hugged me, saying little Lucy was not so little any more. She was a nurse and had two children.

What a small world! I had never known where they had moved to when they left Montevideo, after Friedl's husband had arrived in Montevideo. In order to escape from Hitler, Guenther Sondland joined the Foreign Legion, where he was stationed until the war ended. He came to Montevideo and picked up his family and finally moved to Seattle, where his parents, who had escaped from Hitler via Shanghai, had settled down. Meeting Friedl was such a coincidence, and such a joyful reunion. We quickly became good friends with the whole family. Lucy's mother had had a second child in Seattle, a very nice young boy called Gordon, who became close with Jay. He liked him and considered him as a mentor. Gordi was an extremely bright boy, who had made up his mind that he would not go through the world without money like his parents. He was going to be important and wealthy like his brother in law and sister. I must say he was so successful at fulfilling his aspirations, that he is a very big man now, flying his own private plane and helping his parents.

With Jay at Gordi's Barmitzwah

At one point, we were invited to a party in San Francisco and stayed at Jay's sister, Arlene's house. At the close of our visit, Arlene invited my mother to stay a little longer, as her guest. They wanted to show my mother San Francisco and since it was the first time she had been there, she accepted.

A few days later we had a call from his other sister Francey. Arlene, her husband and my mother had been in a car accident on the Golden Gate Bridge, and my mother was in the hospital. My unfortunate mother—again in a car accident! I took the next plane to San Francisco and Francey's husband, Sol, met me at the airport. He told me, that as Arlene and Herb were returning from his house in San Rafael the prior evening, they had had a head-on collision with a drunken driver on the Golden Gate Bridge. My mother, who was sitting with them in the front seat, was thrown out of the car and had suffered numerous injuries. Fortunately nobody else was hurt.

Sol took me to their house in San Rafael, where the whole family was reunited. Arlene looked guilty and they hardly spoke to me. I asked them whether they were hurt and when she said that they were all right, I unthinkingly said, "Oh, my poor mother!" I was thinking of the many car accidents in which she had been in her life, always being absolutely blameless since she did not drive herself, and I felt sick in my heart. Obviously I said the wrong thing, because they turned away from me and would not speak to me again as long as I was in San Francisco. Actually they ended up hiring an attorney because they were afraid I might sue them. Such an action was far removed from my thoughts and I would never have done anything like that. The word "sue" was not in my vocabulary and even if it had been, I would not have sued my in-laws, whether there was a reason for it or not! However, their insurance covered my mother's medical and hospital expenses so all went well. It was really too bad that Arlene's and Herb's feelings of guilt caused them to distance themselves from us. It was such a waste of time and opportunity.

Finally, Sol took me to the hospital, which was near San Rafael in Marin County and I almost fainted when I saw my mother. Her face was black and blue and she could not move. She was so happy to see me, the poor soul, and I felt guilty that I had left her in San Francisco. After many X-rays the doctors determined that she had a hairline fracture in her hip and explained to us that she should not walk on it for some time.

After staying the night at the Capper's house, I returned to my mother's bedside where I remained all day. Apparently Jay's family considered this absolutely inappropriate and excessive. They felt that such an attachment to one's mother was unhealthy. Astonishing! All I knew was that I loved my mother and would not leave her in a hospital in a foreign country by herself. She did not even speak English well! How my behavior could have been described as aberrant is beyond me.

When I returned to the Capper house, Arlene and her husband had left and gone back to their home. I did not hear from them again until a year later. I guess their attorney must have advised them not to talk to me, or perhaps they felt somehow responsible for the accident. My feelings toward Arlene certainly suffered a big strain. She turned against me when I needed her, behaving in such a strange way.

My mother was supposed to stay another week in the hospital. However, after a few days, the Cappers told me that they were going out of town. They suggested that when my mother was released, I should take her to a motel, since the doctor didn't want her to travel right away. I asked Sol to talk to the doctor and have him keep my mother in the hospital until I could bring her back to Seattle, while I would be able to stay at their house until then.

After the Cappers left I rented a car to go back and forth to the hospital, and when my mother was able to travel, Jay finally came to San Francisco to help me bring her home. Her injuries were still substantial enough that we had to put her in a convalescent home for three weeks. Fortunately it was almost next door to our apartment house. There was a German Jewish lady who lived there permanently because she was diabetic and needed care, and she kindly offered to look in on my mother from time to time and sit with her. They became good friends, and when my mother was allowed to go home, it was my mother who in turn visited the lady.

◆   ◆   ◆

I drove to the plant almost every day trying to get the money out of the butcher shops. I went to their places to talk to them but it was worse than pulling teeth. There was another problem with the plant, however. The manager, whom Jay trusted implicitly, was stealing large quantities of meat. Of course Jay fired him immediately, but things did not improve and I strongly advised Jay that he should close the plant. He couldn't keep it afloat and was losing more and more money every day. But Jay was still hoping for better days and was unwilling to admit defeat. I think he believed that his family and friends would consider him a failure and he was afraid that he couldn't be successful as a veterinarian either. He had had a large-animal practice in eastern Washington and had very little experience with treating pets and small animals. In Seattle, his practice would be strictly small animals.

Despite the fact that Jay was talented and imaginative, often having very good ideas, which were way ahead of his time, he had picked the wrong profession. I think he would have been more suited as a scientist. One of his projects was based on developing a method to feed cattle by recycling their waste. Unfortunately, it was unsuccessful.

After two years of marriage I let myself get pregnant at Jay's fervent request. In spite of the second thoughts I had about my marriage, I felt that my biological clock was ticking and I didn't have much more time. When I realized that I was pregnant, I was very happy and Jay was beside himself with joy. Unfortunately I lost the fetus in my third month. I was devastated. I never tried again, because I felt too insecure about my marriage and I was not getting any younger.

CHAPTER TWO

One afternoon my mother and I were having a nice chat when I received a phone call from the daughter of some friends in Mexico. She told me that my cousin Henry had died in a plane crash in Mexico! I couldn't believe it. How could fate be so cruel? How could it allow my aunt and uncle to lose their last child? My mother and I started to cry, but we immediately realized that we had to think clearly. The only thing we could do at that point was to take the next flight to Mexico. I called to make reservations only to be told that there were no seats available. I told them that this was an emergency, and that a family member had died and we needed to take that flight. Thankfully they were kind enough to give us two first-class seats. Jay took us to the airport, and I told him that I would stay in Mexico as long as was necessary. He understood and hugged me as if he never wanted to let me go.

"Please come back as soon as possible," he said with tears in his eyes. "I love you so!"

During the flight all my mother and I could do was cry and talk about this newest tragedy. We were so worried about my poor aunt and uncle. How could they possibly sustain such a horrendous loss at their age? Henry had been their only solace and hope. My aunt had developed macular degeneration to a point where she could hardly see at all, and Henry would comfort her and try to make life easier for her. What would happen to these two old people now? They certainly could not count on their daughter-in-law, who was busy with her own problems, and the grandchildren were still too young.

We arrived at my aunt's house and it was as sad and chaotic as we had feared. When my aunt saw us, she broke down and cried until her eyes could not take it any more. My uncle, too, was inconsolable but they both were relieved that we had come. They explained that the plane crash had occurred between Mexico City and Monterey, Mexico, where my cousin was going to attend a business meeting, planning to return the same day. He had taken his second-in-command on this flight, which they nearly missed. In fact they had rushed to make the plane. How devastating! All I could think of was how the whole tragedy could have been avoided had they not run! It was never established whether it was bad weather that caused the plane crash, or whether it was human error. Unfortunately there were no survivors.

The biggest problem facing officials was that it was almost impossible to find the bodies. My cousin Emerich helped the search parties with his own planes and it was a horrible job. There were body parts everywhere. The odds of finding Henry's body were slim. In the meantime my aunt and uncle had the sad duty of planning a funeral and we helped them in every way we could. When the day and time were set for the funeral, my aunt's friends advised them to go ahead with the ceremony even though they hadn't found Henry's body. When Emerich heard this he threw a fit. How could anybody be so callous! He couldn't get over the insensitivity and foolishness of people. It was finally decided that the funeral would just have to be postponed until Henry was found. When I was alone, I cried my eyes out, my gorgeous Heini's body parts were scattered on the mountain! Soon, however, the news came that almost all of Henry's remains had been recovered and that was the best they could hope for. Many of the bodies had been burned beyond recognition.

The day came when the funeral was to be held and I was put in charge of caring for my aunt during this painful time. I thought to myself: this is the blind leading the blind. How can I take care of my aunt when I am so distraught. We tried to convince her that she should not go to the cemetery; she was so frail and sick. But she insisted and we had to take her. Beforehand I asked her eye doctor what I should do to protect her eyes from so much crying. He told me to give her Valium before and another during the funeral to help her cope. I managed to get one pill into her before we left the house. Unfortunately at the cemetery she broke down, and despite my efforts I was unable to make her take the second one. After much wrangling, I was finally able to push a pill into her mouth and she was forced to swallow it. Nevertheless, she became so agitated I was unable to hold her. She tore herself free from my arms and tried to jump into the grave. It was heartrending to see her despair. I grieved not only for my aunt and uncle but for myself as well: My dear, handsome Henry, who had charmed me so in Austria when we were children. He had been so full of life and had so much to live for. I could not believe that we would never see him again!

After the official mourning period of one week was over, we heard that Henry's wife, Jean, had taken control of the business, and no longer wanted my uncle to come to the office. It seemed a strange and insensitive act, which hurt my aunt and uncle very much.

Jay called me often, always asking when I would be back, and although I hated to have to leave him alone for so long, I couldn't really say when I would be ready to return. I knew my relatives needed me; they asked for my advice about everything, in addition to needing our emotional support. However, I knew that sooner or later I would have to go back to my own life. We finally decided that I would stay another fortnight and mother would stay with them for the time being since they couldn't manage on their own.

Aside from that, Robby, Henry's son, was to have his Bar Mitzvah soon, which seemed like another good reason for me to extend my stay in Mexico. Although neither Jean, nor Robby himself, wanted a Bar Mitzvah, Henry had insisted, primarily out of respect for his parents. Now the poor boy had to go through something that he felt was an ordeal, and without his father. Robby was moping around my aunt's house and my heart went out to him. When I caught him alone one day, I said:

"Robby, darling, I know how you feel. I lost my father when I was ten years old."

He simply looked at me, turned around and stomped out of the room. He was angry at the world and wouldn't interact with anyone but the maids. I remember thinking that he was such a goodlooking boy with his big blue-green eyes. I was sure he would grow up to be even more handsome than Henry was.

However, we were now faced with having the saddest Bar Mitzvah I had ever seen. The service was at the Reformed American Temple. Robby was standing at the podium and stumbled a number of times during the recitation of his portion of the Torah. He was a pitiful figure standing up there in his old clothes no doubt wishing he were anywhere else. Jean had not even bought him a new suit for the occasion and my aunt was terribly bothered by this. She considered it an insult to Henry's memory. We were all glad when it was over, and I could easily imagine the sigh of relief Robby must have given.

On the day I left for Seattle, my aunt brought me to the safe that was in the study and took out a beautiful diamond brooch. She wanted me to have it for all the help and love I gave them. I hugged her and thanked her a thousand times. I had never owned such a lovely piece of jewelry. How I wished it could have been for a different occasion!

When I arrived in Seattle I found a very depressed Jay. He was shocked about the whole thing and especially bothered that he had had to be without me for so long. The news regarding the packing plant was not getting any better either. We spoke about closing the plant sooner or later, even if he could not sell it as a going business. I guess he was getting used to the idea. In his view, it was a sad solution, but he started to work on the best way to handle it.

Knowing that my mother would not come back to Seattle very soon, I sub-let her apartment to a respectable divorced man. He was a stock-broker and his hobby was painting. After a few months he was unable to pay the rent. He asked me if I would accept a painting as payment. I had seen some of his work and agreed. I really loved what he did and he went ahead and framed it beautifully. I have it hanging in my dining room today.

Jay's cousin, Annette, a widow, who had recently married again, had moved to a pleasant apartment building near us and when we visited her we saw that she had an unusually large apartment. I believe it was two apartments made into one. We found out that there were several of these large apartments and asked the manager to let us know when another one would become available, as we were interested in moving into one.

CHAPTER THREE

One day a German acquaintance of Jay's approached me to tell me that the German Consulate General was looking for a German-speaking person to be executive assistant to the Consul General. She said she had immediately thought of me and had made an appointment for me for an interview.

"Are you crazy, don't you know that I am Jewish?" I couldn't help but shout at her. "How could you possibly do such a thing without my consent? I would not even consider going, and you'd better let them know!"

"Eva, I am very sorry I offended you or made you angry," she replied gently. "But I suggest that you go there yourself and let them know your feelings. I think it would make you feel better and teach them a lesson. What do you say?"

I had the feeling my head was going to split in two, but I could see that some of what she was saying made sense.

"Alright, maybe you are right," I conceded. "I'll go and face them directly."

She was happy and relieved and gave me the name of the person I was supposed to see.

Next day, with a big chip on my shoulder I went downtown to the consulate, which was located on the fifth floor of the IBM building. I took the elevator and my heart was beating so fast that I thought it would explode. With every beat, I wondered what in the world I was doing there. I stepped into the door of the consulate and the first thing I saw was a friendly-looking receptionist who asked me how she could help me.

"I am here to see Mr. Kurrek," I told her. "Somebody made an appointment."

She smiled at me and asked me to follow her. When she showed me into Mr. Kurrek's office I had to hold on to the chair that I was being offered. Mr. Kurrek extended his hand, but I did not shake it. When he asked me to sit down I was happy to; I don't think I could have stood on my feet.

"Well," I started, "I am only here to let you know that you should not count on me. I am sure that this whole thing is a misunderstanding, because I can't believe that you really would think that I, as a Jew, would be willing to work for you!"

"My dear lady, I am sure that you have heard this before, but we have to forgive and forget if we really want to keep peace in the world."

"As I have told the Austrian ambassador before: I cannot forgive and forget!"

"I understand how you feel, but would you do me a very big favor? Mr. Ruscher, the Consul General was not feeling well and therefore stayed at home. Would you consider going with me to his house? I have the car and driver downstairs. It would only take an hour of your time."

I didn't know what was happening to me, but something made me say yes.

We did not speak very much in the car, except remarking on the nice weather we were having or mundane things like that. When we arrived at the house, the driver helped me out of the car and we rang the bell. A beautiful woman opened the door. She was probably in her fifties, looked very pretty and her dress was simple but well cut.

With a big smile she welcomed us in. I thought this was the most attractive house I had seen for quite some time. It was simple but elegant, just like the lady of the house.

Dr. Klaus Ruscher stood up from the living room sofa and approached us holding out his hand, and I shook it. He was pleasant looking, maybe in his sixties. His eyes, looking straight into mine, were a grey-blue and, it seemed to me, unexpectedly honest. His wife offered us tea and cakes and then left. We talked for a long time and what he said made a lot of sense to me. He said that what had happened in Germany was so bad, that it could, and should, never be forgotten. As he talked, I felt the chip on my shoulder get smaller and smaller.

When he explained that one of the main focuses of the consulate was to pay restitution to the German Jews in the area, and to solicit their help to put away some of the Nazis who had been leaders in the concentration camps, I was almost sold. He said that he needed a person to be his assistant and that he would love that person to be me. I recognized that it might well be difficult to find a person with sufficient speaking and writing knowledge of German who also had some administrative experience. It also occurred to me that they really wanted a Jewish employee, in order to be politically correct. When I was ready to go, his wife, Marianne joined us and I thanked her for her hospitality. I told him that I needed some time to think it over, and he said he understood fully. When I told Jay all about this very strange experience which had put me in a great quandary, Jay's reaction was that I should do whatever made me comfortable.

Sometimes it seems that there are bigger forces at work than one realizes. The force at work in that instance was in the form of a German Jewish friend of ours, whom we met at the synagogue the following *Shabbat*. We greeted her and somehow the conversation turned to the job offer I had received. She was surprised and immediately told me that she was from the same town in Germany as Klaus Ruscher, and that she had known his parents and family. During the Nazi era, the Ruschers had done everything possible to help the Jews in their town. She declared without hesitation that she would put her hand in a fire to demonstrate the integrity of this man and that I should, by all means, accept the job. This helped me a great deal and despite the feelings that I was somehow betraying all those who suffered at the hands of the Germans, I decided to accept.

A week later I went back to the Consulate, they gave me a personnel test, which I passed with flying colors and I started my new job. There were about 15 people working there, most of them sent from Germany. Aside from Mr. Kurreck, whose title was Chancellor, there was the Cultural Attache, the Registrar and several young ladies who were German but lived in the U.S.A. permanently. I was hired to be the assistant to Dr. Ruscher, and as I liked him very much I was fairly sure that everything would work out fine. I agreed with my co-workers in the office that he was a fair, understanding and kind boss liked by everyone. The young women who worked there were very friendly and I soon made friends with them. Everybody treated me with respect and kindness, and I have to admit that I enjoyed my new employment.

When I told my mother and my family about this job they were astonished but ultimately were glad that I liked it. The only one who was angry with me was Emeric. How could I have taken a job with a former enemy? Of course I understood his pain and anger, having initially felt the same. Yet I believed that the work I was doing contributed to making up for past injuries to those who survived.

Shortly thereafter, Jay and I were told that an apartment had become available in the building we liked and we decided to move. It had a great floor plan: It was a long apartment with all the rooms in a row. One end had two bedrooms and a bathroom with a separate entrance to that wing. The dining room and kitchen, were separated only by half-walls from the living room and the main entrance. From the living room a door led to the master bedroom and bathroom. Jay decided to take one of the guestrooms as his office and the other guestroom was furnished for my mother. She would only come two months in summer.

It was perfect for us, as we were at opposite ends from my mother's room, giving all of us sufficient privacy. We now were able to bring the French provincial dining room set from Jay's parents' house, and after buying a few extra sofas and chairs for the living room, we still had room for Jay's piano, which he loved to play. He played jazz by ear, quite well, but with one problem: It was always a little too loud. When I think about it now, I think he must have been somewhat hard of hearing, because when he spoke his voice was also much too loud. I called his attention to this several times, which, unfortunately, only resulted in Jay getting angry.

Jay finally closed the plant and his big hope was that he would be able to sell the property. He found a job at a veterinary clinic in Seattle where he took care of the after-hour calls and substituted for the veterinarian when he went on vacation.

Every morning when I drove over the floating bridge to Seattle I would be ecstatic with the view of the lake, Mount Rainier and the city spreading out in front of me. In those moments my happiness would soar and I would give thanks to our Lord for my life. These trips to work were indeed a wonderful beginning of the day. I enjoyed my job, got along with everybody and had an excellent relationship with Dr. Ruscher. He continued to be polite and easy to work with.

One morning he asked me whether I would be willing to sit in on the deposition to be given by a Jewish man living in Seattle. He had been in one of the concentration camps, and the leader of that camp was now in jail in Germany. In order to convict this man of the crimes he committed, it was necessary to have a witness testify to the atrocities that went on in the camp. I said I wouldn't be able to take this deposition; I would be far too emotionally involved and could somebody else do this, please? Of course Dr. Ruscher understood immediately. He asked another young German woman, Helga Hamilton, who was married to an American, and who was too young to ever have heard of or learned anything about the Holocaust. In the early years after the war, schools in Germany did not teach anything about the Hitler era. When Helga was through, she came out crying, devastated by the proceedings. She had heard things that she could not understand.

"What if my parents knew about these things or were even involved?" she sobbed. "I could never forgive them!" She was horrified because she had learned these most troublesome aspects of her country's past and now had, at least in part, to live with them.

Jay was still looking for a permanent job as a veterinarian; in the meantime we lived on my salary. It still seems like a miracle to me that we could live off my income and yet be able to put something in a savings account.

Very often the telephone would ring in the middle of the night and wake us up from a deep sleep. Jay had to get up and take care of a sick animal, and I would not be able to fall asleep again, as I continued to suffer from insomnia since I was a teenager. The next morning it would always be hard to get up and go to work, but somehow I managed.

Jay, having lived in Seattle all his life, knew many people, and I had made friends too, so we had an active social life. We were invited out a lot and of course had to reciprocate. We would often take drives around the countryside; my favorite place to go on a Sunday was to Bainbridge Island, where friends of Jay, an interesting couple, had a little house. They lived there permanently and commuted to their respective jobs. He worked for Boeing, as so many of the people in Seattle did, and she was a teacher. To get to Bainbridge you had to take a ferry and it was so much fun to cross Puget Sound. There were many islands, called the San Juan Islands, one prettier than the next. Nature has really favored Seattle. Sometimes Jay and I would go to Orcas Island, which was a bit further away. There was a beautiful hotel with a swimming pool and we enjoyed staying for the weekend. On the island was a high tower from which one could have a spectacular 360 degree view, and I had the feeling I could see the whole world: There was the city, the mountains, the other islands, the ocean. This view had a wonderful healing power for me and every time I went, I felt grateful and filled with optimism.

When my mother came back to visit, we were very happy to see her, and she was glad to be away from the sad atmosphere in Mexico. My aunt and uncle were getting used to the circumstances, but they were aging and my aunt's eyesight was deteriorating. She would be all right walking around the house and doing her chores, but could not recognize people.

Mother loved our new apartment and liked the privacy her separate bathroom and bedroom afforded her. It was almost like having a whole apartment. It was summer and cherries were in season, which she adored and could not get in Mexico. We took her to Orcas Island, which she thought was fabulous and together with our Austrian friends, the Schmers, we went to Vancouver, Canada, and Harrison Hotsprings, which was not far from Vancouver. We were frequent visitors in Vancouver because we could get things there that we could not find in Seattle—certain dark breads, for instance, as well as imported foodstuffs that we liked. Vancouver was only 1 1/2 hours away, so it was easy to travel there. Harrison Hotsprings was a beautiful resort next to a lake. The hotel was extremely comfortable, had a large pool and all the spa amenities. There were lovely walks one could go on, and there were boats for rent if anybody felt like a ride on the lake. In the evening there was dinner and dancing, which I adored. The people there were well-dressed and in a good mood, and my mother enjoyed the company of the Schmers, especially because she could speak German with them. I have many delightful memories of that time.

One afternoon Mrs. Ruscher invited my mother to tea at their house. Since I was to join them after work, she had the driver pick my mother up at our apartment. It was a wonderful afternoon, we had tea in the garden and everything was enjoyable. Mrs. Ruscher and my mother got along famously and I was grateful for this nice gesture on the part of my boss's wife. She really was a charming lady.

Once a week my mother went to a meeting of a social club called The Jewish Club of Washington. The members were all German speaking, older immigrants and my mother fitted in very well, despite the fact that she asked me several times what I wanted her to do with those old people! Sometimes they would go on excursions with a chartered bus and I couldn't imagine anything better for my mother. She did make several friends there and one of them was an especially nice lady, Charlotte Frank. We remained dear friends until she died a few years ago.

I had joined the ranks of the American career women, and fortunately it turned out much better than I had feared. I worked all week, came home and cooked dinner, and on Saturdays I cleaned the apartment. Frankly, I was quite proud of myself; I had adjusted and assimilated quite well into my new life in America. However, on one occasion Jay, with his inimitable charm, boasted that he could do the housework with both his hands tied behind his back. When I asked him one day to please help me with the vacuuming, he answered that this was women's work and that he was not interested. So much for his ability to do my housework!

The weather started to get cold, so my mother went back to Mexico. I missed her a lot, but I was happy that she did not have to be in the rain and cold of Seattle. It had been snowing a lot and the mountains near Seattle were ready for the skiing season. There was a magnificent area at the Snoqualmi Pass near Seattle where people came to ski; some had weekend houses built around the foot of the mountains and others just came for the day. I was not a skier, but I loved to see the snow-covered scenery.

Robby Jarvis, my cousin Henry's son, enrolled at the University of Washington in Seattle. He was still a very introverted young man, but he was lonely so far from home, (and he didn't like the dormitory food), so for a while he came to spend many weekends with us. He loved to go hiking and would take beautiful photographs, which was his big love. I bought hiking boots and the three of us often went on long hikes. He also enjoyed movies, so we would often go with him. We were happy to have him around. He had turned into a very handsome young man, was very tall and reminded me a little of Henry. His biggest feature were his grey-green eyes with the long black lashes.

In the meantime, my uncle died in Mexico; he had been very sick for quite some time. In spite of the differences they some times had, my mother was the only person who could get him to eat. When he finally died, my aunt in her grief did not want to live any longer, but my mother did not leave her side, and after a while her devastating pain became more bearable.

Because the pollution in Mexico had gotten worse, my aunt decided to sell the house in Mexico City. Therefore she and my mother moved to Cuernavaca where they rented two apartments near the Jewish old-age home. This was convenient because my aunt wanted to be near a synagogue. Cuernavaca had a nice little German-speaking community and soon my mother and aunt had an agreeable circle of friends. Sometimes we visited them for a week and always enjoyed this pleasant little town with its good climate.

When my mother came to visit us, she brought along my aunt, for whom we rented an apartment in our building. Now that my uncle was dead, my mother did not want to leave her sister alone, and from then on would always bring her every time she came to visit. This entailed that we had to buy kosher meat and keep our meals as kosher as possible during her stay. My aunt loved the opportunity to come to the United States. Her biggest pleasure was shopping and her grandson's presence in Seattle was an extra attraction. The two ladies would often go to church sales and were delighted when at the end of the day they were told that they could fill a bag with clothes for one dollar. It was amazing to see the energy they had! I would get tired long before they would be ready to leave. I also had a little extra responsibility because of my aunt's near blindness.

◆　　　◆　　　◆

The time came to apply for my citizenship, so I went to school to study American history and other information with which an American should be familiar. I passed the test and was given a date to appear at the Naturalization Service to get my citizenship papers.

During this time I met the Director of the Immigration and Naturalization Service at a party given by the Consulate, and since I was one of the hostesses, we started to talk. He was a pleasant man, and I told him that I was going to become a citizen shortly. He was very interested and asked me whether I would be willing to give a speech to the other people who had become citizens that year. He explained that there was to be a Citizens' Day celebration, for all the new citizens. Being bashful I started to refuse, but ended up agreeing to do it. Jay helped me write my speech. I remember clearly the first paragraph:

"Becoming an American Citizen is a very personal, human experience. The road has been a long one—from being a little girl of 9 years of age, who had to flee her homeland under the nightmare of facing death, to the memories of loved ones who never made it out of the Holocaust. This was a searing experience! Finally, I am a citizen of the United States of America!"

I went on about what it meant to be an American, ending up by quoting the beautiful song, *"America, the Beautiful."* It was a memorable experience indeed. Jay and my mother sat in the first row and applauded with all the other new citizens. I was now starting the life of an American! Another beginning.

◆   ◆   ◆

At work, my vacation time was coming up. The Germans give employees a much longer vacation than the Americans do, so I was given 4 weeks every year. With such a long break, Jay and I decided to go to Europe since he had never been there, and I wanted to show him my favorite places.

We started in London, where we saw a couple of excellent plays, then went on to Munich where he had some business. From there we flew to Israel, visiting both Tel Aviv and Jerusalem. My mother's older brother, Sylvio the doctor, had died since our last trip, but Uncle Emil, the actor, (whose wife had also died), invited us to stay at his apartment. We arrived in Tel Aviv at a time when he was working, (He also had a window washing company.), so we took a taxi to his apartment, where his neighbor let us in. He had prepared beds on two narrow living room sofas. Since we were tired from the trip we decided to take a nap. Unfortunately, not only were our beds narrow, they were also extremely hard. I was sure that I wouldn't be able to sleep on those contraptions, but I didn't say a word. After a while Jay wanted a glass of water and went to the kitchen. He called out for me to come and look. When I entered the kitchen, I was aghast. The counters of the kitchen were black with ants! We looked at each other and it was obvious what we both were thinking. We packed our luggage, called a taxi and left my uncle a note that we were going to be at a hotel. That evening a very disappointed uncle carrying a big flower arrangement showed up at the hotel. He apologized for everything, explaining how hard it was to keep ants away in the humid heat. I suspected it was more likely that he was not a great housekeeper.

After a lot of sightseeing in Israel, which Jay enjoyed very much, we went to Vienna. I had to show my husband where I had come from. We visited my family in Vienna, and Jay charmed them all. I was gratified when everybody said what a nice husband I had.

I took him to the opera and during intermission Jay noticed that a button had come off his jacket, I told him not to fret; there was a woman in the men's room who would be happy to sew the button on for him. I saw Jay's incredulous face—a woman in the men's room. That he had to see! He came back smiling grandly, a tightly sewn button on his jacket. I think he was more impressed by this service than by the whole opera.

After Vienna we went to Paris, where I showed him around for two days. He loved this city. Then back to London from where we had to take our flight home. All in all it was a great trip and an enriching experience for Jay.

After our return we finally found a buyer for the property Jay was so anxious to sell. Unfortunately he did not get even half the price he had been wishing for. With Boeing, the main business in Seattle, doing poorly and letting thousands of employees go, there was a substantial recession in the real estate market. All the jobless people sold their homes and left Seattle. This, of course, affected commercial real estate and Jay was only able to sell the land the plant was on. In addition, Jay owned a piece of land across the street next to the railroad tracks, which he kept. About ten years ago I sold this piece at a nominal value.

Jay, not being a businessman, did not make the right decisions on how to invest the money he received from the sale. He should have immediately used the money to open his own veterinary clinic, or as he had offered, we should have bought a house. This was the right time to buy a house, and we were shown some lovely homes on Mercer Island. One was a dream, built by an architect for his own use. It was exquisitely located, had a Japanese garden in front and a classic garden in the back. The living room was surrounded by glass and one had a view into both gardens. Because of the recession the sale price was only $35,000 and Jay was willing to buy the house. This is when I made the big mistake. I was so happy with our apartment and so insecure about our marriage that I said that we should wait longer! We never did buy a house together, and the real estate prices in Seattle and on Mercer Island went up tremendously.

Jay had some friends he trusted and together they started a business provisioning ocean freighters and other ships. A lot of the work entailed buying food and other necessities for ships, which docked in Seattle or San Pedro near Los Angeles. It was crazy work with crazy hours. In the end, however, some of the men involved in the business embezzled funds and Jay's money was soon gone. Experiences like this happened to Jay on several occasions. Once he was invited to invest in a play, "Destry Rides Again," which closed the first night!

I was really distressed by this series of bad luck and failure. After all the waiting and hoping, Jay's finances were as bad as before. Fortunately I had my job and we could still live off my salary. However, I had to think about Jay's morale and this was not good for him. It increased his stress and his moods responded accordingly.

Eventually, he heard about a veterinarian who specialized in house-calls and he assisted him for a while to get the hang of it. There was a lot to carry in the car, including instruments, medicines and ointments. But he pulled it together and started the house-call practice "for the customer who couldn't put her Great Dane into the Volkswagen bug."

◆   ◆   ◆

Dr. Ruscher's term as Consul General was coming to an end; he had to leave Seattle and was being transferred to Capetown, South Africa. We at the Consulate were all sorry. He had been such a good boss and we all hated to see him and his charming wife go. I felt that I didn't want to work for anybody else, but in view of our financial situation, I decided to stay on and see what the new Consul General would be like.

Schacco von Estorf, the replacement, was a strange character and I was very disappointed. I missed Ruscher deeply and couldn't get used to this new person. He would come into the office and check what I was wearing, and he would say that I had to be from Hamburg because only women from that city knew how to dress and were as elegant as I was. One day he asked me whether I would invite him to my house and show him all my clothes. Later I was told that he liked to dress in his wife's clothes. I felt very sorry for his wife and children. My feelings that things were not right in the house of Estorff were confirmed a year later, when the 17 year old son committed suicide by throwing himself under a train. As sad and tragic as this was, it was made even more so by the fact that Mr. Schacco von Estorff's hobby was toy trains!

I recognized that I had to leave the office, no matter what. Fortunately, Fate was on my side again. I heard that the Honorary Consul of Austria was looking for an assistant. An Honorary Consul is not a diplomat sent by the government. He can be of any nationality, as long as he has enough money to represent the country and is willing to do so. Mr. Henry Simonson, a Norwegian businessman, was this Honorary Consul. He had an employee who had worked for him in his ski business, a German woman, who had also performed certain functions for the Consulate. However, Mr. Simonson was opening a new office for the Consulate and she was staying with the ski business.

Since he needed help in the Consulate, he approached me and I went to see him. As he did not speak a word of German he was very eager to have me take over. There was one hitch, however, he traveled a lot and I would be the person in charge of the consulate! This meant that I had to sign and certify Life Certificates for the Austrian people who received pensions from Austria. These people were mainly Jewish because Austria had allowed Austrian Jews to apply for a pension from that country regardless of where they were living. This plan was created prior to the government considering paying war reparations. Austria's excuse for not paying restitution was that they had been an invaded land themselves! The truth was they had received the Germans with open arms, an event which I remembered clearly.

Because I was to be in charge of the consulate, I had to be appointed by the Austrian government. Mr. Simonson wrote to the Austrian Embassy in Washington explaining the situation and two weeks later I was appointed honorary chancellor of the Austrian Consulate. Imagine me, being an officially appointed government employee representing the country that had thrown me out! I kept thinking of my encounter with the Austrian ambassador in Mexico. However, as before, I started rationalizing. There were several things that made it easier: Simonson was not Austrian and was a good person. Even more compelling was that the people I would be helping were mainly Jewish.

Most of the time I was the sole person at the Austrian consulate. Mr. Simonson traveled a lot and I had to "hold the fort." People called and made appointments with me, and I served them quite well. When there was a case that I didn't know how to deal with, I would ask the person involved to come back when Mr. Simonson was in town, but more often I just called the Austrian Embassy in Washington to find out what to do.

Jay and I had some serious talks about opening his own hospital, but he had a very strong sense of loyalty to his colleagues and did not want to go into competition with the veterinarians on Mercer Island. To start an animal hospital in Seattle presented similar problems and would be inconveniently far away. We had met a nice man from La

Jolla, California, Adolf Hochstim, who praised that area very much and invited us to visit. Upon accepting his invitation we were quite impressed with the beauty of La Jolla and discovered that there were areas where a veterinary hospital was needed. Jay also had a school friend who had a clinic in San Diego and needed help.

The idea of moving to La Jolla took more and more hold in our minds, and we decided to go ahead and make the necessary plans. We would go down and settle Jay somewhere temporarily and in the meantime, I would quit my job and sell things that we did not need. In Seattle, Jay hired a man who had been helping him with his house-call practice. He was quite good with animals and was strong. So Jay rented a van and filled it with all the things he needed to practice, plus his filing cabinets and desk. The young man was going to drive the van down to San Diego, while Jay and I left in his car.

We stopped in San Francisco to visit his sisters, who tried to convince us that it would be better for us to settle in San Francisco so we used the two days to look at clinics that were for sale in the Bay Area.

The next day we drove to San Diego. We went to La Jolla and looked for a place where Jay could stay for a few months without paying too much. We were told about the Colonial Hotel, which rented out studios with kitchenettes. It was located on Prospect Avenue, one block from the beach and we liked the place immediately.

Jay met his assistant and they stowed all the equipment and furniture in a storage place. Then the man drove back to Seattle, promising to return when Jay was ready to make a move. The first thing on Jay's agenda was to explore the area and see what locations were available for lease, which would also be suitable for a clinic.

I flew back to Seattle where my mother joined me to help me liquidate the things that I did not want to move to La Jolla. I had already quit my job and my mother and I were busy separating all the items we wanted to sell that had accumulated during 11 years. Through an ad in the paper, many people came to our moving sale and business went well. Jay had given me permission to sell his mother's dining room set, which was so big that I did not want it, and we got a very good price for it. However, his piano and the living room furniture had to go with us to La Jolla, as well as his parents' bedroom set and our beds.

Jay had been looking for the suitable clinic; either he would be taking over an established clinic or start one from scratch. Finally he found a small shopping center that was being built in Bird Rock, a little community on the coastal street that ran along the ocean from Pacific Beach to La Jolla. The shopping center was under construction and he picked a place that, according to zoning, was suitable for a small animal clinic. He was able to get a bank loan and put down a deposit. While he had to wait for the completion of his clinic, he made house calls and became well known in the community. When I visited him over the 4th of July weekend he showed me the site of the clinic and I thought he had done very well.

The weather was beautiful and I was looking forward to going to the beach on the 4th of July. Surely animals wouldn't dare to get sick on this important holiday! We had just put down our towels on the sand when Jay's beeper went off, and we had to go take care of a cat. The cat was a neutered male; they tend to have problems with bladder stones that cause a lot of pain. Jay asked me to hold the cat so that he could give it intravenous medication, but though I tried to hold the cat exactly as Jay had asked me to, the suffering animal bit my finger right through the nail. Horrible pain! But we finally managed to get the needle into him and he was out like a light. Many times I was amazed at the diagnostic skills a veterinarian had to possess in order to know what was wrong with an animal. These poor creatures could not talk and show the doctor where they hurt. I felt proud that my husband could help suffering animals, but the beeper was very hard to take. We could not eat dinner or go anywhere without it beeping since Jay was always on call. There was no escape even at night. I told myself that it was the only way he could build his practice, yet it was still difficult to live with.

Through our friend, Adolf Hochstim, we found a nice house to rent in San Diego. It belonged to one of his friends who was taking a sabbatical and would be gone for a year. This was perfect for us; by the end of a year we would know what we could afford to do. The house was located on a hill with a magnificent view of the ocean. It had a large terrace and was surrounded by junipers. We rented it as soon as we saw it. The owners were going to move out in two weeks and promised to leave a double mattress on the floor of the bedroom, so that Jay could move in. Poor Jay, when he moved in and slept on the mattress, he was bitten all over. The owners had a cat and a dog, which they took with them, but the fleas were left behind. Of course Jay called the pest control and I heartily hoped they had gotten rid of the fleas before I moved down there!

Meanwhile, I returned to Seattle, relieved to find that mother had sold a few more things and I could see an end to the process. Pretty soon we would start to pack and be ready to move. As I said goodbye to all my good friends who were very sad to see me go, it occurred to me that I had said "goodbye" a little too often in my life. It is not easy to make new friends over and over again. Although I was happy to move to La Jolla, I felt uprooted again, just like the "Wandering Jew." Would this ever stop? Would I finally settle somewhere and stay?

Jay came up to help me supervise the moving people and my mother went back to Cuernavaca. When everything was in the truck we set out in my little Barracuda car to drive to San Diego. The drive was long and tedious, in spite of our stopping in San Francisco again. My car had no air conditioning, which I had never missed in Seattle but certainly missed while going through California's Central Valley. It was so hot that I thought we were going to melt in the middle of the freeway. We finally stopped at a motel, and entering their cool rooms I felt like I had entered heaven. A new life awaited us. I was determined to greet it with excitement.

PART V
SAN DIEGO

❖

1977–1980

CHAPTER ONE

We finally arrived in San Diego, and as I wasn't keen on sleeping on the mattress on the floor, we decided to spend the night at a motel in Pacific Beach right on the ocean. It was a bad idea. The room, the beds and the other furnishings reeked of mold and we could hardly sleep. Fortunately, the next morning our moving van was arriving and we eagerly went to the house to meet it.

The furniture we had brought fit into the house beautifully. We lacked only a dining room set, and I was able to buy a good one on sale. With everything in place, it was very comfortable and we enjoyed living in a house for a change. Jay had stored all his veterinary equipment and supplies on shelves in the two-car garage, so he had to park his car in the driveway.

The construction of the shopping center and clinic was progressing slowly, and we knew that it would still take a few months until Jay could move in. The house-call practice was coming along quite well and through it Jay made a few friends. I decided to go to school to get a real estate license. I was sure this was a great business with all the expensive houses in La Jolla. After a few months I thought I was ready to take the test. However, real estate tests were unusually difficult since one had to know so many different laws and regulations. In addition, the mathematical questions were quite challenging, especially because, at that time, they did not allow a calculator to be used during the test. A real estate agent could sell or buy a house without an attorney involved, but that meant there were a great many things that the agent had to know. I failed my first test (fortunately, nobody expected me to bribe them in order to pass!). But when I took the test again two weeks later, I passed with flying colors. I was now ready to become a real estate agent in a brokerage firm. I took a job with Century 21, right across the street from Jay's future clinic. I thought this would be convenient, especially because I was so involved with the furnishing and setting up of the clinic.

I enjoyed being in real estate; one could tour the houses up for sale, and I loved to see the different homes that were available. But the unpleasant part of this work was that one had to canvass, which meant that I had to contact people in certain areas either by phone or in person to see if they were interested in selling their homes. This was hard work and I didn't do well at it. I had my own desk at the office and made friends, but business was slow for me. There were two women in the office who were extremely good, they had been in the business for years and made a lot of money. The ones who were the best worked in pairs, which was more successful. Disappointingly, I did not find anyone who was willing to take me under her wings. I was the new one and had to prove myself. I also discovered that I was too shy for this kind of business—it required a level of aggressiveness that I didn't like. Nonetheless, I stayed with it, though it went slowly.

What I liked best about my real estate business was that once a week, all the houses for sale would be open to the agents and we could go from house to house to look at them. Some of the homes were magnificent, and it was fascinating to see how the different tastes and personalities came through the various arrangements and decors. Not only were there single-family homes. Often several condominiums and townhouses were available. Sometimes I would see a townhouse that was exactly what I would have liked for us. But I felt it was too early to think of buying anything, although as far as an investment was concerned, it would have been the ideal time. Prices were going up every month about 10%. More and more developments were springing up, and I wondered how much higher the prices would go. I was afraid of making the same mistake we had made in Seattle by not buying a house.

While I'd been exploring the real estate business, the clinic had been completed and was now ready for business. There was a reception area with a waiting room, two treatment rooms and a backroom with various sizes of cages. Jay hired a young woman who had worked at an animal clinic before to be the receptionist, bookkeeper and assistant when necessary. Word of the new clinic spread quickly and the people in the area were happy that they now had a clinic in their neighborhood. Some of the clients that Jay had made with his house call practice still wanted house calls, but many of them brought their pets to his hospital instead.

It was a lot of work, and I could see that Jay was proud of what he had created. There was one recurring problem, however, which negatively impacted his practice. Jay was comfortable with giving local anesthesia, as well as short-acting general anesthesia by giving a narcotic through the vein. However, when he had to perform major surgery he became nervous and insecure because he lacked experience with general anesthesia and intubation. Therefore, he frequently had to bring in another veterinarian to handle it. He did not like to do so and this increased anxiety created a lot of stress for Jay, which in turn caused me some real concern for his health. Jay had had a problem with high blood pressure for quite some time yet refused to take medication to treat it. Despite my entreaties, he would not see a doctor about it, pushing aside my worries by saying he had everything under control. Nevertheless, I could see the toll the increased stress was taking on him and I remained uneasy.

After some time my mother and aunt came to visit and stayed in the second bedroom at the house. I took them around La Jolla, San Diego and Coronado and in my role as guide I felt as if I had lived there for ages. How fast one adapts to new surroundings! San Diego had an interesting Old Town. It was a picturesque area with Spanish-style houses and lively Mexican restaurants with music and dancing. Balboa Park in San Diego was also one of my favorite spots. The park was beautiful and had a lot to offer, from theater and great restaurants to one of the best zoological gardens in the country. Aside from the zoo in Balboa Park, there was also a wild animal reserve near San Diego. It was a very large natural park fenced in, in which all kinds of wild animals could freely roam around, not minding the little train that took tourists around to view them. It gave one the illusion of being in Africa.

Jay's sister Francey's son, David, came to San Diego to study at the University of California and we saw a lot of him. Of the three brothers he was the most extroverted and affectionate, and he called me Auntie Eva. He loved his uncle Jay and enjoyed helping him whenever he could. He also liked to listen to Jay play honky tonk and jazz on the piano. Jay played by ear and had a hard time reading music so he decided to take lessons from one of his clients. After several months she organized a concert with a few of her students and I was pleased to see Jay's progress.

We joined a Reformed synagogue in La Jolla and met some wonderful people, little by little making new friends. A couple of Jay's women clients were very taken with him and he became a big success with the ladies. I was happy; Jay needed admiration and success, and I was convinced that we had made the right choice in moving south.

My mother's youngest sister, Franzi, who had emigrated to Australia with her family, had gotten a divorce from her husband quite early on, and when her daughter, Ruth (Uti), came to study at UC Berkeley she came with her daughter and settled in Los Angeles. This was the cousin I had loved so much when we were children, but we became so estranged that, although she now lives very close to us, we do not see each other at all. The relationship between mother and daughter had always been a close one, but when Uti decided to get married, her fiance did not meet her mother's approval. Fireworks exploded, resulting in a rift between them that was insurmountable, with Ruth determined never to have anything to do with her mother again. Franzi was hard to get along with, and although I would never have broken with my mother, I did understand. I had stayed with Franzi in Los Angeles for a week soon after I had arrived in Mexico. She had a mean streak and I came to the conclusion that staying away was better. However, Franzi felt very alone, and after living in Phoenix for a while, where she had her cousin Martha and children, she decided to move to San Diego. This was not something I was excited about! I found a room for her and hoped that I wouldn't have to see too much of her. Unfortunately, she started showing up every evening right before dinner. What could I do but invite her to stay? She was not very fond of Jay, and somehow she always found a way to anger him, and invariably the biggest fights occurred at the dinner table. Her unpleasant behavior created tension and I could see Jay's stress level begin to rise as soon as he saw her. I warned her repeatedly, but she simply paid no attention and I was forced to tell her to leave more than once.

Our landlords called us to tell us that we could extend our one-year lease to two years. So now, much to Jay's happiness we had another year before we would have to make a decision about buying a house. Jay was too afraid of committing himself to buying something at that time. His practice was just starting and he was waiting for the crazy real estate bubble to burst so he would not have to pay such an inflated price.

One day somebody from the Humane Society brought a young male tabby cat into the clinic who was obviously lost and had been in a fight. His face looked pitiful from the many bite marks on it. Amazingly, the cat did not fight back while Jay took care of him, understanding immediately that he was being helped. He was so well behaved that Jay asked the person to let him know if nobody claimed the cat, because he was interested in keeping him for himself. A week later Jay brought the cat home, and although I had never had a pet before, (nor would I have picked a tabby), I immediately liked him and named him "Kitty." Jay named him "Tom Mix", but Kitty it was for me.

This was a whole new experience for us. Suddenly, we had a tiny being to take care of! Jay didn't want the cat to roam around and cry in the middle of the night so we made a soft bed for him in the garage. During the day, however, Kitty had the run of the house when we were there, but when nobody was at home, he had to be confined to the garage.

Soon I had become very attached to Kitty, and sometimes waking up in the middle of the night I would think of him and smile with happiness. What a wonderful feeling it was to know that my little friend was there, safe and sound. Kitty was not an average cat, he never cried or got angry. He behaved so well, that I was sure he understood every word I said to him. As a matter of fact, I was certain he thought he was a dog because he would follow us around like a puppy, sitting by our feet when we sat reading in the evening or jumping in my lap to be petted. He came when I called him, and if I bathed him, he would only fight me a little bit and then with a big sigh would give in. Jay taught me how to clip his nails and Kitty would let me do it without scratching me. He never clawed or bit anyone. He was so loyal and was such good company. When Jay and I had a fight, Kitty would look at us with big frightened eyes, until I would take him on my lap and hug him to my chest. He was a great comfort.

One afternoon, after having been gone only for an hour, I drove into the garage and noticed that the door leading to the interior of the house was open, with Kitty standing in the room looking over his shoulder. I knew that Jay had been home to pick up something he needed; however, I was also sure he always closed the door. Walking into the house, I felt a shiver of apprehension a moment before my heart stopped in shock. I couldn't believe what I saw! The horror hit me in the chest and I could hardly breathe. Every item that had been in drawers or cabinets had been strewn all over the floor. It looked like a burglary but instead of running to the neighbors and calling the police from there, I was seized with the idea of seeing what the rest of the house looked like. Not even thinking that the burglars could still be in the house, I went from room to room and was met by the same chaotic jumble everywhere. Every drawer had been emptied, every box and even perfume bottles opened. Every piece of clothing had been tossed on the floor! I had heard of breaking and entering, but I had never heard of anything like this! The level of vandalism was staggering. Finally my good sense caught up with me and I realized that I should not be in the house. Screaming I ran to my neighbors, who were absolutely horrified and immediately called the police. Then they escorted me back home to see if I would be safe in the house until the police arrived. They were angry with me that I had entered the house in the first place—the intruder could have still been there and for all I knew he could have had a gun. I started to cry, who would do a thing like this? I felt violated, and I couldn't imagine how I would ever put everything back where it belonged. It reminded me painfully of the devastation I witnessed on Kristall Nacht so many years before. The extent of the willful destruction that ran through the house made me feel very frightened and insecure.

I called Jay, who was making a house call, and told him that we had been burglarized and to please hurry home. I was so frantic on the phone that he was home in 10 minutes, and when he took me into his arms I began to feel a little better. The police were checking everything and found a bottle of Chivas Regal hidden in the bushes. When they were through investigating, they decided that it had to have been done by teenagers who were either looking for money or drugs, or just engaging in sheer vandalism. The strange part was that they took only two things of value: A gold necklace with a gold coin that I had left on my night table and a magnificent, hand-hammered antique silver box that I had on the coffee table in the living room. It was one of my most precious possessions and I was heartbroken. Of course they never found the perpetrators or the stolen items. Apparently, the burglars had broken the bedroom window to get into the house. They were probably interrupted by my return while in the middle of the crime and had to flee through the sliding glass door.

CHAPTER TWO

I don't know whether it was due to the break-in or because the clinic was doing better, but Jay decided that it was time to look for a condo or townhouse. We saw some lovely places, which I liked, but those needed an immediate decision and Jay's insecurity could not be overcome that easily. He opted for going with one that was being built, since decisions did not have to be made in the immediate future. Unfortunately, the site was in an undeveloped area with the only buildings being the ones they were putting up. Nevertheless, we went ahead and made a small down payment knowing that there were many months of construction ahead. At the same time, we found out that the price for this condo was higher than those I had looked at earlier. In addition, it became clear that the new property would not be as pretty as the earlier ones, yet we went with it, hoping for the best.

Jay needed some rest so we decided to visit my mother and aunt in Cuernavaca and then take them to Acapulco with us. It was good for Jay to get out a little bit. He had been working hard and he really needed the time off. He arranged to have another veterinarian who specialized in covering the practices of vacationing vets to take care of the clinic. I was sure it was in good hands and I tried to keep Jay from worrying too much.

On returning home we found out, our condominium was nearing completion and we had to come up with the rest of the payment. Jay went to the bank across from his clinic and applied for a mortgage.

He was scared that they would not approve it because the clinic wasn't making that much money and we had no real assets. However, after a couple of weeks the mortgage was approved and Jay was relieved.

As we met more people, we were invited to a variety of parties. One time we met Prince Alfonso de Bourbon, cousin to the King of Spain, who was permanently living in La Jolla. His title was Goodwill Ambassador of Spain, but it appeared that he lived off people inviting him to dinners and lunches because of who he was. We talked a bit and because we had a language in common, he opened up to me. Sometimes I would see him sitting on a bench in front of a deli on the main street in La Jolla. When I asked him what he was doing there his answer was:

"I am waiting for somebody to invite me to a meal."

He said it jokingly, but I knew that there was a lot of truth in this, so I invited him to my birthday party in August. Each time I saw him, I would think: Here is a member of what used to be one of the most important royal families of Europe, related to the Hapsburgs, no less, and he is practically living on the street! It seemed a sad fate.

We went to San Francisco where my sister-in-law, Francey, gave a big party, inviting all of Jay's old friends who lived in the area. Clearly, seeing these friends was one of the happiest moments of Jay's life. His face was radiant and he joked and laughed with everybody. In his good spirit, he wanted to embrace the whole world.

Back at home I received a very sad phone call from my mother. Uncle Emil, my mother's youngest brother, who was visiting them from Israel, had suffered a stroke and was in the hospital in a coma. She asked that I come to Mexico immediately, they needed me. Once again I flew to Mexico on a very sad mission. My uncle stayed in the coma for two days before he died. My aunt was inconsolable.

When their mother had died giving birth to Emil, my aunt, who had been 15 years old, took care of baby Emil as though he had been her child. Emil was grateful to her and insisted that she had saved his life, thus there was a very close bond between them. Once again, I had the very sorrowful duty of attending the funeral of a loved one. My aunt Franzi had joined us the day before, so she was also present, behaving better than she had in San Diego. After the funeral my cousin Emerich invited us to have dinner at his house, where, thankfully, everything went well.

I stayed in Cuernavaca for a few days and then went home, where I told Jay everything about the stroke my uncle had suffered. I was trying to drive home how dangerous high blood pressure was and that he should be taking his medication and seeing a doctor regularly. Though he promised to do this, he never did. I grew tired of constantly harping on these things with no results. Not only was his attitude frustrating, it was worrisome in the extreme.

My real estate business was going slowly, I rented an apartment for some clients, sold a townhouse for some others, yet I had not had a big sale, and I was becoming anxious. On the "plus" side, there was no pressure from the managing broker, and it gave me something to do outside the home each day.

The clinic was going quite well and months went by without any problems. It was spring and we enjoyed the weather, going to the park and taking walks along the beach. Since the clinic was becoming more successful and we had decided to buy a townhouse for which Jay had been able to get a mortgage, he had become more relaxed and was looking at life in a more optimistic way. In July we would move to the new townhouse and I began to believe that everything would finally fall into place. I, too, was also feeling more upbeat, hoping that now that all the problems of moving and starting a new business were out of the way, we would have a better relationship.

Jay's aunt and uncle who lived in Seattle were going to celebrate their 60th wedding anniversary in San Francisco, where one of their daughters lived. So we planned to go to San Francisco for the occasion and stay at Arlene's house, while she was away on a cruise with her husband. Although we had made up our differences a long time ago, she had left because she didn't want to be around so much family, but had given us the use of their house.

Jay's uncle, who had been at our wedding, decided to fly to San Diego with his wife, visit with us for a couple of days and then fly together with us to San Francisco. Jay was very exited; he hadn't seen this uncle since our wedding and he was really looking forward to the visit. We met them at the airport and Jay in his enthusiasm picked up three heavy suitcases at one time.

I was appalled. "Jay, don't carry so much, please!" I shouted, but to no avail. He had to show off how strong he was!

We had a nice evening, Jay brought out all his photo albums and we joked and laughed. They retired early because they were tired from the trip and we did the same. The next day Jay got up very early and went to the clinic. He wanted to take care of the animals and send the ones home that could be released, since we were going to San Francisco that afternoon. In the meantime, I had packed our suitcases, and was having a nice chat with his uncle and aunt, when the phone rang. I lifted the receiver and heard Jay whisper hoarsely that he was so sick he had thrown up three times and was coming home. I put him to bed right away but he started complaining of a terrible headache, telling me that he had never felt so awful in his life. I felt sick to my stomach. I knew he was showing symptoms of a possible stroke, and I was so scared that I couldn't think straight.

However, I called a doctor who was willing to make a house call. I remember Uncle Julius kept saying: "This is nothing; all he needs is a laxative." It was an inane comment, but I could only hope he was right; yet Jay's blood pressure had been too high for so long and he had been so unwilling to have it treated I feared the worst.

The doctor, after examining Jay, said that he needed to go to the hospital right away and called 911. By now I was really frightened and just kept praying. After the paramedics put Jay into the ambulance, I followed in my car to the hospital, where they admitted Jay. I was not completely comfortable with the hospital, because it was a small community hospital. So I wondered if I should have him taken to Scripps Memorial, but the doctor said that he should not be moved.

It turned out that Jay had indeed suffered a stroke, so they gave him blood thinners intravenously. Through my years of experience and having seen so many mistakes made in health care, I was doing my best to trust the doctors and nurses, at the same time praying earnestly for God's help. After I took Julius and Ida to the airport, I returned to the hospital and was terribly distressed to find Jay's body cold to the touch and dark spots all over his arms. When I asked the doctor about it he answered that perhaps Jay didn't need a blood thinner after all. I was shocked—what exactly did that mean? First they give him the blood thinner and then he shouldn't have it? Did they know what they were doing? I called Francey and Sol to tell them what had happened and they asked me to keep them informed. I stayed with Jay as long as I could that evening. He had had a CAT scan and they told me the damage was at the base of the brain, explaining that if you had to have a stroke, it was the least dangerous spot. By this time I was so upset I found it difficult to make sense of their prognosis. However, I took them at their word because he had been able to speak and move all along. So, I kissed him goodnight at 10 p.m. and went home.

The jarring ring of the phone woke me from a deep sleep—it was 1 a.m. My heart was racing when I lifted the receiver. "This is the hospital, your husband has had another stroke and is not doing so well. Come right away." How I got dressed, into my car, and to the hospital, I never knew. Jay was unconscious, they had put him on a respirator and he had tears in his eyes. When I saw that, I broke down and began to sob. How could he have deteriorated so quickly? Then I remembered the blood thinner and I was certain that it had caused a hemorrhage. I was appalled; what was I going to do now? My first instinct was to get him out of there, but I felt helpless. Could he even be moved? I didn't care how late it was, I needed help. So I called our friend Adolf Hochstim, who had encouraged us originally to move to La Jolla, and he came immediately. He took a look at Jay and then gently told me to go home. This was not exactly what I had expected from him, but I let him put me in my car and drove home. Once at home I called Francey and told them that they needed to come quickly. Then I called my aunt Franzi, explained what had happened and told her that I didn't want to stay alone, I was too scared. I have to give her credit, in spite of all her problems she immediately came to the house and slept on the sofa in the living room. I wasn't able to fall asleep. I just lay there counting the hours until I could go to the hospital again. I was in a complete fog. When they told me he was in intensive care and I could only see him for 5 minutes every hour, I was devastated. He hadn't changed in the last few hours, but when Franzi and I looked into the room I saw his foot move. I am sure he wanted to tell me that he was aware that I was there, but Franzi told me that this was only reflex movement and pulled me out of the room. I still regret that incident. I should have talked to him and held his hand at that moment.

Francey and Sol arrived on the earliest flight from San Francisco, and I was relieved that I could share the responsibility. We were going to the hospital every hour but his condition didn't change. Fortunately the hospital was very near our house. Sometime during that day Arlene and Herb arrived. They had been reached on their ship in Hawaii and they caught a plane back from their next stop. The house was buzzing with people and I walked around in a daze.

We remained in this state of limbo for another week, until the doctor reported that Jay's condition was deteriorating, the damage to his brain was extensive and he would not recover. We were now faced with the decision of taking him off the respirator. After an anguished consultation among all of us, we decided it was the merciful thing to do. An hour later, on May 8, 1979, Jay died. All I could think of was that I wanted to die with him!

I felt so sorry for him I couldn't breathe. As far as I could tell, my poor husband had never experienced the satisfaction of success in his life, or in his relationships. And now when he might have slowly seen his practice building up and us moving into our own home, he was gone. The futility of it ached in my heart.

I told Sol that I wanted to bury Jay in Seattle so he could be near his parents, and it was arranged. The next morning we took the same plane that carried Jay's coffin and went to Seattle. Before the funeral there was a very touching memorial service at the synagogue to which Jay, and his parents before him, had belonged. The rabbi, who had known Jay for many years, gave a wonderful eulogy for which I was very grateful, and the synagogue was packed with all our friends. Everybody embraced me with tears in their eyes; Jay had been loved and he would be missed!

After the service we all gathered at the home of Jay's cousin and I couldn't get over how much joking and laughter there were as people remembered experiences they'd had with Jay. I could not stop the tears from running down my face. In spite of the fact that we had had a difficult marriage, we had been married for 13 years. I missed him and felt great compassion for him. The pain seemed almost unbearable.

When I went back to San Diego the next day, I called my mother and aunt who had been planning to come visit later that week. I didn't tell them what had happened, but simply asked them to come as soon as possible. I didn't want mother to receive this shock over the phone.

My mother and aunt arrived and I met them at the airport. When I finally had them at home I gave them the bad news. They were stunned and couldn't believe it. My mother started to cry and we tried to comfort each other. However, I knew that I could not show them the extent of my grief. I had to take care of my mother's heart and my aunt who had already lost so many of her loved ones. My aunt Franzi came and cooked for us and helped in whatever way she could. I went to my real estate office and resigned. I had too many other problems to take care of to have time and energy for that work.

Despite my grief, I knew I had to take care of Jay's business. I went to the clinic and arranged for the temporary veterinarian to stay on as long as necessary, since I wanted to sell it as an active practice. I was nearly brought to tears when I entered the clinic, which Jay had built and furnished with such love and expectation.

Somebody recommended a broker who specialized in selling medical practices, and after he assured me that he could sell this clinic for a good price, I quickly signed a contract with him. In the meantime

I paid a weekly salary to the receptionist and the veterinarian in charge, hoping that this would not go on too long.

I was so busy during the day that my pain only lifted its ugly head when I sat down to lunch or when I went to bed at night. The moment I feared most was waking up in the morning and facing reality. I would feel overwhelmed with the enormity of the situation. Sleep was almost impossible, but fortunately my mother slept next to me. We would sometimes talk for hours during the night. She was such a solace to me!

Two weeks went by before I finally heard from the broker. He brought an offer, saying that it was the best I would be able to get. I looked at the offer for a long moment. Then I raised my eyes to his face and slowly tore up the piece of paper he had given me. With a firm voice, I thanked him for his endeavors but told him he was fired. I would take care of selling the practice myself. He practically laughed at me.

"Good luck, lady," he sneered. "You'll come back to me. You don't have a clue where to advertise or how to go about it. I am a professional and I always have my client's best interests at heart."

I didn't bother to argue with him. "Thank you very much, but I will take it from here!" As I said this, I showed him the door. I was disappointed and angry. "This is what happens to a woman alone," I said to myself. "But I'll show them all!"

Of course he was right, I had not the faintest idea how to sell a medical practice, but I was sure I could do better than he. The first thing I did was put an ad in the local paper. I also wrote a letter to the local office of the Veterinary Medical Association, explaining what had happened and that I needed to sell this lovely new clinic. Within a week I received calls from three different veterinarians who were interested in settling in the area. One of them sounded promising on the phone and I made an appointment to see him. I showed him the clinic and he said he would like to think about it. Two days later he made me an offer that was three times larger than the offer I had received from the broker! I grabbed it. It occurred to me that maybe I could have gotten a better price, but I didn't want to be greedy.

Jay had life insurance, not a lot, but enough for my purposes. Together with what I received from the clinic sale plus a little loan from my mother I paid cash for the condominium. Now I owned it outright and although people thought it was crazy not to have a tax deduction, I figured that with no income I needed no tax deduction. I was able to put a good amount of cash into the bank and was set for the time being, not having to worry about working.

I had to leave the house by the end of June, so I started packing and my mother helped a lot. My aunt tried to do as much as she could, but this of course was very limited as she could barely see. A daughter of friends also helped, and we began to transport clothes and small things in our cars. We made many trips and slowly got the smaller things into the new townhouse. On June 30th the moving van picked up the furniture and boxes, and by that afternoon we had the two bedrooms completely furnished and ready for the three of us to sleep. With all the furniture in place the only thing that remained was to unpack the boxes. I decided to open the box with the dishes and glasses that we would need immediately and leave the rest.

My townhouse was one of several completed in the new development, which had a swimming pool, tennis courts and a clubhouse already constructed. The condominium's front entrance led to a nice size living room, with stairs that led down to the garage and up to the next level, which contained the dining area, den and kitchen. From that level stairs led up to the first bedroom with its own bath, and a few more steps led to the upper bedroom with its own bath. This, being the bigger room and facing the back, I chose for myself. I felt like a million dollars; this was the first time I owned my own place! What a feeling! However, when my mother saw how isolated this development was, she was worried; how could I come home alone in the evening in this wilderness? I did not feel uneasy at all with the situation. I had neighbors on both sides and I tried to calm my mother's fears. She should have seen that place a few years later. It was bustling with additional condominiums, high-rise office buildings, hotels and shopping centers. She would never have recognized it.

Kitty got used to his new surroundings, but I still had his litter box and bed in the garage. I did, however, have a pet door installed in the garage door, hoping that he would not run away.

Mother and aunt Elsa wanted to go back to Cuernavaca and asked me to join them. Other than emptying the boxes, I had nothing pressing to do. I was not looking forward to starting my new life alone, so I decided to go with them. Friends, who had taken care of Kitty before, agreed to take him for as long as necessary, so I had nothing to worry about.

In the peaceful surroundings of Cuernavaca I realized how exhausted and stressed out I was. The quiet beauty of the place allowed me to regain some equilibrium. Mother and aunt Elsa were delighted to be able to spoil me a little and for a while I just lounged in the garden with a good book. Gloria, the maid, would bring me little refreshments from time to time. After an enjoyable lunch we would all take a nap, and in the afternoon one or two friends would come to visit at time for tea. The pace was slow and relaxing: just what I needed. The weeks slipped by very quickly and before long my birthday was coming up. Of course we decided that I should stay over for my birthday; I knew I couldn't face it alone.

To celebrate my birthday we went to lunch at my favorite hotel in Cuernavaca. Las Mananitas was one of those incongruous places that have an uninviting exterior, yet once you go through the entrance you exclaim "Ooh!" as you find yourself surrounded by beauty. The cool and inviting Spanish-style hotel lobby led to a magnificent terrace and a glorious garden with exotic plants and sculptures by famous Mexican artists. Peacocks roamed around displaying their colorful plumage. To one side there was a fenced in swimming pool surrounded by lounge chairs and cabanas. Tables were set on the flagstones in the gardens, where they served drinks and brought the menu so that we could order from there. When we went to the tables, which were set for lunch on the terrace, everything was ready to be served. We had a delightful lunch and they even brought me a birthday cake with candles. At the same time, a Mariachi band appeared and sang "Las Mananitas," which is the Mexican birthday song. It was a wonderful surprise and I was very touched and sadly nostalgic. The last time we had gone there had been with Jay. It had been barely three months since his death and I still suffered from losing him.

A week later I was thinking that I could not bury myself in the wonderful love and peace that surrounded me in Cuernavaca. I had to face life and I had to face it alone. I needed to stand on my own two feet emotionally. When I explained this to my mother she understood, although she was sorry to let me go.

Coming home and seeing all the boxes that still needed to be emptied I felt the need to unpack and get settled in my new home. I wanted the house to look nice and cozy. When I had everything in place and the pictures hung, I finally felt proud of what I had done.

CHAPTER THREE

The weather in September was lovely, and living in La Jolla had its advantages. I was near the beach and the quaint village of La Jolla, and I would meet friends for lunch at one restaurant or another. Sometimes I took my aunt Franzi to the Valencia hotel, an old hotel, where all the film stars of the twenties stayed. It was great for having lunch on the terrace. The future was something so vague in my mind that I couldn't focus on when and where I would be doing anything. In the meantime I just lived each day, one at a time. Every morning I swam in our pool because the waves at the beach were a little too high for my taste. The pool was a good place to relax and reflect upon my life: past, present and future.

Weeks went by and I was starting to feel a little less sad and a little more comfortable being alone for the time being. One day I had a call from my friend Adolf Hochstim, who asked me whether I would be free for dinner the next day. He had a friend he wanted me to meet and they would pick me up at my place at 7 p.m. the next evening. They arrived at my house punctually, and when I opened the door I knew my life had suddenly changed. Standing next to Adolf was a handsome man, 6 feet tall with brown hair and glasses. He looked a little bit like Jay, but his personality and manners were completely different. He smiled at me and said, "How do you do?" He said it in such a musical way that I started to laugh. I think just hearing the four words made me happy!

Adolph introduced him, saying his name was John Ross, and that he was Professor of Chemistry at Stanford. We went to one of the nicest hotels in the area not far from my home and had dinner.

As we talked, we noticed how many things we had in common. John was 3 years my senior, was born in Vienna and had also been forced to emigrate because he was Jewish. His father was the first to leave because he was in the most danger. He went to San Remo, Italy, where the rest of the family were to meet and from where they would try to get a boat to France. (Fortunately this did not work out and thus they were saved from eventually ending up in a concentration camp, which happened to many French Jews).

John's mother, who had been a Catholic and had converted to Judaism when she married John's father could still be considered a Catholic if she so decided. However, although she had been approached to leave her marriage and come back to the fold, she had ardently refused to do so. She would stick with her family. The second to leave was John, who at the age of 13 was put onto a plane to Italy where he was to meet his father. The plane was an old aircraft, the kind where you could still open the windows. The poor boy was airsick during the whole flight. The last to leave was his mother, and she left the day the war was declared. After some time in Italy, they were finally able to get their visa to the United States where they settled in New York.

We had the same mother tongue and the same roots, we laughed at the same jokes and were brought up with the same songs. It was uncanny. It was a memorable evening indeed and I was overcome by the feeling that I had found a soulmate. The feeling was mutual because John immediately said that we had to see each other again. When we parted for the evening we stood a long time looking into each other's eyes.

When I arrived home I felt that I was floating on air. What a lovely man this was. He was kind and attentive and very good looking. He had large grey-blue eyes, which looked deeply into your eyes and brimmed with understanding. I couldn't wait to see him again, and was very grateful to Adolf for having had the wisdom to introduce us. I called my mother and told her that I had met my future husband. She laughed, and I had to join in when I realized the wishful thinking I was expressing. That night I went to bed happy and had a wonderful dream.

However, we each had adjustments to make and knew it would take time. He had recently left his position as professor of physical chemistry at MIT, was separated from his wife, and had begun the initial stages of divorce proceedings. We needed to get to know each other, get used to each other's way and to appreciate each other. I also needed a substantial period of adjustment, due to my mourning for Jay. I felt a little guilty for starting a relationship so soon after his death. Again, as I had felt with Hans Kronberger, I had fears of not being able to fit into academic life. After all, I had not gone through formal university training.

John had two children: Betsy, who was 25 years old and studying for a college degree, and Bobby, 22 years old and a medical student. He was very close to them and I was glad that he confided in me with many discussions about them.

Fortunately, John was on a governmental committee and had to come to La Jolla frequently. We saw each other as often as possible and I had the feeling from the start that this was a man I could live with. He was interesting, self-assured, cultured, very understanding and considerate. In spite of his great success as a physical chemist and professor, he was quite humble and had a wonderful sense of humor, which he sometimes turned on himself. His visits to La Jolla were delightful and served to form the foundation of a relationship studded with joyful events and memories.

After a few months, John invited me to go with him to a meeting in Cocoyoc, Mexico. Since this was very near to Cuernavaca, I invited him to visit my mother and aunt. It was a wonderful trip. My mother was absolutely enchanted with John. Not only could she speak German with him, he was such a charmer that he had both my mother and my aunt in his pocket in no time. He was not putting on an act, but was being himself and the truth be told, in spite of my efforts to take things slowly, I was already very much in love with him. The two days we spent in Cuernavaca were like a fountain of youth for the two elderly ladies; there was a lot of laughter and lively conversation.

Cocoyoc was beautiful. It used to be a sugar mill but had been converted into a resort, which was surrounded by rivers, ponds and trees that had enormous roots. While John attended his meetings, I walked around getting acquainted with some of the wives who had joined their husbands at the conference. It was a marvelous and romantic time for us, and I got to know John from yet another side: his interaction with fellow scientists. I hadn't realized just how distinguished he was in his field and I enjoyed hearing them talk about John as a renowned scientist.

After some time, my mother and my aunt came again to stay with me in La Jolla, and we were invited to the wedding of my friend Nanette's daughter Gigi, who had been studying at Stanford and was now getting married there. Unbeknownst to John, my mother, my aunt and I traveled to Palo Alto and checked into a hotel. I called John, but was told he was out of town and would not return until that evening. He didn't get back until 10:00 that night, but he didn't wait until the next day to call me at the hotel we were staying, he was so delighted that I was in town.

The next morning he picked us up to take us to the house that he had bought on campus, and which he now shared with a post-doctoral fellow of his and his family. When I saw the house I was charmed to see the nice location, the interesting architecture of the living room, and the large garden and patio. The furnishings were nothing to look at, since they were only temporary, and the walls were completely empty, ready for a feminine hand. My mother declared that it was like a little house in the woods, for it was quite hidden by trees, and one could not see any of the neighbor's houses. I thought it quite idyllic.

The next evening was the wedding, to which John had also been invited. It was formal and looked very elegant in the garden of the young couple's beautiful house. However, it was a chilly March evening and in spite of the heaters placed throughout the area, we were so cold that we decided to go inside after the ceremony. We sat with Hanni Lustig, my dear childhood friend, her husband Dave Hochman (also from Vienna), and her daughter Monica with her husband, who all lived in the Berkeley area. After all these years, I was overjoyed to be close to them again! Many years ago Hanni had divorced her husband and married Dave in Buenos Aires. While we were in Mexico they had moved to the San Francisco area. Living very separate lives, we had finally ended up in the same place!

John and I left early because his son, Bobby, was arriving from New York and we wanted to meet him at the airport. We arrived, clad in our formal wear, to meet John's son, who was studying medicine at Einstein University in New York. As he departed the plane, I saw a tall, good-looking young man, with the same ready smile as his father. I knew that he couldn't have been too thrilled meeting me, knowing that his father and I were serious about each other, but he was friendly and pleasant. I believe he knew that his parents' marriage had been a difficult one and he wanted his father to be happy.

After 11 months, things between John and me had progressed to the point that we were ready to make a commitment. We decided that I would move to the house at Stanford in September of that year, and John told the family who was living in his house that they had to move out as soon as they could find something suitable.

Once again I found myself having to pack up all my belongings for a long distance move, but this time it was with joy in my heart. I was so happy I couldn't think straight. I decided to take everything except a few small items, which I would not need. In May I started to pack, leaving enough time so I could do it slowly and by myself. In August I held a little garage sale in an area at the back of our bank, where anybody who was interested could sell things. I also flew to San Francisco with Kitty, whom I didn't want to take in the car in September because we were going to stop in Newport Beach, and we couldn't have a cat. I arrived in Stanford with Kitty and stayed a few days to see if he would get acclimated to his new surroundings and not run away. His first time out in the garden was very traumatic for him. A number of blue jays swooped down from the trees, cawing loudly and scaring him, and he ran away, trying to get back into the house. This was all so new to him that I felt sorry for him. After a few days, however, he got used to the birds and the different noises and was happy to be able to go into the garden and roam around. He could have easily run away, but thankfully he didn't try.

In the meantime, Bobby had used the influence of his father's friends to transfer from Einstein University to Stanford Medical School. When he achieved this, he asked us whether it would be all right for him to live with us for a while. We agreed that this would be fine, although we explained that we could not get married until the divorce was final. Bobby had no problem with that. Fortunately Bobby loved Kitty and promised to take good care of him until I moved up.

At the end of August John came down to help me with the move. I had left all the-hard-to-move things for when he would be able to help me. Unfortunately, Murphy's Law had gone into effect: "Whatever can go wrong, will go wrong." John threw his back out the evening before he came to La Jolla, so when he arrived he couldn't do much. The movers were due to arrive in two days and there were still many things that needed to be done. Luckily a friend of mine, a young woman from Buenos Aires, was willing to help, and we managed to get things ready in time for the movers.

For the umpteenth time in my life I said goodbye to my friends, but this time I was happy to do so. Certainly I would miss them, but I was heading toward a future that I was looking forward to with every fiber of my being. I finally had found the man I had been waiting for all my life. My Prince Charming on the white horse! So many times over the years I had reproached myself for always making the wrong decision; I now had to retract that. Clearly every decision I'd made was the right one, for had I not made them I would never have met John!

I am sitting in front of my town house for the last time.

PART VI
STANFORD

◆

1980–2000

CHAPTER ONE

On September 1, 1980, at the age of 51, I arrived at Stanford to start a new life. I felt like a young bride arriving at her new home with a husband she was very much in love with. However, there was a difference: My new son, Bobby, welcomed us with a wonderful meal he had prepared. I was very touched by this and was certain it augured well for the future. Part of the welcoming committee was Kitty, who seemed overjoyed to see me again after a separation of three weeks. That night I fell into bed exhausted and grateful that Fate had been so good to me. However, I knew that there was plenty of work ahead of me. The house needed a lot of attention and my furniture and belongings were coming the next day.

Due to the financial settlements of his divorce, John had moved to the West Coast with limited funds, forcing him to buy the house at Stanford with a substantial mortgage. Although a loan from one of his friends from the East had helped enormously, and he had an excellent position at Stanford with lucrative consulting arrangements in the private sector, I still thought I should go to work for a while until we saw how our finances went. Fortunately, Raychem, one of the companies for which John was consulting, offered me a job as Liaison Officer for foreign visitors since they knew I spoke four languages, German, Spanish, French and English. My main responsibility was arranging the right accommodations for the visitors and seeing to their schedules.

However, after a short time, John and I realized that there was no need to pursue my work any further, so I devoted myself to John and the house. There was much to be done to get our home to the level commensurate with the type of entertaining and hosting John and I would be doing as part of his work. The garden had good landscaping but was thoroughly neglected and desiccated. John had a long-running joke that we specialized in the diseases of plants. The interior of the house required a lot of renovation, yet we could not afford to make major changes right away. So we made the immediate ones necessary and over the following years upgraded much of the house.

With new carpets, a new oven, my furniture and the artwork I brought from La Jolla, the house began to look quite livable and inviting. We had three bedrooms, two and a half baths, a great room, (living and dining), a small kitchen and a family room. In addition there was also a storage room next to the attached garage, which became the Kitty's room.

The garden took longer to take shape, and since this was the first garden I was responsible for, I had no experience to guide me. My approach was to go to the nursery, see a plant that I loved, buy it and plant it wherever there was an empty spot. It didn't occur to me to check whether the plant needed sun or shade. I learned my gardening lessons the expensive way!

During the week I was alone in the house, as John and Bobby were both very busy. Bobby was studying medicine and trying to decide what field to specialize in. He seemed to change his mind every month, but in the end, decided on anesthesiology. My darling John worked very hard. He would leave at 8 a.m. and return at 6 p.m. and then work even more after dinner. This required adjustments on both our parts. He carried a heavy load of teaching, including graduate students in his research group, as well as the time he spent enthusiastically working on his own research. As I found out later, he was considered a leading authority in the world in his field of physical chemistry, which included esoteric topics such as chemical kinetics, the determination of complex reactive mechanisms and non-linear behavior. However, I didn't need to be aware of this to be proud of him. He was a great scientist, a wonderful teacher, and a beautiful human being. Throughout the years I have met former students of John's, who went on to develop their own careers. They can never say enough about John's positive influence on their lives and how much they loved and respected him. Truthfully it has never been a surprise to me, I know what a great person he is from my own experience!

As time went on, we were able to furnish one bedroom for my mother and aunt, so we invited them to spend some time with us. Watching John guiding my mother through the garden and holding her hand when they had to climb a hill, my heart just melted. What a different relationship my mother had with John than with Jay. I believe the most important factor was that John was not jealous of the close relationship between us. In addition, of course, there was the language and background they had in common. Sometimes John would talk with a Viennese dialect that would make my mother and aunt laugh. It was so cute. Laughter was very common those days. At meals Bobby entertained us with stories from medical school, while casually helping himself to some salad off my mother's and my aunt's plates, which they could not finish. The relaxed atmosphere cemented the comfortable relationships we all shared.

My mother, John and my aunt.

◆   ◆   ◆

Shortly before I left San Diego, my aunt Franzi complained about her health, and went from one doctor to another without finding a diagnosis. Finally, she went to the Scripps Institute, which was famous for check-ups and diagnoses. After a lot of tests and X-rays, one of the doctors said that she had an enlarged liver. When Franzi asked him what the reason for this could be, he answered, "This is the way God made you." Not satisfied with this, she went to another hospital in San Diego, where they diagnosed cancer of the liver and the lung! She called me to give me the horrible news and once again I found myself doubting the credibility of the medical system. How Scripps could have made such a mistake was beyond me. By this time she was already very sick and was losing weight quickly. I went to San Diego to see what I could do for her and hired a caretaker to be with her in her house. My mother and Aunt Elsa had returned to Mexico, and I did not want to ask them to come back to the United States to look after their half-sister. They had enough of their own health difficulties. Franzi's relationship with her daughter had, if anything, deteriorated, and she asked me not to tell her that she was sick. I was tempted to go against her wishes, but she made me swear that I would keep this information to myself. Franzi was very ill and I had to travel to San Diego quite often while she still survived. Her wish was to be cremated and her ashes to be scattered over the ocean. John and I did this in La Jolla with a prayer, and I felt really sorry about the sad circumstances of her life. Her daughter was not even able to be present at her mother's funeral because her mother did not wish me to tell her. After it was all over, I finally called Ruth to tell her about her mother's death. She did say that she was shocked and sorry, and I think she finally felt guilty that she hadn't treated her better during her lifetime. Yet she did not offer to come and take care of her mother's belongings. We had to clean out her apartment, and it was a sad duty. We ended up throwing away most of Franzi's things, and the rest we put in bags for Goodwill. This was a very regrettable end to an unhappy life.

John and I were getting impatient to start our life as a married couple, but the divorce proceedings dragged out interminably. However, we loved each other very much and there was no question in our minds that sooner or later we would marry. In the meantime, we decided to live each day making the best of it. We spent happy days and passionate nights.

John was invited to a conference in Florence, so we planned a trip to Italy with the intention of going to Vienna and England as well. In those days we flew coach and we were lucky that the flight from New York was not crowded. We had three seats to ourselves—so what did my John do? He prepared a bed for me on the three seats, and when I worried about where he was going to sleep he showed me the bed he had made on the floor between our seats and the row ahead of us. What chivalry! With enough blankets for both John and me we really had two long enough areas in which to lie down. The lights went out and we took our respective positions for the night. Suddenly we heard a meow, and we both became alert wondering where it had come from. It didn't take us long to find out that on the floor behind our seats, a cat was sitting in its cage, looking right into John's eyes! After the two of them "talked" to each other, everything calmed down and John fell asleep. Of course with my lifelong insomnia I couldn't sleep in spite of my having the whole three seats made into a bed. I had a hard enough time sleeping in a bed, much less on a plane. Poor John had made his sacrifice in vain! After a while, he woke up and saw that I was lying with my eyes wide open. He insisted that I had to close my eyes to go to sleep; it wouldn't happen otherwise. I closed my eyes but never did drop off.

Fortunately John slept well and arrived well rested in Milan. I, however, could not say the same. I was so tired that I was dizzy; all I could think of was how much I wanted a shower and a bed. No such luck! John had not planned to stop over in Milan, but was going to go on to Florence right away. So we rented a car and he poured me into the passenger seat. The three-hour drive to Florence was a torture. The freeway was full of big, fast trucks whose drivers seemed to make a special effort to push us off the road. They honked their loud horns and startled me so that my heart froze with fear. Arriving at a long tunnel, we desperately tried to find the switch to turn the headlights on, but to no avail. The European signs on the dashboard were so different from what we were used to! In darkness we drove through the long tunnel. Once in daylight again, we finally discovered the switch. How dumb can one be? Of course we decided that it was the Italian car industry, which was dumb. But even bad situations eventually have their end, and we finally arrived in Florence.

John's friends and colleagues had reserved a room in a beautiful villa on top of a hill, which had been built by a disciple of the famous Renaissance scientist, Galileo. Run by nuns, it was a pension as well as a home for elderly people. The elegant villa was surrounded by a magnificent park, which had an abundance of flowers, cypress trees, fig trees, fountains and sculptures. We were given the nicest and biggest room, which had five windows with views into the garden and down to the city of Florence. When we checked in with the Mother Superior, we were a little worried that she would be shocked that we were not married. However, she looked at our passports, saw the different last names, asked us for our address, and said: "Since you both have the same address, you are obviously a married couple." And that was that.

The nuns were lovely and treated us like family. In addition to breakfast, one meal a day was included with the room. Each day we would let them know whether we would eat lunch or dinner. The food was wonderful and the portions were so big we could not eat everything. This made them worry that we weren't eating enough or that we didn't like their food.

From Florence we took the train to Vienna, where we met Uncle Noldi and Ilona at the best Viennese pastry shop. When we came in, my uncle got up and said to John in a very formal manner:

"In the name of the family, I bid you welcome!"

John and I were both surprised and pleased by this ceremonious reception. I believe that as the oldest living brother of my mother, Noldi felt it his duty to thus welcome John.

We enjoyed Vienna, going to all the places which were meaningful to us, and taking all the common tourist pictures, such as the two of us sitting in front of the monument of Johann Strauss. We went to some concerts with my aunt, who had season tickets for the family, as well as to the theater, where we saw a rather heavy play about the Hapsburgs. John and I share a deep love for classical music, art and theater so we took every opportunity to go to concerts, museums and plays. At home we have a large collection of classical music and operas. John's favorite composer is Bach, though not mine at the time; it took me a little while to truly appreciate his music.

Sitting in front of the monument of Johann Strauss

From Vienna we went to England, where John had to meet some people at a branch of Raychem. They had made reservations for us in a charming place in the Cotswolts, called Whatley Manor. This was an impressive stone mansion surrounded by a beautiful park and bordered by the Avon River. The inside was very luxurious with wood-paneled walls and eighteenth-century furniture. The salon had comfortable chintz sofas and chairs, and though the guest rooms were of different sizes and styles, they were all comfortable. During the day while John drove to Swindon for his meetings with the company, I would explore the surroundings or sit and read in the stately park. When John came home we took walks and dined at the manor or went out with the people from Raychem. There were a number of excellent restaurants in the area, most of them French. The closest village to the mansion was Malmsbury, a quaint old town with stone houses and a cross from the eleventh century. The fields and meadows were divided by picturesque stonewalls, which transported me to "Olde England."

We went to London for a few days where we saw a number of great plays. From there we returned back home to California. The trip had been wonderful; John made an excellent travel companion, and he was the kindest and most considerate man I had ever met. He was loving and caring, and tried to make everything as smooth and pleasant as possible. My love and admiration for him increased from day to day, and I couldn't imagine being any happier than I was at that time.

When we arrived home, Bobby informed us that he had decided to take an apartment and move out. He said a year was long enough to intrude on us. We were sorry to see him go, as he had been a pleasant addition to our household, but we understood that he needed his privacy too.

It was time that I met John's daughter Betsy, so we invited her to come and stay with us for a while. Unfortunately, Betsy suffered from bi-polar disorder. Her disease had started to manifest itself when she was 17 years old and she and her parents had suffered and worried throughout the years. I have to admit, I had misgivings: Was she going to resent me for having her father's affection? What would her behavior be, considering her illness? It turned out I needn't have worried so much. When she walked in, it was like a ray of sunshine had appeared at the doorway. She came into my life with a big smile and open arms declaring: "Here I am!" Betsy was lovely and full of life. Her face was beautiful with a straight, small nose and a small well-shaped mouth. The color of her smiling eyes was a lovely green-blue. She was a little embarrassed by this new situation, but eager to please and accept me. We bonded quickly and throughout the years, we rarely had any difficulties between us.

Betsy struggled with her illness on a daily basis, sometimes becoming terribly depressed and desolate. It broke my heart to see and hear her so despondent. So I tried to give her as much love and understanding as I could. After that first visit she promised to call me whenever she needed to talk, and we had many hour-long conversations.

Bobby and Betsy

During that first year at Stanford, I got to know John's colleagues in the Chemistry Department, and we became very friendly with some of them. I also met many of his undergraduate and post-doctoral students. Summers we would have a big barbecue in the garden for his students, which was great fun though a lot of work. Each year, we hosted Thanksgiving dinners for his post-docs and students, so we would cook for days to prepare enough food for these seemingly always-hungry young people. I remember one year, a student arrived at our dinner a little late, apologizing for being tardy because he had had to eat a turkey dinner at some friend's house. To our amazement he ate another complete meal with us! Where did he put all that food? He was tall but did not seem to have an ounce of fat on him.

Slowly but surely I was making new friends and acquaintances, settling into this new community. My fear of not fitting into the academic life was unfounded. John kept assuring me that I was smarter than many scientists and intellectuals. This was one more characteristic of his wonderful personality: Realizing that life had dealt me with a few blows, he kept building me up. He finally convinced me that I was stimulating and engaging, and would tell me repeatedly that he was perfectly happy with me.

I audited an art class at Stanford and took a correspondence course in interior design, which I had always liked. My intention was to take this up as a profession. It turned out however, that I really did not have the time to pursue this as a career.

◆   ◆   ◆

John had been serving as a member of the Board of Governors of the Weizmann Institute in Israel, and it was time for him to make an inspection trip. There was also a meeting at the University of Bordeaux in the fall of 1981 so we combined the trip to Israel and Europe.

Returning to Israel was exciting, especially meeting all the Israeli scientists and visiting the Institute, which was a very successful research facility. It had produced a number of compelling insights into different health issues, establishing itself as a world-renowned organization. It was also interesting to see how they received John and the respect they showed for his comments and suggestions. As if I hadn't been proud enough of my John already! One of the scientists who had been a post-doc with John at Stanford, Itamar Procaccia, was especially enthusiastic in his praise. We were invited for dinner at his house and it was a pleasure to meet his wife and two boys. Their home was like a museum. Itamar was an avid collector of Oriental carpets, Japanese scrolls, Pre-Colombian and Chinese art, and had accumulated quite a few exquisite pieces.

The next day we all went to Tel Aviv to have lunch at a restaurant on the beach, and then we went on to Bordeaux.

From Bordeaux we went to Paris for a day and saw my cousin Grete, who was thrilled to meet John. In Paris we rented a car and drove to Goettingen in Germany. John was friendly with the director of the Max Plank Institute and we stayed at the Institute's Guest House, which was located on top of a hill. Amazingly, it was the first time I experienced a good night's sleep since I had been 15 years old. I think it was because I was so happy and looking forward to our wedding in the coming spring. The divorce was going to be final in February, and we were planning to have a March wedding. Life couldn't get any better.

I slept well until February 1982: The divorce became final, but the attorney informed us that there was a stipulation that forbade John to get re-married for six months. I was crushed. At that point I went back into my insomnia mode; I was so disappointed and angry I could have strangled somebody. We already had the invitations printed, and had invited my mother and aunt to come up. I had to cancel everything. Nevertheless, I asked the ladies to come up anyway, knowing we would still have a lovely visit with them.

So we were forced to set the wedding date for August 15, 1982. When the time finally arrived, I was so excited I could barely wait. At last we were getting married. I eagerly dove in to making all the preparations, having the invitations reprinted and finding a rabbi to perform the ceremony. Aside from family and friends, we also invited all of John's colleagues in the Department and his research group. I purposely set the date two days after my birthday on August 13. This way I would have my mother and aunt present for our wedding as well as my birthday.

Unfortunately, life's problems never disappear entirely, and in June, much to my dismay, John started showing symptoms of what turned out to be atrial fibrillations, scary but not uncommon. Nonetheless I worried a lot. The fibrillations would come and go in spite of the medications that were prescribed. One never knew what would cause them to come, and they would occur at very inopportune moments—like the evening before our wedding! We were sitting in a restaurant having dinner with my mother, my aunt and some friends talking about the wedding and how joyful we were. I looked at John's face and suddenly I knew that he was experiencing an episode of fibrillations at that moment. I was beside myself. Had somebody jinxed us? Would John be well enough for the ceremony? What were we going to do? It seemed that life had condemned me to be in a permanent state of worry and although I have tried to fight this predisposition of mine, I've never quite succeeded.

Fortunately, everything turned out all right! The next morning John was feeling well again and we were able to have the wedding. We had invited the rabbi's wife, who had recently had a baby and who had asked us whether we would mind if she brought him. Of course we said that we would be happy to have baby Avinoam come.

Our wonderful wedding.

The religious ceremony was held in our garden and we had only my mother, my aunt, John's son Bobby and our closest relatives and friends. Sol Capper, my former brother in law, was our witness. The ceremony was wonderful, and both John and I were very nervous but elated. After the ceremony, Rabbi Lewis told us a delightful story: There was a man who owned a very beautiful, large diamond. One day to his chagrin he noticed that there was a crack through the middle of it. He was devastated and called every well-known diamond cutter to come and tell him what they could do with this precious piece. Each one told him that the only thing they could do was cut the diamond in two. The man did not like this because he wanted to keep the diamond in its original shape. There was one more expert he could consult, who, upon looking at the diamond asked the man to trust him and leave the diamond with him and he would do something to improve it. After a week he brought the diamond back and the man could not believe his eyes: The diamond cutter had carved a beautiful rose into the diamond and used the crack as the stem. The piece was now lovelier than before.

"You both have cracks," the rabbi continued, "now it is time to make a rose!" We, as well as everybody present, were very moved; it was so fitting to our situation! A rose was made in spite of the tragic blows we had survived, and we knew it would hold us in good stead for whatever destiny might still have in store for us.

After the ceremony we all went to the Faculty Club at Stanford, where we had our wedding dinner. We sat near the rabbi and his wife, with two-week old Avinoam. In John's inimitable way, he lifted the baby in the air and with an impish gleam in his eye announced to all:

"You see how fast we worked?"

Everybody applauded and laughed, shouting *"Mazel Tov."* The party was a success. We were with family and friends, who were all truly happy for us. Bobby made an especially gracious speech welcoming me into the family. I was in seventh heaven: I was now married to the man I loved more than life itself. There were no doubts and no disappointments; how different from my first wedding!

Since my mother and aunt had made the journey to California specifically for our wedding, John said that we could not very well let them go back to Mexico after only a few days with us. I felt the same way, so we decided to take them on our honeymoon. Perhaps this sounds a little unorthodox, but it was one more proof of John's kindness. Furthermore, when it came down to it, we had had several honeymoons already. I also think we felt so blessed that we wanted to share it with everybody. We went to Carmel and stayed at the Quail Lodge, where we had a wonderful week. That time we all spent together is one of my most cherished memories.

The first morning, John called my mother into our room and showed her the bed, which had broken during the night.

"Mutti," he said laughing, "look what Putzi did!"

My mother took one look at the bed, then one at my blushing face and giggled delightedly. "Congratulations!" she said, and the two of them had a good laugh together.

When we returned from Carmel, my aunt wanted to get back to Cuernavaca, and I wanted my mother to stay with us a little longer. So we arranged for somebody to meet my aunt at the airport in Mexico, and we put my aunt on the plane here, having the stewardess take care of her during the flight. It worked well and we used this system quite often from then on.

My two ladies with me.

The following weeks we spent with my mother were almost as good as our honeymoon. Because it was summer, John could take time off and we would go on little trips into the mountains or the woods. While she was visiting us, we were invited to a meeting and formal dinner and dance given by the friends of the Weizmann Institute. The event was at the Century Plaza Hotel in Los Angeles, so we brought her with us. She did not have a formal gown, so I gave her a lounging robe of mine, which was made of a lovely fabric and had a zipper in the front. It looked smashing with her mink stole, and no one would guess it wasn't intended to be a gown. She was so excited and cheerful, the hotel was the nicest she had ever stayed in, and I was thankful for this opportunity to provide some pleasure for her.

We had such a great time on that visit that when the time came for my mother to go back to Mexico, she was rejuvenated and elated.

Though her life was beset by upheaval and tragedy, I was so grateful that she was finally able to see me happy and well taken care of. She no longer had to worry about what would become of me.

In our garden.

The year 1982 was kind to us. Life became more complicated later, but our love for each other grew from day to day and we felt that we were each other's best friend as well as lover. As time went by, I noticed several changes in me. The anger and frustration, I so often felt in earlier years, was gone. I had nothing to be angry about.

Also I started to feel more confident and self-assured. I felt I belonged, and was accepted by John's friends and colleagues. Most important of all: I had the love of my wonderful husband, who showed me what love should be like. Nevertheless, I kept worrying about my mother and what the future might bring. This is something I was never able to shed, however hard I tried.

◆   ◆   ◆

We liked the rabbi who had married us very much and decided to join his congregation. John started to go to the synagogue every Saturday and became more religious. He learned how to read the *Torah* in Hebrew and dedicated more and more time to his prayers. Not having had a bar mitzvah at the age of 13 because of his emigration to the U.S., he decided to have a bar mitzvah-like ceremony at the ripe old age of 60. It was an exciting and profound experience for him, a re-dedication to his faith and culture.

At the end of September we took John's research group to Napa Valley, where we visited different wineries, ending up at the winery, which was owned by the father of one of John's students. They had invited us to have a picnic dinner there, and we had a barbecue, drank wine and played music. John had brought his accordion, and after all the wine and the tasting beforehand, everybody was in a mellow mood. The day had been very hot and everybody was a little tired at the end. But we still were able to listen to John's funny jokes, of which he has a seemingly never-ending collection. We drove home very carefully in our separate cars, and it was a story the students talked about for quite a while.

For many Christmases we joined the ladies in Cuernavaca, which I loved so much. We were always invited to the homes of their friends and had wonderful times. It turned out that John and I had a common weakness: We loved to buy shoes in Cuernavaca. The leather was good and the price for a good pair of shoes was a third of the price in the U.S. When one day we came back from shopping with 11 pairs of shoes between the two of us, the ladies were speechless.

Bobby and I on one of our Mexico trips.

In 1983, John became Chairman of the Chemistry Department. He had served in this capacity for five years at MIT and thus he was well prepared for this job. However, it meant that he would be busier and, of course, have more responsibilities. We had to go to more dinners, and invite more people to our home, but it also gave us, and especially me, the opportunity to meet many interesting visitors.

CHAPTER TWO

That year, when the ladies came back for a visit, my mother wasn't feeling well. This time, instead of taking her to her old doctor, I decided to take her to John's doctor who didn't know my mother. Big mistake! The new doctor gave her a medication that was too strong for her. The result was that she got an arrhythmia called Brady-tachycardia; her heart went from too slow to too fast, and they ended up having to install a pacemaker. We were devastated. The pacemaker had to be regulated and monitored. How could I possibly send her back to Cuernavaca? We begged her to stay permanently with us, but she didn't want to leave my aunt alone. Finally we decided that she would stay a few months and then we would go back with her to Cuernavaca to make sure she had a good doctor and the right attention there.

My aunt left California by herself in August, and we kept mother here until middle of December, when we all went back to Cuernavaca. While we were there, I ran all over looking for a suitable doctor and making sure we would be called in case of an emergency. However, the night before we were to leave Cuernavaca I began to cry, telling John that I was too worried to leave my mother. My good husband replied that if I needed to take my mother back with us, I should do so. It was a bit harder to convince my mother. She didn't want to return to California with us; however, she gave in when she saw my anguish. So to my aunt's big disappointment, all three of us went back home.

Things went quite well and all our friends were happy to invite my mother together with us. However, I had the feeling that she was lonely for her friends. As she was doing quite well, in February I took her to the airport and delivered her into the care of a stewardess, knowing my aunt and a chauffeur would meet her in Mexico.

In May, I went to Cuernavaca for her birthday, but I didn't find her in good condition at all. For some reason, she was very down, even with me there. We took her to the Mananitas for lunch and Emerich and Nanette joined us to celebrate her birthday. She was listless throughout the meal and I began to worry. Again it was hard for me to leave her, but the ladies promised to come to Stanford the following month.

After they arrived, my mother experienced episodes of arrhythmia, sometimes so bad I had to take her to the emergency room. Then she would be better again until the next episode. I was sure the pacemaker was not doing its job, but at the hospital they never tried to find out. In addition, I was certain that had she not taken the medication given her by John's doctor, she would never have needed the pacemaker in the first place. Nevertheless we tried to live as normally as possible and we had some good times. Mother and Aunt Elsa loved to go to rummage sales, and they had the patience and energy to stand there for hours looking at everything. I would get tired long before they did, begging them to call it a day. Mother loved to go to the movies, but since my aunt couldn't see, we didn't go. However, I promised my mother that as soon as my aunt left we would take her to the movies. With that in mind, we continued on with life, doing our best to provide the ladies with an enjoyable time.

The bathroom my mother and aunt shared had a very low bathtub with a glass enclosure. However, when my mother's pacemaker had been installed, I had the glass removed, and replaced it with a shower curtain so that I could help my mother take showers. What a horrible mistake that was—for which I will never forgive myself. The bathtub was an accident waiting to happen, but one I didn't antici- pate: One day my aunt fell into the tub. Since her head was bleeding, I took her to the doctor immediately; he said that it was only a super- ficial flesh wound and not to worry. Before we left, I had asked my mother to clean the blood spots from the shower curtain, and when we came home she had cleaned it to perfection. My poor mother had put a lot of effort into the curtain! It was then that I should have acted. This had been a warning, and as I stood in front of the tub and looked at it, I couldn't think of what to do to make it safe. Why does the mind go blank when one most needs it? I closed the curtains and told the ladies to be careful. I also told my mother that she should call me if she had to go to the bathroom during the night. I didn't want her to navigate that room on her own.

On the morning of August 10, at 3 a.m., John woke me up and told me that he had heard a big thud. We ran to my aunt's room, thinking that she could have fallen again, but she was in bed. Full of panic, we ran into the bathroom and saw a horrible sight, which has never left my mind since: My mother had fallen into the tub and was unconscious. I was so horrified, I could barely think. Mother opened her eyes and started to whimper, so we pulled her out of the tub and led her to her bed. It was only then that we called 911. Of course we shouldn't have moved her at all, but we couldn't leave her in that awful position!

After several X-rays, they diagnosed a fracture in her neck and said she needed to wear a "halo." I don't think these horrible contrap- tions are used any more, but it was what they insisted she must have. Four holes would have to be drilled into her head where they would put the screws which would hold a steel ring with steel rods coming down and then eventually be fastened into a tight fitting vest. When I explained this to my poor mother she cried and said she didn't want to have this done, that she wanted to die. I begged her to accept this procedure for my sake and she finally consented to it.

The vest took days to be produced and in the meantime my mother had to be tied from the ring on her head to the head of the bed. She was thus immobilized! I should have stayed with her, but John was worried about me and took me home. I should not have moved from her bedside as long as she was in the hospital, but I did. Her roommate told me that my mother had nightmares at night and was very scared. Nevertheless, I couldn't stay with her all the time. Thinking back on that terrible time, I have the feeling that I was so scared and shocked my brain stopped functioning, causing me to make poor decisions. During the day my aunt was with her for a few hours and I was there for a few hours, but what about the rest and the nights?

When the renowned orthopedic surgeon made his rounds with his entourage, he didn't even approach my mother's bed; he just shouted from the door asking where the vest for that woman was. John went to talk to him and introduced himself as Chairman of the Chemistry Department. This made hardly any difference in his degree of arrogance. Once again, my distrust of the medical establishment reared its head,

When the vest finally came, the doctor said she could come home, so I prepared a hospital bed for her in her room. Before she was released the blood test showed that all the intravenous fluids she had received had washed out her electrolytes—yet one more health complication. They told me not to give her any water, as well as other instructions, which I believe were counter-productive. My poor mother was in horrible pain, and she got a bladder infection, which only got worse. The doctor finally came and said he would send a nurse to take another blood test so we could see what was going on, yet the nurse only came the day she died. Each day, I forced my mother to get up and sit at the table with us, thinking that if I could just keep her mobile, she would not lose too much of her strength during her recovery. With a walker she could barely manage, but she was terribly depressed and kept telling me that she didn't want to live. I arranged for assistants to help her and be with her, but she just couldn't take the toll the injury caused and her body gave up. I sat with her most of the last night of her life, and in the morning she died. It was August 21, 1984. The blackest day of my life!

I was so devastated and so full of guilt, I could barely function. There were so many things I could have done differently during the last days of my mother's life! What I had feared all my life had finally happened and I couldn't handle it. My great sorrow and guilt took my breath away. How could I live this way? My pain was so all-encompassing that for a while I forgot that life had to go on and that I had a lot to live for.

John was very kind during these hard times, but the painful grief was overwhelming. It never really went away although I knew, in time it would ease and become more bearable. However, it went slowly with me. I mourned my mother deeply for many years. I still miss her terribly. My birthday on August 13 as well as our wedding anniversary on the 15th is always mixed with the sad memory of my mother being in the hospital during that time. However, the fact that she had been able to see me happily married to John for two years was a great consolation for me. What made me so terribly sorrowful was that my mother had had a very difficult life, with very few moments of pleasure. I realized that all through the years my greatest satisfaction came when I saw my mother having joy through my life.

I had wanted her to feel and share the good experiences I had, because she did not have similar opportunities herself.

CHAPTER THREE

One month after my mother's death, John needed to take a trip to Canada and Europe. Since we have always traveled together he did not want to leave me alone at this stage, and everybody insisted that the trip would be good for me. So I decided to go, but with great misgivings. Poor John had to drag me around, it was so hard for me to function and not show my deep sorrow. We started in Toronto, where John had attended an International Conference. While he was busy I visited some friends from the Weizmann Institute, who were very kind and invited us to dinner with them. Since it happened to be a Jewish holy day we were able to go to the synagogue with them. During the prayers, I couldn't keep from crying and thinking of other holidays when we all had been together. I had the feeling that I had lost my soul and would never find it again.

From Toronto we went to Munich, Germany, where John had a business meeting and a very kind woman showed me around. She was a chemist and she took time off to take me to some lovely stores where I bought a black Valentino suit on sale. We also went to the best store for down comforters and I bought two lovely comforters, which they promised to ship to us. I felt like I was so fragile, I needed something warm and soft to wrap myself in. My gracious hostess couldn't do enough for us and took us to a concert given by the great pianist, Vladimir Ashkenazi, who played Schubert. It was wonderful and for the first time I found a little peace.

Our next stop was Israel. The Weizmann Institute was honoring John by awarding him the Doctor of Philosophy Honoris Causa. This was a wonderful celebration with a big banquet; I was very proud of my husband and very sad that I could not tell my mother about this. This is a feeling that I have had ever since her death and no doubt will have forever.

Life had to go on and John was kind, considerate and loving. I woke up one morning and realized that he was all I had in this world. He was everything to me. I tried to keep my grief to myself and not burden him with my sadness. I was successful most of the time, but once in a while I just broke down and cried in his arms. Finally I decided to get help and saw a psychiatrist. When he saw how much guilt I felt, he asked me to write a letter to my mother telling her everything that I regretted and felt guilty about. I did this and in a small way it made me feel better. I had gotten it off my chest, but only for a short time. At the next session the psychiatrist asked me whether I had written the letter and if so, he wanted to read it. My answer to him was that I had written it in German, as my mother wouldn't understand it in English. When he asked me to translate it for him I refused. There are things between mother and daughter that have to be private. My mother had been my best friend; I could tell her everything and she would be understanding and supportive in every respect.

◆   ◆   ◆

When John told me that he had been invited to give a talk at the University of Sydney I was enthusiastic. My mother's favorite cousin, Mira Hafner lived in Sydney, and I had always loved and admired her. She and her husband were the people I had had the most contact with in my childhood in Pernegg. After her husband's death in Australia, she had come to visit us in Mexico and then in Seattle. As she got on in years, however, she decided not to travel any more. Since Australia was so far away I had not seen her in a number of years.

Mira and her husband Fritz were another example of the changes refugees had to make to survive. Fritz had been a successful lawyer in Graz, Austria, but could not practice law in Australia. Before leaving Graz, Mira had taken a course in making leather handbags, so she went into partnership with her sister-in-law, with whom she started a handbag factory in Sydney. With her taste and resolution the factory soon became successful, but she had to work hard. Fritz was devastated by the fact that he could not be the breadwinner, and to overcome his depression he started to make ceramics. I never knew whether he had always been artistic but the ceramics he created, mainly animals, were stunning. After his death one of his nephews organized an exhibit of his pieces in the Museum of Art in Canberra.

Unfortunately after some years in Australia, Fritz had a stroke and was bedridden for a long time. Mira gave up the factory because she wanted to take care of him herself. The need to move him and turn him in bed was a strain on her back. By the time he died she was exhausted, and it took a while for her to get her strength back. Her friends and relatives told her that she would be very lonely if she did not have a hobby. So at age 70, she took up painting. Again I have no idea whether she always knew that she had a talent or whether she was inspired by her husband's artistic success, but she turned out to be a very good painter. She specialized in oil painting, mainly flowers and landscapes, some of which are hanging in my home today.

When we arrived in Sydney we found it to be spectacular. The city is so beautiful with its many bays, the Opera house, and the hundreds of sailboats on the ocean. The reunion with my dear Mira was a tearful one on my part. I really felt close to her; somehow I never felt as close to my Aunt Elsa in Mexico. Although I felt very sorry for Elsa, I always had the feeling that she was resentful of my relationship with my mother, perhaps because of her own tragedies.

Mira was very kind and consoling to me, and she was extremely happy to meet my darling John. She never liked Jay and was glad that I had finally met the right man. They got along famously and she made him laugh a lot with her comments and insight into our family. She was a charming and gracious lady with a great sense of humor. One time she was telling me of a certain member of our family, and when I told her that I had never met him, she responded: "you have missed nothing!"

Mira was very close to her nephew, Eric Bonyhady, with whom I had bonded so nicely when he visited us in Mexico. He had also visited me in La Jolla before I moved to Stanford. He came on a weekend when John said he couldn't make it, but when I told John that my cousin from Australia was coming, he showed up unannounced at my place. Was he jealous? Perhaps. Yet it turned out to be a fun weekend. Eric and John liked each other, and Eric was happy that I had found such a wonderful man. Eric himself was divorced and had a woman friend in Australia who was not yet divorced, but he didn't give up hope that this would happen some day.

We, Eric and his brother Fred, had dinner at Mira's home in Sydney, which was a comfortable but small house surrounded by a lovely rose garden. She loved to do gardening herself and took good care of her roses, of which she was very proud. After a tour of her garden and her home with the many paintings she had done, she served us a nice meal. We talked about old times and were overjoyed to be together. She told us that she took the bus several times a week to go to the Art Museum, where she took more classes and viewed every new exhibit. I admired her great drive and independence. On the other hand, she relied on Eric for all her shopping and taking care of her finances.

The next day John gave his talk at Sydney University and was happy to see his ex-student Bob Gilbert, who was a professor there. Gilbert was a very smart and ambitious person, but when he invited us to his apartment for dinner I was shocked at the way he lived. The furniture was falling apart and the walls needed paint throughout the entire apartment. Knowing that he had a good salary and came from a wealthy family I asked him why he did not move to a nicer place of his own.

"Of course you are right," he said "I have been wanting to buy a condominium for a long time." Years later he was still in the same run-down apartment! However, he invited us to the opera, where they were showing Carmen. Before the opera he took us to dinner at the elegant restaurant in the Opera House, but did not let us order dessert, he wanted us to wait for the intermission. Sure enough, during the intermission he took us back to the restaurant and we were served a very special dessert, which he had ordered in advance. This was something that the restaurant usually did not allow. The man had class in spite of the way he lived! Upstairs at the Opera House, food and deserts were also served, and we were amazed at how much people ate in intermission! It was a memorable evening. The Opera House, built like a seashell sitting on the shore, was very impressive and the view from there was delightful.

Sydney reminded me of San Francisco, except it didn't have the hills and there were more coves along the shore with beautiful homes built right on the water. I decided that I must come back to this place; I needed to see Mira again.

We did go back again while Mira was still alive but, unfortunately, she had entered a nursing home and had lost her tremendous energy. Her nephew Eric had met a nice lady, whom he decided to marry and he had moved into a beautiful home. Vera, his bride, was a gray-haired woman with a clean-washed face, very blue eyes and a great sense of humor. She was the salt of the earth. We stayed at their home and Mira came over for dinner from the nursing home. It was sad to see Mira so frail, but she had not lost her sense of humor and regaled us with amusing stories. An amazing lady! She didn't want to attend her nephew's wedding because she felt she didn't look well enough. Fortunately, Vera convinced her that there could be no wedding without her presence.

Mira died soon after and I was saddened to hear of it. John and I did go back to Sydney one more time and stayed with Eric and Vera, but I missed Mira very much. Eric's sons visited us in California with their families on separate occasions, and so did Vera and Eric. We were always happy to see them. Unfortunately Vera has health problems and they cannot travel any more, so they often beg us to come to Sydney.

The last time we saw Mira she had given us a wool throw-blanket to take to her sister Martha in Phoenix. She decided that it was high time that we met Martha's children, who were also living in Phoenix, and whom we had never met. So when John had a meeting in Phoenix, we called Dr. Henry Reuss, Martha's son. It was wonderful to meet my cousin Henry and his wife Diane, as well as their son Eric and daughter Michelle. Henry, a gynecologist, was a tall, good-looking man. He sported a beard, which made him look very interesting, and with his ready smile and merry eyes gave the impression of a bon vivant. He was married for the second time and he also had three daughters from his first marriage. Diane was a lively young woman with lovely blue eyes, a cute nose and a pretty smile. She had a lovely figure and dressed well. They made a handsome couple.

We spent a few great days in Phoenix, meeting the family. We visited Martha in an assisted living residence, and she was delighted to see us and hear from Mira. We also met Martha's daughter, Eve, who is a psychologist and who was kind enough to drive us around a bit. Since that trip, we have seen a lot of the Reusses. We have visited each other and traveled together, and although they are not first cousins we are closer to them than many siblings are. It so happens that Judy, one of Henry's daughters, lives very near us and we see a lot of each other. I have come to love her very much. She is a sensitive, lovely and charming woman, who decided to convert to the Episcopal religion, and dedicate herself to helping others.

In 1987 we went to Europe again and ended up in Bordeaux, where John received the Doctor Honoris Causa, from the University of Bordeaux. This was an absolutely wonderful occasion. After a long and laudatory introduction by one of his colleagues at the University of Bordeaux, John gave a carefully prepared expression of gratitude in French and then continued in a more relaxed fashion in English. After the ceremony we had a three-hour feast at the official festival hall of the University.

CHAPTER FOUR

The house was now very homey and comfortable. We had enlarged our bedroom and remodeled the master bathroom. Everything was beautiful and convenient. However, we had to suffer a few months of noise and dust during the renovation. There were also the difficult decisions John and I had to make when faced with the hundreds of possible different bathroom appliances and fixtures.

While John was busy during the week, I would meet friends for lunch, go to my once-a-week French conversation group and my once-a-month investment group. I also joined an exercise class to keep in shape. I was so busy that I asked myself: "How did I ever have time to work?" There were frequent day-trips to Half Moon Bay, San Francisco and some weekends we spent in Carmel. We also had season tickets to the San Francisco Symphony and sometimes went to the Opera.

Evenings at home, John and I read, listened to music or talked about our respective days. John always had something interesting to say about his students and his research. My reports were not quite as exciting, but John was a very good listener and always had a good comment or constructive advice. We enjoyed those quiet evenings and thanked God for having brought us together.

The happy couple.

◆   ◆   ◆

For the last few months since returning from Australia in 1988, John had been feeling short of breath when walking a lot. After several tests and an angiogram it was decided that he needed angioplasty. It worked for a time but unfortunately John's case was one of many, which didn't respond to this treatment for more than a few months before the blockage would re-occur. We had already packed our suitcases for a one-month trip to Paris, where John had been invited to lecture at the College de France, when we were told that he needed by-pass surgery immediately.

The surgery was set for next day. I was horrified to learn how blocked one of his main arteries was and I was very frightened. I kept praying, "Please, dear God, don't let me lose my loved one, I couldn't bear it!" Bobby came up from Palm Springs, where he was working as an anesthesiologist, and sat with me waiting for the surgeon to come and report after the surgery. I was so nervous I had to knit the sweater I had started in order to keep myself from falling apart. Finally one of the surgeons came and reported that John had had a double by-pass and that everything went well. He was now being taken to recovery and we could see him soon. I was so relieved that I embraced and kissed the surgeon. When we finally were allowed to see John, he was hooked up to all sorts of medical devices in the Intensive Care Unit and could not speak because of a tube in his mouth; but he could write on a pad and told me to pray. This I did, with all my heart.

When I was allowed to visit him the next hour all hell had broken lose. Apparently, when one of the nurses was trying to clear his nose by putting a tube in, she had punctured a blood vessel, resulting in a nosebleed that couldn't be stopped. Finally they brought in a specialist who packed his nose with yards of material, but my darling had lost so much blood he needed a transfusion. All I could think was that during the whole difficult surgery there had been no need for this, but now because of an accident that could have been avoided, he needed a transfusion, a dangerous procedure because of the AIDS virus. I was so furious I couldn't see straight. However, I decided that I wanted to keep peace and didn't say a word, but suddenly nobody was talking to me. The nurses who had all been very kind and forthcoming all clammed up. They were afraid that they would be held responsible for what had happened and I was the enemy. At one point the doctors even tried to blame Bobby for being an anesthesiologist. They said they had taken shortcuts just so that he would not have to see his father with more tubes. They were afraid of looking bad in front of their colleague.

So much blood had gone down John's throat that he was forced to vomit it all out, which took a great effort and made him terribly sick. This whole incident kept John in intensive care longer than normally necessary, but finally he was moved into his own room. I begged them to put in a bed for me. I was determined to stay with him. I had learned enough from my previous experiences, and I was not going to leave him alone.

John was weak and not feeling well when one of our friends brought a bag of special, home made cookies, which John loved very much. During the night when he couldn't sleep we talked a bit and I told him that we had these lovely almond kisses. "I would love to try one," he said, so I gave him one. His reaction after eating this little cookie was unbelievable. His depression was gone and he started to recite funny poetry. Relieved, we both started to laugh and thus fell asleep again. From that day on he improved very rapidly, and on the eighth day after surgery I brought him home.

I had been warned that depression could still follow along with other problems. Yet John came home, sat himself in his chair and started to conduct business by telephone. He was so busy that he never had time to get depressed. Each day we walked a little more, and soon he had regained much of his strength. Six weeks after his surgery we went to Zihuatanejo, Mexico, where we swam and lay on the beach and where he became his old self again. I really admired him for his positive outlook during this whole ordeal. For me it had been a terrifying blow from which I did not recover so easily.

◆   ◆   ◆

The trip to Paris, which we had had to cancel, was set for next spring. We were looking forward to it—springtime in Paris! It was the perfect time. The College de France had given us an apartment on the Left Bank, which though slightly simple, was a dream. It was in a lovely building, which had a beautiful garden in the back, and was built around a courtyard. Our apartment was one story up overlooking the patio. There was a ledge outside our windows, which ran around the whole building, and on that ledge we had the daily visit of Plumeau, a beautiful, white, Angora cat. With her fluffy long hair she looked like a feather duster, thus the name Plumeau. The building was on the Rue Universite, a street with many interesting delicatessens and antique stores, and the neighboring streets were filled with good restaurants. We often ate out, but always prepared breakfast at home as well as some dinners, which we bought at the delicatessen.

John went to the University every day, walking a different route each time, thus getting to know the surrounding area. A place we both loved to visit was a street market where one could buy exquisite fruits and vegetables. I also enjoyed walking along the streets and looking at the antiques, linens and clothing shops. Of course I could not resist buying a few things.

Bobby came to visit with a friend of his, and stayed nearby in a hotel. We took them to the Louvre, which made a big impression on Bobby and his friend. Although we had been there many times before, John and I could not get enough of the beautiful paintings, especially the Impressionists.

At the end of our stay John was awarded the Medal of the College de France for the distinguished lectures he gave. Another beautiful feather in his cap, which was already very colorful indeed!

When we first arrived in Paris, John had asked me to do all the talking since my French was better than his. I was very happy to do as he requested, and although I had forgotten much of my French I managed to do most of the interpreting when necessary. On our last evening in Paris, we were invited to a big dinner at the Hotel Plaza Athenee, and after drinking two glasses of wine John started to tell stories in French! I was dumbfounded; I would never have been able to tell a joke in French. Just you wait, John Ross, just you wait!

◆　　◆　　◆

Betsy came to visit us at least once a year in California and we in turn visited her quite often, usually combining it with some trip to the East Coast. Sometimes we would go to a Gordon Conference, one of many scientific meetings, which were always held in the summer in one of the many colleges in New England. The nicest place was at the Salve Regina College in Newport, Rhode Island. The so-called Summer Cottages in Newport were worth seeing for in reality they were mansions built by the very rich just to spend the summer. Of course, one had to outdo the other and the homes got bigger and bigger. Now they are open to the public as museums and sometimes there are concerts. We also went to Cape Cod to visit a secretary of John's, who had been with him for over 25 years and had retired there.

Other times we attended the annual meetings of the National Academy of Science in Washington. It was always held in the spring when the trees were in their full bloom and everything looked like a picture out of an edition of Beautiful Gardens. These meetings were always lovely affairs with luscious buffets offered in a large tent, along with concerts, dinners, and dances, in different places. On one occasion Betsy joined us for one day. She had such a good time, she felt in seventh heaven.

Once we happened to be in Washington, when a friend of John's, a real estate developer, held his housewarming party. They had bought the top floor of one of his buildings and had constructed it exactly to their specifications. The result was magnificent. A Renoir sculpture graced the entry hall and the apartment was furnished in the Empire style. The spacious living room had a domed ceiling and each room had a spectacular view of the Potomac River. The master bathroom was done in dark green marble and was so outstanding that everyone flocked to see it, oohing and aahing. The waiters, hearing the acclaims, came right in and served appetizers!

At one point, as I went to the powder room, I met a woman also waiting to use it. As we spoke, I detected an accent so I asked where she was from. "Oh," she said, "you wouldn't know the place, it is a small country in South America called Uruguay." Bingo! It turned out that her house was across the street from the house I had lived in! I had often seen children playing there but had never talked to them. I was astonished to find out that she was one of them. That was not the first time that I've been tempted to use the trite phrase "It's a small world!"

This interesting encounter must have sown seeds in John's and my minds, and we decided to go to South America that winter. John had never been to any of those countries. I wanted him to see the place where I grew up, and meet my cousins in Buenos Aires, my "little sister" Dorita in Montevideo, and my good friend Hanna in Sao Paulo. We planned a trip to Buenos Aires, Montevideo, Sao Paulo and Rio de Janeiro. I must admit that it is true that one cannot go home again. I had not been back in 30 years and everything seemed so different. Buenos Aires, which had been such a cosmopolitan city, often compared with Paris, looked like an old lady who had once been beautiful and elegant, but had faded over time. One could still imagine her past splendor, but saw that much had been lost. Florida Street, which once was filled with lovely boutiques and expensive coffee shops, was now filled with cheap tourist shops. I couldn't believe what had become of all the famous streets and avenues. When my cousin Ernesto came to the hotel, I had another surprise upon seeing what he was holding under his arm.

"This," he replied to our question, "is the radio of my car. I have to take it with me every time I leave the car to avoid having it stolen."

Obviously things were worse than I thought! He took us to his apartment, which he and his wife owned, and although small, it was very pleasant and well appointed. He was in the banking business, and there were many problems with what had become the steady decline of the Argentine currency.

That evening they took us to the typical "*asado*" restaurant, where they grill steaks, chickens, pork and sausages on charcoal. This is very delicious. There was one restaurant next to another on that street, all very crowded with lively and seemingly happy people. People did not seem to worry about the country's financial situation.

We visited my old cousins who had been so good to me, and providing lunch for me every day when I first lived near them (before the revolution which ousted Peron). They were still in the same little condominium and were very old, but delighted to see me and meet John. One evening we went to the old quarter "La Boca" and watched a show of tango dancers. It was a wonderful performance. As we walked along the streets, I tried to explain to John what the city had been like, so he would understand just how beautiful it used to be.

After a few days we went on to Montevideo, and stayed in Pocitos, where I had lived, at a hotel that had been new and very chic a few years before I left. It was disappointing to find that it, too, had deteriorated, (what did I expect after 30 years?) but the location was still good, only one block from the beach. It was very hot and humid and although I wanted to walk on the famous *Rambla* it was a little too hot for that. We were told that the water was not as clean as it used to be, so we decided not to go to the beach. In the evening we took a taxi and went to Dorita's condominium, which was located almost downtown. Dorita had married a Uruguayan pharmacist, and had a 12-year-old boy. She was now divorced and was financially in a precarious situation. Although, she was working for a health care organization, as a psychiatrist, the salary she earned was meager, and her ex-husband, who had moved to Venezuela, never met his alimony payments. Because of this I had been sending her money for some years, after having received a call from a friend of hers, apprising me of her sad financial situation.

When she opened the door I had to look twice to recognize her. She appeared so run down that there was no sign left of her former beauty. Poor Dorita had suffered a lot through the years. Miguelito, her son, was quite cute and smart, but I couldn't help but remember his mother's letters in which she kept complaining about how difficult he made her life. He was disobedient and obstreperous, apparently more so than the average child of a divorced family. We went to a restaurant near her apartment where we all ate steak of course, since Uruguay, like Argentina, has a large beef industry and specializes in steaks. The weekend was coming up and we saw Dorita several more times, but then she had to work again. So we invited her to come visit us during our next summer.

One Saturday morning, a crown from one of John's teeth came loose so we had to find a dentist. This was not easy on a weekend, so I contacted the hotel receptionist and asked her for help. Ten minutes later she called and said that she had a dentist on the phone, who had agreed to see us. Once again it was a "small world" because we discovered that the dentist lived in the building that had been erected where our house used to be! However, his dental office was downtown. Very kindly he offered to pick us up at the hotel, take us downtown, fix John's tooth and then drive us home again. We very gratefully accepted this kind offer and just couldn't believe our luck in finding such a wonderfully helpful person. It makes one believe in the goodness of humanity again. Once at his office, he fixed John's crown and absolutely refused to take payment. Of course we did not accept his magnanimous gesture and did pay him for his time and effort. He then offered to take us back to the hotel, but we decided to stay in town and walk around a little. We stopped by the bus company that went to Punta del Este, the world famous beach resort, where many wealthy Argentinians had built their villas, and decided to buy two tickets for the next day.

Punta del Este for a few days would be pleasant but it was March and the summer season was over. All the tourists had gone home and it was quite empty. I also saw a lot of changes in this once lovely place. The shoreline had been built up with high rises and the original beauty of the place was changed. We looked up some friends who had a condominium in one of those high rises since they spent their summers there. They were due back in Buenos Aires the following week, but their daughter kindly took us around in her car, showing us many new sites and things I had not seen before. We really enjoyed those few days. When we went to the bus depot to go back to Montevideo, we saw many dogs barking and running after the cars and buses. When we asked what this was all about, we were told that people adopted dogs at the beginning of the summer, but would abandon them when they left at the end of the season. We couldn't get over this heartbreaking lack of feeling and responsibility.

Back in Montevideo I called some of my old friends, but there were very few around. Some were on vacation and some had left the country. Walking on the streets and going into coffee shops, which we had frequented when I lived there, I was very disappointed not to run into somebody I knew, the way it used to be. We walked by the house we had lived in and a high rise was in its place. I felt like a stranger in the town where I had grown up and spent my youth so many years ago. It was an interesting experience.

When we arrived in Sao Paulo, my friend Hanna met us at the airport, and again it took a few moments to recognize each other after so many years. But it was a very joyful meeting. We had so many fun memories. Hanna was the girl with whom we had lived and with whom I had gone to school. She was the one whom I visited in Rio so many years ago. She had gotten married to a German Jew and had two sons with him. Unfortunately he died very young and Hanna got married again to an Austrian aristocrat, Herbert Stukart. He was a tall and interesting looking man and I could very well understand that Hanna had married him. She was wealthy in her own right since she had inherited from her grandmother, who had lived in Brazil many years before 1939, and her father, who got his factories in Germany back after the war. The day we arrived in Sao Paulo there was a currency problem there too, and the banks froze all the accounts. At the same time they stopped changing the dollar into cruzeiros and it was with great difficulty that we paid our hotel bill. Fortunately, Hanna and her husband picked us up to take us to their country estate, which was absolutely magnificent. They had a lovely home with a swimming pool, and beautiful land surrounding all of these amenities.

Hanna's pride and joy were her roses. There were hundreds of different varieties and colors, and she took care of them herself since she did not trust her gardener with them. They also had two boxer dogs who were the friendliest and most affectionate of dogs, but who, in their exuberance, tended to knock you over when they showed you how much they loved you. They were friendly to a point of not discriminating between family and thieves. For that reason they had a watchdog who was only let loose at night to roam the estate. They did not trust this dog to meet us and not attack us, so they kept him in the kitchen while we were there.

As we sat around the pool one day, talking with them and with some of their children who had come up from Sao Paulo, the main subject was the financial situation of the country. The bank accounts were still frozen and nobody could withdraw any cash. It was very annoying for everybody, but it occurred to us that there was a dark humor in this situation. Here we were sitting by a beautiful pool on a luxurious estate and everybody was worried about how to get some money!

We stayed a few days in this lovely paradise and while sitting by the pool John wrote a very good scientific paper. He is always very productive when on vacation and sitting in lovely surroundings. When he published the paper he mentioned where he had written it and thanked my friends for their hospitality, sending them a copy of the published paper. I was very sad when it came time to leave. When one grows older it is not as easy to make good friends like this.

Rio de Janeiro was as lovely as ever when viewed from a distance. Unfortunately, however, when one got closer and saw the poverty and crime, which had increased dramatically throughout the years, the picture was a dismal one. Gone were the days where I could walk alone at night on the Avenida Atlantica in Copacabana without a worry. Now tourists were at risk from pickpockets and thieves during the day and night. On every corner of the Avenida Atlantica there was a police kiosk staffed by officers with machine guns. On the beach itself, policemen would patrol in bathing suits carrying holsters with two guns. When we decided to sit on the beach, the people next to us warned us not to leave the towels alone if we wanted to find them when we got back. Sad indeed, but the water looked so nice and inviting that although I knew that the waves and the undertow were very strong, I told John that I would just go in with my feet. That looked easier said than done. No sooner did I hit the water, the waves sucked me in and threw me down. I tried to get up but couldn't and was turned around several times in the water. I was panic stricken; every time I tried to catch my breath I was thrown under water again. Luckily John and a passer-by, who had seen me, came running to help and pulled me out. I was very grateful and very embarrassed.

We took in some of the shows in the evenings, and they were still lovely to see with the colorful costumes and lively music. We also went to some outdoor markets where vendors were selling arts and crafts and one of the saleswomen told me to be careful with my ring (I had left my diamond at home and only had a wedding band), since thieves have been known to cut fingers off! I thought this was a bit of an exaggeration, but it was another sign of the changes that had occurred in the country, which had once been so lovely and prosperous. With a heavy heart, I left my formerly beloved continent, and was only sorry that I wasn't able to show John the countries the way I had seen them and come to love them in my youth. The countries had changed a lot but so had I.

CHAPTER FIVE

In the meantime, our son Bobby was facing serious problems. With a genetically predisposed bad spine, he had had surgery on his cervical vertebrae, which left this area in a weakened state, and from time to time he suffered bouts of pain. To make matters much worse, someone crashed into his car from the side. The result was that he suffered a complication in his cervical area and because surgery in this case would have been dangerous, he was left to heal on his own. This resulted in damage to the nerves that run down the left arm and hand. This made Bobby's hand too weak to intubate patients when he put them under anesthesia.

To Bobby's great disappointment and pain he could no longer be an anesthesiologist. We all were devastated. Bobby had been an outstanding anesthesiologist, had accepted a new position in a big hospital in Los Angeles and was now forced to give up his career for which he had studied so long and in which he had been so successful. As unhappy as we were with his disability, we encouraged him to seek other possible activities. He was able to function and live a quasi-normal life, except he wasn't able to practice in his field.

After Bobby recovered and adjusted to his new condition, he studied business management and administration especially for physicians, and received his MBA. He was also interested from time to time in public policy issues concerning medicine and medical care in this country. A sideline activity has been his interest in houses, and over the years he has done very well moving into a new house, renovating it, selling it and then repeating that process.

That summer we went to Europe as usual, starting in London where we visited Lord Marcus Sieff, Chairman of the Weizmann Institute, who also was CEO of Marks & Spencer, the department store, which had been started by his father. Lord Sieff was a tall, imposing man with very intelligent blue eyes and handsome features. He was very active, a born leader, enthusiastic fisherman and sportsman, and very charitable. He was with his second or third wife, who was a very intelligent and charming woman. We visited him in his office and he showed us a room full of new merchandise that had been imported from Israel. It was fascinating to see the lovely underwear, bathing suits and leather jackets that had been produced there. I tried on a beautiful antelope jacket, which Lord Sieff immediately said was mine. I was just about to thank him very enthusiastically, when John said that under no circumstances would he accept this gift. He was so adamant about it that Lord Sieff had to respect his wishes; however, he made him promise that he would buy me one of these jackets since it looked so nice on me. John never bought it for me, nor was I about to forgive him for this!

One Saturday we were invited to the Sieff estate in the country. His chauffeur picked us up in the Rolls Royce, and took us to their country place. It was near a river, where Lord Sieff liked to go fishing, standing almost waist deep in the water. We all frolicked around in their pool, which was warm and inviting. Afterwards a scrumptious lunch was served in the dining room. They had a young and beautiful daughter who entertained us with her charm and wit, and in the middle of the meal their butler brought her a cordless phone to the table. It was the first of these phones that John and I had seen used, and we were very impressed with it.

◆   ◆   ◆

After we returned that summer, we awaited Dorita's visit with excitement, looking forward to showing her a good time. Her life was so challenging and I wanted to give her a little pleasure. I couldn't help thinking about her privileged childhood, which, although she had had to leave her country of birth when she was five years old, had still been a very happy one. Her doting parents were wealthy and Dorita was given everything money could buy. She had tennis lessons, dancing lessons, rode horses, and had her own car when she was seventeen. She had everything but a healthy psyche. I often asked myself how a life can change so radically and came to the conclusion that perhaps things would have been different had it not been for Hitler. In spite of the good beginning as refugees, there were deeper and more complicated issues in her family that only came to the surface later on, but might not have, had it not been for the radical changes they had been forced to go through. It is likely neither her grandmother nor her mother would have committed suicide had they not faced such severe challenges.

When Dorita finally arrived, she was in a bad state, complaining about the terrible flight and how sick she had felt the whole time. She was very tired so we put her to bed. I could tell immediately the next day that there was something radically wrong with her. When I asked her why she had such a large abdomen, she simply said that she must have gained weight. I wanted to take her to a doctor here, but she wouldn't hear about it. So I tried to let it go and we took her sightseeing. We went to San Francisco and I showed her my favorite places there. Afterwards we visited Hanni (Lustig) Hochman, my friend whom she too had known since she was born, but somehow I could not lighten her spirits. We went shopping, we went to a play, but nothing really helped. She would talk continuously about her problems but would not even stop to listen to a reply. She was tired a lot and could hardly walk around our neighborhood because it was "hilly".

With a heavy heart I took her to the airport and watched the plane carry her away, asking myself whether I would ever see her again. My premonitions were right; she died of an abdominal cancer two years later. Her son called me to give me the sad news, telling me he was joining his father in Venezuela, and promised he would keep in touch with me. I never heard from him again. I was terribly sad; I had lost my "little sister" and the poor woman had had a very unhappy life.

CHAPTER SIX

The following year brought an exciting opportunity: With great curiosity and expectation I boarded a plane, which was taking us to Japan. This was my first trip there and I had heard so much about it, mainly from John. He had been there before, not only as tourist and lecturer, but also as a 19 year old second lieutenant in the army during the Occupation.

Our first stop was at Fukuoka on Kyushu, which is the southernmost island. Fukuoka is a bustling city, and John attended an international conference there. I went on a walking and sightseeing tour to become a little bit acquainted with a Japanese city. Of course I went shopping at a department store and saw a fantastic display of shoes covering an entire floor. The next day I happened to be back in the same store and the shoes were gone. Overnight they had changed all their displays! I have never seen this happen, and was very disappointed. I had hoped that I might find a pair of shoes.

From Fukuoka we took the express train to Kyoto. The train moves so quickly that it is difficult to focus on a particular scene in the countryside. We were served a typical Japanese box lunch of fish, rice, salad and a sweet. On leaving this impressive train we found ourselves with our luggage on the platform and had to find a porter. Only later were we told that on the train one could order ahead for a porter to help with the luggage. The train stops at a precise spot, departing and arriving at exactly stated times. In Kyoto we were tourists mostly on our own. We visited the best-known temples, which are magnificent. The days we were there were quite crowded with Japanese tourists, each group following guides who were distinguishable by different colored flags they held.

One day we went to a shrine located a distance away from the center of Kyoto. There, as in every shrine, we removed our shoes, and sat in awe contemplating a stone garden with its carefully raked pebbles. When we left the shrine we had difficulties finding transportation back to our hotel. A Japanese couple stood near us and when a taxi came to pick them up we begged to share the ride with them. They knew about as much English as we knew Japanese, but amazingly we exchanged friendly information, including the name of our hotel in Tokyo where we would be in two days. John, in Japanese fashion, took out his calling card and embarrassed our Japanese host because he had none with him. His wife quickly opened her purse, took out a lovely handkerchief, and gave it to me as a present. We were touched and grateful. Despite our entreaties, they would not allow us to share the cost of the taxi; we said goodbye with no hint that we would ever hear from them again.

When we arrived in Tokyo I was pleasantly surprised. From what I had heard about the overpopulation of the city I was prepared to see crowded streets, cars honking and people pushing each other. However, I saw none of this; it seemed just like any other large city, at least the areas we saw. When the taxi brought us to the Imperial Hotel, where we were staying, my mouth fell open: The hotel bordered a verdant park which seemed like an oasis in the middle of the downtown area. Its wide areas of green grass and beautiful trees led to the stunning Imperial Palace where the Emperor lives. The hotel was a very modern and luxurious building, which had replaced the original one designed by Frank Lloyd Wright.

The staff was very polite and treated us like royalty. When we took the elevator to our room, a young woman made sure that we were comfortably placed in the elevator, and bowed as the doors closed. Our room was well furnished in Western style. A former Japanese student of John came with his family to meet us at the hotel, and we walked with them through the streets in the neighborhood to a lovely family restaurant. I enjoyed Japanese food very much, though I had to admit that I was starting to get tired of what seemed like similar fare during the past ten days. One of my big cravings was bread. Thankfully I was able to get a roll or toast at breakfast at the hotel.

The next day we received a telephone call in our room. It was an English speaking man asking for John Ross. He was from Holland and was an accountant for the Japanese gentleman who had so kindly given us a ride in his taxi in Kyoto two days before! On his employer's behalf he apologized profusely for what turned out to be a misunderstanding. His employer thought they had taken the taxi from us instead of the other way around. John was correspondingly profuse in assuring the caller that his employer had behaved with great civility, courtesy and hospitality, and reiterated our gratitude for the ride. We were delightfully surprised with the call, and it reflects just how hospitable the Japanese are.

John had an appointment with the Chairman of the Board of Cannon, which was arranged by a dear friend, a lawyer in Washington, D.C. During the meeting, which had to be mediated by an interpreter, the Chairman invited us for dinner and gave an option of either a French or a Japanese restaurant. Without consulting me, John chose a Japanese restaurant, which was probably the more gracious response.

That evening, we were picked up by a limousine and taken to a very small Japanese restaurant, one, which accommodated only a few parties at a time, and those had to be well known to the owner. The table at which we sat was set up both for Japanese and Westerners who could not sit in the Japanese position. The banquet was magnificent in its novelty and visual splendor. We were told that we would be having blowfish and it was explained to me that this fish could only be prepared by a licensed chef because of its potential toxicity. I was hoping that a license required a practical test and that the chef knew how to remove the poisonous gland. When the first course was served in the form of a magnolia blossom with the white translucent petals made out of the fish, I was thrilled; it looked so lovely. When the second course came and I was told that this was also blowfish, I started to think of all the people who had probably died from eating blow fish and my appetite began to wane. When the third course turned out to be blowfish also, I stopped eating. However, I think we were served at least seven courses of the same fish all in a variety of decorative forms. By the time dinner was over, I was glad to have "experienced" blowfish but I don't need to have it again anytime soon. Our hosts were very gracious and during part of the evening the owner of the restaurant joined us for about an hour. Cannon had no doubt given her substantial business before.

On the way from the restaurant back to the hotel, accompanied by the interpreter, John discreetly remarked that the meal must have been very expensive. He mentioned an extraordinarily high figure per person, which was met with gentle laughter by the interpreter. We never did find out the facts but were sure the meal was more than $600 per person. In juxtaposition, on another occasion, the two of us went for a walk to seek a place for lunch and had a very satisfying meal for about $12 per person.

The next day we flew to Hong Kong. for our first visit. Everything pleasant that we had heard about the city was indeed so. Shopping fever strikes every visitor to Hong Kong whether in the thousands of jewelry stores, tailor shops, and lovely boutiques on Nathan Street in Kowloon or the open booths and shops in Hong Kong. One day we went to a section of town in which there was a jade market. On the way we stopped in an antique store and saw some lovely, and consequently highly expensive jade. The man running the store understood our search for a cheap souvenir and showed us the way to an open jade market. There were hundreds of stalls each tended by one or two people, mostly women who came from Mainland China every day. They were not only selling to customers but also heavily trading with each other. For no reason we picked one stall and I found a very nice pendant. We asked about the price and the woman, who probably understood more English than she admitted, wrote a very reasonable number of US dollars on a piece of paper. We were told to bargain and when we initiated this process, the woman took out packets of cards each with an English phrase on it. The first one she showed us said: "I am an honest business woman." Nonetheless she lowered the price a little and we agreed. When it came time to pay, John handed her a US fifty dollar bill and she took out a very fat roll of US dollars and gave us exact change! The whole event was worth the price of the jewelry.

There is amazingly effective and cheap ferry transportation between Hong Kong and Kowloon, where most of the elegant hotels and the wealthy homes are located in the area called Tsim Tsa Shui. Regular tickets on the ferry are about 10 cents and first class tickets on the upper deck are 12 cents. The view of the harbor from the ferry is memorable, during the day or at night. From the ferry in Hong Kong it is only a few minutes walk to a tram, which takes one up to the Victoria Peak overlooking magnificent villas on the mountain and the entire harbor.

We took a number of trips on the ferry and used one to view the fish, meat and other consumer goods markets in Hong Kong. To show a prospective purchaser how fresh the fish was the seller would reveal that the fishes' hearts were still beating, demonstrating how recently they'd been killed.

The following day we took a plane to Sydney, Australia, where we wanted to visit my cousins. It was October 2, and when the stewardess learned that it was John's birthday, she brought us a lovely cake and a bottle of champagne to take with us. My cousins met us at the plane and that evening we had a wonderful dinner at a delightful fish restaurant where we celebrated John's birthday. As usual we had a very relaxing and pleasant stay with Eric and Vera. After all the excitement we had had on our trip, we were ready for a rest with the family.

◆   ◆   ◆

Back in the United States the country had been enjoying a robust economy under President Clinton. The Government had a big surplus, people were making money on the stock market, technology was doing great, there were many new millionaires due to being at the right place at the right time, and taxes flowed into the Treasury. I belonged to an investment group of fifteen ladies who met once a month, and we were not complaining either. It was rather easy to make the right investment at that time, but it was hard to get 15 members to agree. Although we were a nice group of women who usually got along very well, one couldn't help but have somebody's feelings hurt. Our daughter Betsy, who happened to be visiting when I hosted the group at my home, sat in on the meeting and to my astonishment gave us some great stock advice. Everybody loved her and when the ladies left, Betsy sweetly said:

"You were the most beautiful." Darling Betsy! Of course that was not so, but I appreciated her kindness. Unfortunately our club was not wise enough to sell before it was too late and so we, as did so many thousands of people, lost quite a bit. However, we were resigned to hold on and have not done so badly since.

CHAPTER SEVEN

My dear husband had been invited to lecture in several cities in Spain. This lectureship tour of four weeks was being sponsored by a bank in Spain, and was part of a program to improve science in the country. We started in Madrid, where we were assigned a lovely apartment just outside of downtown.

John gave a lecture for high school and college students, which was well received. After the lecture many of the students came to ask him for his autograph and John acted like a rock star besieged by groupies. With a wave of his hand and a twinkle in his eye he told me he would talk to me later.

We alternated days of our activities: One day we spent together visiting museums, and the next day John would spend at the University while I poked around in stores. One evening John surprised me with the news that the next evening we would go to a symphony concert, which did not start until 10:00 p.m., somewhat past his bedtime. However, that was not all; in addition we were invited to go with some of our friends to hear Flamenco singing after the concert. We arrived at the Flamenco Club at 1 a.m. It was located in a basement of a house, and when we entered we could see nothing because of the thick cigarette smoke hovering in the room. The singer was excellent and we wondered how she preserved her voice in all that smoke. We soon learned, at least a little bit, to chime in with the response of "Ole!" together with the audience at selected vocal phrases. The guitar player, a young man, was excellent as well. We came home at 3:30 a.m. with a feeling of having participated in a revered local tradition.

From Madrid we went to Barcelona, which was a real surprise: Their primary language is Catalan and Spanish is the second language. Street and store signs are written in Catalan. This is a language that has no similarity with Spanish, and I didn't understand a word.

We stayed in a hotel on the square across from the Cathedral to which we walked when the sun was setting. The light was wonderful and on the steps a young man was playing a guitar. We asked him to play our favorite song called *Romanza*, by an unknown composer. He played it beautifully, and with the music and the fading sunlight we were carried away into utter bliss in this romantic setting. The next day we climbed Gaudi's unfinished Sagrada Familia. What a pleasure it was to visit his wonderful architecture and buildings: The spectacular designs, unbelievable colors and shapes, an incredible imagination.

Our next city was Granada, which was an unbelievable experience. The Alhambra is one of the most remarkable fortresses ever built. It has a magnificent view over Granada and the snow-covered mountains of the Sierra Nevada. Its Moorish architecture and gardens have been admired since the American author, Washington Irving, reminded the world of this splendor. Many buildings, connected through beautiful garden passages with many fountains, are built in an architectural style so rich and with such a variety of decorations that it is hard to imagine. The most magnificent one was the Alcazar, the Kings Castle, built in the 14th century. The geometric arrangements and patterns of Moorish tiles show their engagement in the art of symmetry. It was hard to decide where to look first as we were impacted by so many visual impressions. At the end of the day we were still far from having seen it all. There were so many places we had to see again that we decided we had to come back.

In the evening we were taken to a very interesting restaurant by the university people, who were so proud to have such an important professor from the United States visiting. They were kind and lovely people and I had a wonderful time talking to them in their own language, which quite intrigued them, since I am blonde, and, as I have been told in Mexico many times, look like a "*Gringa*" (an American).

We were driven from the university in Granada to Cordoba. The road led us along marvelous fields of sunflowers, and we stopped several times to take pictures. The whole countryside was magnificent. Arriving in Cordoba we checked into our hotel and walked around the town. The city has substantial evidence of the three great cultures of the Moors, the Jews and the Christians. The narrow streets of the old sections of town are all picture post-cards: Flower pots hanging from windows, iron-wrought lanterns, interestingly shaped doorways and windows, with alleys leading everywhere.

The next day we made the mandatory visit to a famous site where a sixteenth century church had been built into a mosque. The extent of the mosque was vast, with hundreds of columns of marble, each of different colors. The church was built into the mosque after the Christian conquest of Moorish Spain. When Emperor Charles V saw what had been done, he was far from pleased. "You have destroyed something unique," he said, "to build something commonplace."

Everything in this twin monument was beautiful and interesting, but as a whole, points to the folly of humans.

One afternoon we were invited to visit a couple whose home was built against a wall of the medieval part of the city. From a hot street we entered a courtyard cooled by sprays of water and shaded by greenery. The lady was a Moslem, and her husband was a Spanish writer. The house was filled with exquisite furniture and objects of art. She took us down to the basement of the house and we were speechless: When our eyes got used to the dark we could see that the entire floor was a two-thousand-year-old Roman mosaic. We were in awe in the presence of such history. She gave us a present of a Roman clay oil lamp, which had been found in her home. We were fascinated: Who used this lamp two thousand years ago and what were their lives like? She then took us across the river to a museum, which she and her husband were active in founding; the museum was devoted to the three great Abrahamic religions that helped to make Spanish history, and to the ideal of the brotherhood of all humanity. We were overwhelmed with her gracious hospitality.

◆   ◆   ◆

Over the years, John and I had become good friends with our neighbors Alba and Luca Cavalli-Sforza, a very sophisticated Italian couple, who live half their time at Stanford and half in Milan and Beluno, Italy. Luca is a prominent genetic anthropologist who has traveled all over the world to gather specimens and study the migrational patterns of people. They invited us many times to visit them in Beluno, a small town where Alba's mother had a large country estate, and in the summer of 1995 we decided to accept their invitation. We asked our cousins the Reusses to join us on the trip to Italy, and they were very enthusiastic about going.

We started in Florence, where we took them to the beautiful pension run by the nuns and they were as impressed with the location, the service and the kindness of the sisters as we had been. I was having problems with my stomach and the ladies insisted on cooking special meals for me. Through their kind treatment I started to feel better very soon.

From Florence we traveled by car to Ravenna to visit the 5th and 6th century churches with their magnificent mosaics. After driving around the north of Italy, we went to Beluno to visit the Cavalli-Sforzas. Our trip was interrupted for a couple of hours due to a rock slide blocking the main highway. Though we arrived a bit late in Beluno, we were warmly welcomed to their estate, which consisted of several houses and a 12th century octagonal chapel. Alba's mother was well over 90 at the time, and presided over an extensive and delicious lunch. The environment was so grand we felt we were actors in some Italian movie filmed with romantic splendor.

It seems to me that we were constantly traveling to different countries those years, which is not far from the truth, for this is the life of scientists in academia. But of course most of the year we were home in Stanford and John was teaching and doing research. Our house was open to visitors from around the world and in turn we were often invited to visit them. I was busy as always and was proud that the garden had finally improved to a degree where I did not have to be ashamed any more. I even got many compliments.

The calendar is entirely predictable, yet an event like John's 70th birthday came unexpectedly quickly. A large party was arranged for his former students and co-workers with a day of scientific presentations and a dinner to celebrate his birthday. The day was a great success and his students said many wonderful things in regard to John's scientific abilities and his care and devotion to his students. At the same time a special issue of a scientific publication, the Journal of Physical Chemistry, came out to honor his birthday. Many outstanding scientists contributed original research articles in honor of John's scientific contributions. Such an issue is called a *Festschrift,* (a writing on a festive occasion), and is bestowed upon leading scientists. Also each of John's former students and co-workers wrote a laudatory letter, all of which were collected in a volume. The dinner, for which we had rented a lovely restaurant, was magnificent. Aside from all the scientists we had also invited many of our friends. There were more speeches and Bobby made some very kind remarks about his father.

Through the years, John had been receiving a number of awards and life had been good.

Of course we were always worried about Betsy, who struggled so hard with her bi-polar disorder. Before John had left Boston to come to Stanford, she was hospitalized several times, each time a painful experience for everyone involved. With great effort on her part she returned to school to obtain a B.A. degree and then a M.S. in social work. We were all impressed with her accomplishments and looked forward to her life becoming more stable. She went on to obtain her license to practice in Massachusetts where she worked in several institutions. She got married and lived in a very nice townhouse in Westford. We held our breaths, hoping her life would even out. Her episodes of depression were especially difficult because all the light and joy in her sunny personality would disappear, and each time we worried about whether she would be able to come back from them.

In spite of all efforts, her life began to spiral down, especially when some key medications she had been taking were discontinued by her Psychiatrist. More hospitalizations followed, each one worse than the one before. She finally could not bear the pains of life any more, and in February 1998, our dear Betsy took her life.

We were all devastated. We searched our minds and hearts in vain for how and when we failed her. Surely there must have been something else we could have done to save her! No words to the contrary from the doctors or clergy, could soothe our consciences. We ached with such despair. The loss of Betsy was a deep and painful wound, especially for John. Betsy had been his little girl and his grief took the light out of his eyes for a very long time. The irreversibility of death never seems acceptable, especially to a parent. It is a terrible blow to lose a child; she was not my own but I had gotten to love her very much. Over the years I had tried to support her in various ways during our many telephone conversations, which were carried on even when we were traveling.

Betsy the day before she died.

Bobby returned immediately from a trip to Bali and we all attended a memorial service conducted in the Chapel at Concord Academy near Boston, from which she had graduated with honors years ago. Her mother arranged the service in a very short time, and we found solace for our grief in being together. Bobby read a most thoughtful and passionate letter partly in grief and partly to help the mourners present.

Nevertheless, life was never quite the same after that. My heart was bleeding for John, Bobby and Betsy's mother, but all I could do was to be there for John. Our love had grown and intensified over the years; we were very close and dependent upon each other, frequently finding ourselves having the same thoughts at the same time. We played many roles for each other: Lover, husband, wife, father, mother and child. I am certain that if my father could have seen us he would have ceased to worry about his daughter; we feel that our parents would be pleased.

CHAPTER EIGHT

One day wee received some truly spectacular news. The highest honor awarded to scientists in United States is the National Medal of Science bestowed by the President. The award is given almost annually to five to twelve scientists for the outstanding body of their work. At the end of 1999, John was informed that he had been awarded this distinction. The ceremony was to take place at the White House in March of 2000!

We were thrilled and I was so proud of my John. Every day we received congratulatory letters and emails from John's friends, colleagues and ex-students from all over the world. Of course once the initial excitement eased, came the question of what I would wear for the several affairs scheduled. An extremely important issue in my mind! Fortunately, I finally solved it to my satisfaction by buying a new gown for the banquet and deciding to wear a black suit, I owned, to the ceremony at the White House. We invited our son Bobby, his mother and our cousins Henry and Diane Reuss to join us. We met in Washington, and it was a pleasure to see a few of John's friends, who had also been awarded this medal, and their families at the hotel.

On Sunday, March 12, the National Medal of Science awardees and the National Medal of Technology awardees were invited to the large apartment of the President of the National Academy of Sciences for a reception. Each of the medalists was asked to make a few comments about his or her career. John reached back to the past and reminded the people attending the reception that today was March 12 and 62 years earlier on that date Austria was taken over by the Germans. John recalled, with gratitude to the United States, the admission of his family to the country in the early 1940. In a few sentences he sketched his education, stressing the almost continuous help he received from various sources including the City of New York, Queens College, the G.I. bill of Rights, and the National Science Foundation in the form of fellowship and research grants for nearly 50 years.

The next day we were invited for lunch at the home of John's good friend, David Ginsberg and his wife. David was still active in law, which he had practiced since the New Deal days when he wrote laws and speeches for Roosevelt. David was already in his eighties, but still going strong. He had married a pretty and intelligent younger German woman, who had an interesting job in Washington. We enjoyed showing our relatives the stately colonial home the Ginsbergs owned in Alexandria.

That evening there was a formal dinner for the medal recipients and their guests, sponsored by the Secretary of Commerce and the Director of the National Science Foundation. There was a military honor guard, and outstanding high school students from Washington with interests in science and engineering attended as escorts. It was a magnificent affair, and after dinner, short films about each recipient were shown.

The award ceremony was held the next day at the White House, and was a most impressive and exciting event. All the invited guests assembled first outside the White House, passed through inspection and then were guided by a number of military officers, who volunteer at the White House to be aides. The awardees and their spouses were led to the State Dining Room to await the President. We had to wait a bit and the wife, of one recipient, who was pregnant, took her shoes off to be more comfortable, saying "Here I am in the White House, barefoot and pregnant!" It was good comic relief. I was so excited I could not stand still. I was so proud of John and it was exhilarating to watch John's joy and happiness. During our whole stay in Washington he kept saying that he was so happy that he could share this great experience with us.

After a while President Clinton walked into the room. He was better looking than on T.V. and radiated his special charisma. He went from couple to couple shaking hands with the awardees and their spouses, staying with each for a few minutes. When he shook my hand and looked into my eyes, I was shaking a little from the magnitude of the occasion. When President Clinton talked, he would look directly in your eye, giving you the impression that he was concentrating on you. It was a heady experience.

When the President had finished speaking to the awardees individually, the White House photographer took a picture of the group with the President. We then went to the East Room where the other guests had assembled. The President entered to the sounds of "Hail to the Chief" played by a marine band. The audience stood and I had the opportunity of taking a photo of the President as he passed by.

The President gave an excellent address, short by his usual standard, yet very engaging. He then asked a military officer to announce each Medal recipient, and read the citation of the award. The recipient stepped on a small platform and the President put the National Medal of Science on his or her neck, and then shook hands. Many photos were taken of the process.

John receiving his medal from President Clinton.

When all this was done, the President thanked us for our presence and invited everybody, to join him for refreshments in the State Dining Room, quickly departing in that direction himself. We followed and saw the President signing an invitation card of a 10-year-old boy, the son of one of the awardees. The boy had asked the President to write him an excuse for missing school that day, and the President cheerfully obliged. The Reusses, Bobby, John and I just then passed the President, and John introduced our party to him. President Clinton said, "Well, we have to have a family picture here," calling for his photographer who took several pictures of us. We were absolutely delighted with this event. We couldn't have imagined anything better. Everyone thought that our great President was charming and I even heard a few academic matrons say, with a nod to his reputation: "Well, if he had asked me, I would have said yes!"

The reception was joyful and festive, the food and drink excellent. In addition to the marine band there was a marine string ensemble and a marine jazz band that entertained us. We were allowed to visit a number of the public rooms in the White House, which were shown expertly by military aids. We lingered because we knew we would leave with the feeling that a truly wonderful and awe-filled occasion had come to an end. We all felt it was one of the great experiences of our lives.

At the reception in the White House.

Since that visit, we have watched the movie "American President" several times and have enjoyed it. There is a scene in which Annette Bening attended a banquet in the White House at the personal invitation of the President to be his escort. After the banquet she is being driven home in a limousine and looks back at the White House with an expression of awe, joy and glorious memories. That is exactly the way we felt when we left the White House.

The next day we were in a hurry to see what had been reported in the newspapers and saw the wonderful photo in the New York

Times. You can see John's right ear, the rest hidden behind a colleague, and I am on the left elatedly smiling while taking a picture of the President.

◆   ◆   ◆

This was the year 2000 and I think a good time to close this book. We were happy, the country was in good shape, and considering the fact that we had both started as refugees and were part of the Jewish Diaspora, we had much to be grateful for.

EPILOGUE

We all carry the past within us and our characters and personalities become formed in part by the circumstances. I had to change my life many times and that may have contributed to my persistent insomnia and worries about the future.

I recall the many events described here with both pleasure and sadness, but I am pleased that I retain so many memories despite never having kept a diary. Fortunately, I feel settled and have now been living in our home longer than I have ever been anywhere before in my life. The same is true for John, whose career had taken him to many different universities until finally he settled here.

John and I came from middle class families in Austria. Though we became frightened refugees, we took hold in our respective new lands, became educated and had the opportunities of free people. As we celebrated in Washington, we recognized that we had taken good advantage of those opportunities. There were many sorrows along the way but even more joys.

Considering the dreadful fates of so many people in the twentieth century all over the world, we, survivors, must indeed be grateful to the Lord for the blessings given us. John and I followed the rabbi's instructions well and made a beautiful everlasting rose.

CPSIA information can be obtained at www.ICGtesting.com
Printed in the USA
LVOW10s0107151113

361194LV00001B/9/P